CONTENTS

Abbreviations and Acronyms 2
Preface 2
Introduction 2

1 Overture: The Struggle for Kharkiv in 2014 5
2 The Kharkiv Defensive Operation (24 February–14 May 2022) 8
3 Combat Operations in the Kharkiv Oblast in the Second Half of May – August 2022 26
4 Slobozhanska Offensive Operation (September–December 2022) 30

Conclusions 54
Bibliography 54
Endnotes 62
About the Authors 72

MAP OF EUROPE SINCE 1992

Note: In order to simplify the use of this book, all names, locations and geographic designations are as provided in *The Times World Atlas*, or other traditionally accepted major sources of reference, as of the time of described events.

Helion & Company Limited
Unit 8 Amherst Business Centre
Budbrooke Road
Warwick
CV34 5WE
England
Tel. 01926 499 619
Email: info@helion.co.uk
Website: www.helion.co.uk
Twitter: @helionbooks
https://helionbooks.wordpress.com/

Cover image: One of dozens of abandoned Russian T-72s and BMP-2s, captured by Ukrainian troops at the high point of the Slobozhanska Offensive, in the Izium area, around 14 September 2022. (ZSU)

Designed and typeset by Mach 3 Solutions (www.mach3solutions.co.uk)
Cover design Paul Hewitt, Battlefield Design (www.battlefield-design.co.uk)

ISBN: 978-1-806722-99-0

British Library Cataloguing-in-Publication Data
A catalogue record for this book is available from the British Library

We always welcome receiving book proposals from prospective authors.

ABBREVIATIONS AND ACRONYMS

ATO	Anti-Terrorist Operation
BTG	battalion tactical group
DPR	Donetsk People's Republic
LPR	Luhansk People's Republic
MANPADS	man-portable air defence system
MLRS	Multiple Launch Rocket System
VDV	*Vozdushno-desantnye voyska* (airborne forces) (Russian)

PREFACE

Why did I decide to write this book? In the past, during my peaceful life, I have visited Kharkiv only a few times. Thus, I felt no sense of kinship with the city before the war. But due to the relentless war, my family and I found ourselves forever connected to Kharkiv. On the morning of 30 August 2022, my son, Lieutenant Taras Kharuk, callsign 'Aizec', a coordinating physician in the medical company of the 14th Separate Mechanised Brigade, was killed by Russian artillery fire in Kharkiv (on Kultury Street, in front of the military hospital). This study is therefore a tribute to my son, his fallen comrades, and all the sons and daughters of Ukraine who paid the ultimate price for our freedom.

Andrij Kharuk

Taras Kharuk (5 September 1995–30 August 2022). (Authors' collection)

INTRODUCTION

The current Russian-Ukrainian war is an unprecedented phenomenon in European history in recent decades. For the first time since the Second World War, full-scale combat operations involving large numbers of troops and all types of conventional weapons have unfolded on our continent.

In planning a large-scale invasion of Ukraine, the Russian military and political leadership set itself several goals. In the north, the key task was to capture Kyiv, Ukraine's capital. In the minds of Russian leaders, this would lead to the disorganisation of our state's administration and the replacement of the legitimate leadership with Kremlin puppets. The strike from the south was intended to create the land corridor to Crimea, restore the North Crimean Canal, and, ideally, occupy the southern regions of Ukraine, cutting off its access to the Black Sea. The attack from the east and north-east was intended to capture Ukraine's industrial centres, primarily Kharkiv. As we know, the Russians failed to achieve this goal, although the fighting for the Kharkiv Oblast was long and fierce. The fighting is still taking place – as the author writes these lines (in the summer of 2024), the Defence Forces of Ukraine are repelling the aggressor's attempt to break through to Kharkiv from the north, from the direction of Vovchansk, and Russian pressure on Kupiansk continues.[1] However, the decisive battles, during which the Russian offensive was initially stopped and the occupiers were later driven out from the Kharkiv Oblast, took place in 2022. This study is devoted to these events.

The author's initial idea was to study the battles for Kharkiv as a key administrative, industrial and scientific centre of eastern Ukraine, the second most populous city in our country and a large urban agglomeration. However, at the very first stage of studying the problem, it became clear that it would not be possible to limit the study to Kharkiv alone, as the defence of the city cannot be considered separately from events in the nearby and distant approaches to it. Therefore, we had to expand the territorial boundaries of the study to the whole Kharkiv Oblast. But even this is largely arbitrary, because in a number of cases we have to consider events in neighbouring areas of other oblasts.

In determining the chronological framework of the study, the author was guided by the periodisation developed by experts at the Centre for Military History Research of the Armed Forces of Ukraine.[2] According to this periodisation, the large-scale Russian-Ukrainian war, which began with the invasion on 24 February 2022, is considered the third period of the Russian-Ukrainian war that began in 2014. Several stages can be distinguished in this period:

- the preparatory stage (December 2021 – 23 February 2022) – preparation of the military and political leadership of the Russian Federation for a large-scale invasion, and of Ukraine for its repulsion;
- the first strategic defensive operation (24 February – April 2022) – the invasion of enemy troops in many directions with the intention of implementing a 'blitzkrieg' scenario and the disruption of these plans by the Defence Forces of Ukraine;
- the second strategic defensive operation (May – August 2022) – the enemy abandoned its initial plans, withdrew and regrouped its troops, and focused its main efforts on the final seizure of the Donetsk and Luhansk oblasts and the maintaining control over the occupied territories;

- the first strategic offensive operation (29 August – December 2022) – Ukrainian troops carried out a large-scale strategic offensive operation in the Kherson and Kupiansk-Lyman directions, as a result of which most of the occupied territory of the Kharkiv Oblast was liberated, and in southern Ukraine, enemy troops were pushed back beyond the barrier line of the Dnipro River.

This periodisation, in the author's opinion, has one drawback: in reality, the Russian Federation's preparations for a large-scale invasion began not in December 2021, but much earlier. The starting point should be the publication of Vladimir Putin's article *On the Historical Unity of Russians and Ukrainians* on 12 July 2021, which effectively marked the start of ideological preparation for a large-scale invasion.[3] However, for our study, this shortcoming is not significant, especially considering that the periodisation of the actual hostilities does not raise any objections.

When analysing the events of the Russian-Ukrainian war, researchers inevitably encounter the problem of source base. On the one hand, modern electronic media and social networks allow combat operations to be tracked in near real time. On the other hand, such information is usually personalised. It may be far from an objective coverage of events and sometimes it can even distort them. Access to official materials is extremely difficult – when hostilities are still ongoing or have just ceased, archival documents relating to the war are not available to researchers. This is quite understandable given the need to maintain an appropriate level of secrecy. In such circumstances, the solution for researchers is to use official chronicles of hostilities. The information contained in these publications reflects the official position of one or another side in the armed conflict. In combination with the aforementioned unofficial sources, such as social networks and mass media, it allows for a fairly complete reconstruction of the course of hostilities, although it certainly requires a critical approach.[4]

Several chronicles of military operations were used in writing this work. The most informative is the monthly *Military-Historical Description of the Russian-Ukrainian War*, published by the Ministry of Defence of Ukraine and the General Staff of the Armed Forces of Ukraine.[5] A significant part of its issues concerns military-political and military-economic factors, as well as a general description of the strategic situation. However, in most cases, the description of combat operations at the tactical level is presented in a fairly generalised manner, without detailed elaboration. These publications can assist in reconstructing the overall situation and the sequence of events when examining a particular operation.

Based on a synthesis of the materials included in the issues of *Military-Historical Description of the Russian-Ukrainian War*, the work *A Year of War for Freedom: A Military-Historical Essay on the Russian-Ukrainian War* was published (in four volumes). The period relevant to the subject of our study is described in the first three books, which are devoted, respectively, to the first and second strategic defensive operations and the first strategic offensive operation. At the same time, the description of the course of hostilities itself is given relatively little space in the books. For example, in the first book, the section 'Description of the main combat operations in the Kharkiv direction' takes up less than four pages.[6] The second book deals with combat operations in the Slobozhanska direction, and the entire description of events from May to August 2022 takes up just over two pages.[7] The course of the Slobozhanska Offensive Operation is covered in much greater detail in the third book.[8] It should be noted here that the term 'Kharkiv counteroffensive (or offensive) operation' is used in this work and in the vast majority of other studies. However, in our opinion, the term 'Slobozhanska Offensive Operation' is more rational and logical. The explanation for this point of view is given in the relevant section.

The second monthly chronicle publication is the *Chronicle of War*, whose issues are prepared by researchers at the National University of Defence of Ukraine. It is positioned as an 'information bulletin developed in accordance with the requirements of guiding documents through the indirect collection of operational information, reconstruction of the chronology of events […]'.[9] The publication contains daily reports on the operational situation, which are characterised by several features. On the one hand, it is quite detailed. On the other hand, it provides information only about the actions of the aggressor and says nothing about the actions of the Armed Forces of Ukraine. In addition, the reports contain information not only about actual events, but also about possible operations predicted by intelligence data. Such data should be used with caution in historical research, especially if such predictions have not come true.

Another official source is the brochures published by the Centre for Military History Research of the Armed Forces of Ukraine. They are compiled according to a thematic principle – most of them are devoted to a specific operation of the Defence Forces of Ukraine. Among them, the work *Eastern Gate of the State* stands out, which describes the Kharkiv Defensive Operation.[10] This work reflects the general course of the operation and highlights its stages, but it also contains a number of factual errors – for example, regarding the composition of Russian troops operating in the Kharkiv direction. In 2023, these brochures were published as a single book.[11] However, the content of its sections is quite similar to the brochures, so we will use them as primary material in our citations.

Important sources of information about the operation are reports from analytical centres, in particular the daily reports of the Institute for the Study of War (ISW). Reports from the General Staff of the Armed Forces of Ukraine were also used. They contain significantly fewer details and often reflect the course of hostilities with a certain delay. However, these reports serve as official confirmation of certain actions taken by the Ukrainian Armed Forces.

A significant group of sources used in our study consists of memoirs by participants in the events. Although they are not always clearly structured, they nevertheless make it possible to clarify many important details related to the course of combat operations. As an example, one may cite the book by A. Trystan, which highlights the participation of officers of the Kharkiv National Air Force University in the defence of Kharkiv.[12]

In this study, the author used the work of historians and military experts, which can be divided into several groups. The first group consists of descriptions of combat operations published in periodicals (mainly foreign) almost simultaneously with the development of events. For example, the course of the Kharkiv Defensive Operation was covered by M. Cielma.[13] The Slobozhanska Offensive Operation is reflected in the works of P. Batacchi and A. Mottola, as well as M. Gaweda.[14] Separately, we should highlight the publications of M. Stembski, who consistently covers the course of the Russian-Ukrainian air combat, including in the Kharkiv Oblast.[15] The chronicle of air combat in February–May 2022 is also covered in the publication by M. Zhirokhov.[16] The works included in this group are characterised by a minimal degree of generalisation (especially in the case of M. Stembski's works). D. Rovenský's article on Ukrainian offensive operations in the Kharkiv Oblast and the right bank of the Kherson Oblast stands out for its unique approach,[17] unlike most researchers who consider these two offensive operations separately, albeit in relation to each other, D. Rovenský resorts to a parallel presentation of events in the Kherson and Kharkiv oblasts. This technique allows for a clearer understanding of the interdependence of these events. Some pretty interesting conclusions and generalisations can be found in an article by a group of Italian researchers, which analyses the key events of the first weeks after 24 February 2022, including the defence of Kharkiv.[18]

The second group consists of articles written with the benefit of temporal distance. They are characterised by attempts at a more in-depth analysis of either the course of operations as a whole or their individual aspects. An example of the first approach is works devoted to the Kharkiv Defensive Operation and the first stage of the Slobozhanska Offensive Operation.[19] As an illustration of this second approach, one may cite an article on the employment of modern forms of offensive manoeuvre, drawing on the experience of the Slobozhanska Offensive Operation.[20] In an article by D. Komarov and D. Kruglyak devoted to the same operation, the main focus is on the significance of the operation for the further course of the war.[21] It is also necessary to note another characteristic – or rather, a shortcoming – of the approach adopted by some researchers: the downplaying or complete neglect of combat operations in the Kharkiv Oblast. For instance, in the work by O. Boiko devoted to the course of the main phases of the war, the analysis of the first strategic defensive operation focuses on the battles for Kyiv and in southern Ukraine, while the defence of Kharkiv is not mentioned at all. The Slobozhanska Offensive Operation is likewise only briefly noted.[22]

Unfortunately, domestic historiography still suffers from a critical shortage of studies devoted to the history of individual military units. Such research is clearly warranted, at the very least, for the 92nd Separate Mechanised Brigade, which played an exceptional role in the fighting in the Kharkiv Oblast, as well as for the Kharkiv territorial defence brigades. Currently, there is only one such work – that of A. Shevchenko, who studies the participation of units of the Main Directorate of Intelligence of the Ministry of Defence of Ukraine in the defence of Kharkiv and the Slobozhanska offensive.[23] The main focus is on the actions of the special unit 'Kraken'. However, A. Shevchenko's work cannot be regarded as a fully-fledged scholarly study, as it has a pronounced journalistic character.

The third group of publications consists of monographs devoted to the Russian-Ukrainian war, in which combat operations in the Kharkiv Oblast appear as one of several narrative strands. First and foremost, mention should be made of the substantial study by V. Golovko, *Invasion. 2022. Russia's Large-Scale Aggression Against Ukraine*, published by the Institute of History of Ukraine of the National Academy of Sciences of Ukraine.[24] In this work, events in the Kharkiv Oblast are covered in an extremely uneven manner. The Kharkiv Defensive Operation is described in only a few paragraphs, which are not consolidated into a single subsection but scattered across different pages. In general, this can be explained by the author's intention to focus on the key events of the war; during the first strategic defensive operation, such an event was undoubtedly the battle for Kyiv. Somewhat more attention is devoted to the offensive in the Slobozhanska region in September 2022. However, when examining the first strategic offensive operation of the Defence Forces of Ukraine, V. Golovko focuses primarily not on events in the Kharkiv Oblast but on the Kherson Offensive Operation.

Another noteworthy comprehensive work devoted to the events of 2022 is a collective monograph published by the National University of Defence of Ukraine.[25] In our view, it contains one of the best and most detailed descriptions of the Kharkiv Defensive Operation available to date (pp.165–176). The monograph also characterises the events of the second strategic defensive operation in the Slobozhanska operational area (pp.198–203). At the same time, disproportionately little attention is paid to the Slobozhanska Offensive Operation (pp.254–260). In contrast to the fairly detailed accounts of the defensive fighting, the analysis of the offensive operation is marked by schematic treatment and the absence of many important details.

Along with Ukrainian works, foreign publications also deserve attention, such as the study by T. Cooper (with co-authors) on the first days of large-scale Russian aggression.[26] In a chapter with the telling title 'Fortress Cities', the authors devote a separate subsection (small in size but sufficiently substantive) to the battles on the approaches to Kharkiv and within the city itself in February 2022 (pp.48–50). Special consideration should also be given to works by Russian authors. It is evident that most of them are far from objectivity and serve the purposes of propaganda rather than research. Nevertheless, some articles – particularly those published in the journal *Voennaia Mysl* – were used in this study. These materials can be employed in several respects. First, they allow for an analysis of the Russian Federation's preparations for the large-scale invasion of Ukraine and for assessing the influence of geopolitical and strategic concepts held by the Russian military-political leadership on invasion planning. Second, they enable the study of the planning and execution of individual operations. Third, they make it possible to examine how the lessons of the war against Ukraine are interpreted in Russian sources, which in turn allows for a retrospective assessment of the effectiveness of the aggressor's military actions in relation to its initial plans and expectations. Finally, a critical examination of these publications provides additional material for refuting Russian disinformation and distortions in the portrayal of the Russian-Ukrainian war.[27]

1
OVERTURE: THE STRUGGLE FOR KHARKIV IN 2014

The Russian-Ukrainian war began long before 24 February 2022. In fact, since Ukraine regained its independence on 24 August 1991, the Russian Federation has been conducting hybrid actions aimed at bringing Ukraine under its complete control. The intensity of these actions has fluctuated, with periods of escalation (the Crimean crisis in the first half of the 1990s, gas and other trade wars, the conflict over Tuzla Island in 2003) and periods of relative calm. The Russian-Ukrainian war entered its phase of armed aggression in February 2014, when the occupation of Crimea took place. However, the plans of the Russian military-political leadership were not limited to the peninsula alone. Seeking to extend its influence across the entirety of eastern and southern Ukraine, Russia instigated the implementation of the so-called 'Novorossiya project'.[1] The myth of the 'Novorossiyan' character of eastern and southern Ukraine was drawn from the imperial past and revived as a counterweight to Ukraine's Revolution of Dignity. The project envisaged not direct annexation (as in the case of the Autonomous Republic of Crimea and the city of Sevastopol), but the creation of puppet quasi-state entities termed 'people's republics', which would remain under the full control of the Russian Federation. The implementation of the 'Novorossiya project' would have allowed Russia to avoid a direct armed invasion of mainland Ukraine. At the same time, it would have opened avenues for hybrid influence over Ukraine's internal situation, enabled the establishment of a land corridor to Crimea for Russian expansion, and made it possible to deliver a serious blow to Ukraine's socio-economic situation.[2] Notably, Russian military theorists even substantiated their plans with corresponding mathematical calculations. In an article devoted to the modelling of military operations, Russian authors calculated the resilience of Ukraine's oblasts as of 2013. Significantly, the Autonomous Republic of Crimea does not appear on this list. According to their calculations, the oblasts with the lowest chances of remaining within Ukraine were Donetsk, Luhansk, Odesa, and Kharkiv, while the highest chances were attributed to Ivano-Frankivsk, Ternopil, Lviv, and Rivne.[3] It was precisely those oblasts regarded by Russia as the least resilient that were subjected to a hybrid attack by the Russian Federation in 2014.

The Russian leadership assigned a key role to Kharkiv in the implementation of the 'Novorossiya project'. It is Ukraine's second largest city, and it is located only 40 kilometres from the border with the Russian Federation, where the border-crossing regime at the time was extremely liberal and border control largely nominal. This enabled Russia to infiltrate its agents without difficulty. A significant proportion of the Russian-speaking population in Kharkiv and the surrounding oblast, also, in the view of the Russian leadership, simplified the task of establishing control over the area. The city and regional leadership were likewise pro-Russian – namely, Kharkiv Mayor Hennadii Kernes and Head of the Kharkiv Regional State Administration Mykhailo Dobkin. At public rallies, they openly appeared wearing St. George's ribbons (which became one of the key identifiers of pro-Russian forces) and under Russian flags.[4]

The seizure of Kharkiv was intended to carry symbolic significance, as between 1919 and 1934, the city had already served as the capital of the Bolshevik-occupied part of Ukraine – the Ukrainian Soviet Socialist Republic. In this capacity, it was framed

Rally of Euromaidan supporters in Kharkiv near the Taras Shevchenko monument. 1 December 2013. (Photo by Serhiy Petrov)

as a kind of alternative to 'Euromaidan' Kyiv and was well suited to the role of the 'capital of Novorossiya'.

The first step toward this goal was the congress of deputies at all levels from the pro-Russian Party of Regions, which took place at the Kharkiv Palace of Sports on 22 February 2014. It was intended to be chaired by Viktor Yanukovych, who had already arrived in Kharkiv, but at the last moment abandoned this plan and left the city. It should be recalled that on that very day, the Verkhovna Rada of Ukraine adopted a resolution stating that Yanukovych had unconstitutionally withdrawn from the exercise of his constitutional powers and calling early presidential elections.[5] About 3,000 Yanukovych supporters arrived in Kharkiv, including members of the Party of Regions faction, which at that time had a majority in all regional councils in eastern and southern Ukraine.

The congress essentially ended without the results that the organisers had hoped for. However, it became a catalyst for further events in Kharkiv. Two rallies gathered in the square in front of the Palace of Sports – supporters and opponents of Euromaidan.[6] After the congress ended, a column of thousands of Euromaidan supporters marched to Freedom (Svoboda) Square with the intention of dismantling the Lenin monument. However, they did not succeed in doing so immediately, and in the evening, representatives of pro-Russian organisations began to gather at the monument with the intention of preventing its dismantling. Representatives of 'Oplot' (a pro-Russian fighting club and public organisation) attacked Euromaidan activists who had barricaded themselves in the building of the Kharkiv Regional State Administration (RSA).[7] At night, supporters of preserving the monument began to take turns guarding it.

The confrontation on Freedom Square lasted for several days. On 1 March 2014, at the initiative of Hennadii Kernes, a large rally of pro-Russian forces was held there. Kernes and Mykhailo Dobkin addressed the crowd beneath Russian flags. Inflamed by the speeches, the crowd stormed the building of the Kharkiv Regional State Administration, forcing out the Maidan Self-Defence units.

Russian flags were then raised on the building. As a result of the assault, at least 97 Maidan supporters were injured.[8] Among the victims was writer Serhiy Zhadan, who described the events of 1 March as follows:

> Friends, I'm fine. Two cuts on my head, a cut eyebrow, a concussion, and a suspected broken nose. They hit me on the back of the head with bats. They attacked as a group. When they demanded that I kneel, I told them to f*ck off. The police pulled me out. Gennady Adolfovich [Kernes], how are things with peace and quiet in the region? Mikhail Markovich [Dobkin], for which country's presidency will you be running? Arsen Borisovich [Avakov], how are things with our internal affairs agencies? Many Kharkiv teenagers were beaten up by Russian citizens today. And most importantly, when will you all be put in jail? Kharkiv residents, I love you. Don't be afraid of them – you can't break someone who isn't afraid.[9]

The building of the Kharkiv Regional State Administration, seized by pro-Russian forces, 7 April 2014. (Depo.Kharkiv)

One consequence of the assault on 1 March was the dismissal of Mykhailo Dobkin from the post of Head of the Kharkiv Regional State Administration the following day. The corresponding decree was signed by the Acting President of Ukraine, Oleksandr Turchynov.[10] On the same day, Ihor Baluta was appointed to this post.[11] G. Kernes remained in office as mayor, as this is an elected position. After some time, the pro-Russian forces left the Kharkiv Regional State Administration building, but the situation in the city remained extremely tense, with fights breaking out from time to time. An eyewitness to those events recalls: 'On weekdays, it was relatively calm. But on weekends, buses brought 'tourists' from Belgorod and fights broke out'.[12]

A new escalation began on 6 April 2014 – the day on which pro-Russian forces seized the building of the Donetsk Regional State Administration and the building of the Security Service of Ukraine in Luhansk. On the same day, pro-Russian forces gathered for a rally outside the building of the Kharkiv Regional State Administration, and at 21:00 launched an assault. The police guarding the building offered no resistance. Negotiations then began between the local authorities and the protesters. Meanwhile, one of the pro-Russian activists read aloud an 'Act on the Proclamation of State Independence of the Kharkiv People's Republic', which virtually replicated the text of a similar document issued by the so-called 'Donetsk People's Republic'. A total of 150 activists registered as members of the 'Council of Deputies of the Kharkiv Territorial Community'.[13]

Participants in the pro-Russian uprising detained after the liberation of the Kharkiv Regional State Administration building. (apostrophe.ua)

The situation in Kharkiv – as, indeed, in Donetsk and Luhansk – was slipping out of control. By decision of the Acting President of Ukraine, Oleksandr Turchynov, authorised representatives and additional law enforcement forces were dispatched to all three cities. The particular importance attached to Kharkiv is evidenced by the rank of the officials sent there: the Minister of Internal Affairs of Ukraine, Arsen Avakov, and the Commander of the Internal Troops of the Ministry of Internal Affairs, Lieutenant General Stepan Poltorak. The choice of these figures was far from accidental: Avakov as a Kharkiv businessman and politician, had close ties to the city and the region, and served as head of the Kharkiv Regional Council from 2005 to 2010; Poltorak, meanwhile, had been head of the Academy of the Internal Troops of the Ministry of Internal Affairs – located in Kharkiv – since 2002.

The force component was provided by the special purpose unit of the Separate Special Forces Regiment of the Internal Troops of the

Ministry of Internal Affairs, 'Jaguar', which was urgently redeployed from Kalynivka (Vinnytsia Oblast). On the morning of 8 April 2014, this special unit cleared the building of the Kharkiv Regional State Administration. Without a single shot fired and without casualties, 70 offenders were detained. According to Oleksandr Turchynov:

> They [the Jaguar fighters] expelled the insurgents, restrained them, forcing them face down onto the asphalt. In this way, we localised the uprising in Kharkiv. From Donetsk and Luhansk, I was informed that it was not possible to carry out the task because there were too many civilians and there would be many civilian casualties, and they could not assume such responsibility. Despite my pressure, I was told that attempts were being made to free the seized buildings through a negotiation process.[14]

The recapture of the Regional State Administration building was a turning point in the armed confrontation in Kharkiv. In the following weeks, fights between pro-Russian forces and Euromaidan activists continued, but overall, the situation in Kharkiv remained under control. A decisive role was played by several factors, foremost among them, in our view, the presence in Kharkiv of a strong and cohesive pro-Ukrainian majority. An illustration of its determination was provided by the community of football supporters of the local club Metalist Kharkiv, noted for their high level of organisation and their well-known anti-Putin chant. In addition, it proved possible to isolate pro-Russian forces in Kharkiv relatively effectively from external support. Local law enforcement agencies were reinforced by units deployed from other oblasts.

On the evening of 8 April, pro-Russian activists attempted to seize the Kharkiv Television Tower, demanding the restoration of Russian television broadcasts. This attempt was, however, suppressed by law enforcement agencies. On 13 April, pro-Russian elements once again gathered with the intention of storming the building of the Kharkiv Regional State Administration, but subsequently redirected their actions toward the pre-trial detention facility, seeking the release of previously detained insurgents. This attempt likewise failed.

When the Anti-Terrorist Operation (ATO) was announced in eastern Ukraine on 14 April 2014, the corresponding legal regime was introduced across the territories of Donetsk Oblast and Luhansk Oblast.[15] In Kharkiv Oblast, however, it was applied only within the city of Izium and the Izium District, which directly bordered the northern part of Donetsk Oblast.[16] The oblast also became a logistics base for supplying troops operating in the ATO zone. The ATO regime remained in effect in Izium and the Izium District until 7 September 2014.

The Metalist football club fan community proved to be one of the most organised and determined in opposing Russian aggression in Kharkiv in 2014. (nakypilo.ua)

Kharkiv's proximity to the region where active hostilities were already underway by late April 2014 created a certain degree of risk – especially given the continued activity of pro-Russian forces within the city itself. The focal point around which these forces coalesced remained the Anti-Maidan tent camp. On 27 April, football supporters of Metalist Kharkiv and FC Dnipro marched through the city streets with slogans affirming the unity of Ukraine. An Anti-Maidan column moved to confront them, and a mass fight erupted. Among those injured were members of police special units who were attempting to restore public order.[17] The next day, the police dismantled the tent camp of pro-Russian forces on Freedom Square.

By 1 May 2014, pro-Russian forces had announced plans for a mass demonstration in Kharkiv, intended to become the apogee of the so-called 'Russian Spring'. In response, pro-Ukrainian forces declared the holding of a 'Ukrainian May Day', thereby demonstrating their readiness to suppress a pro-Russian mobilisation by force if necessary. Ultimately, the mass demonstration announced by pro-Russian forces did not take place. At the same time, pro-Russian activists were preparing to hold a pseudo-referendum in Kharkiv and the surrounding oblast on issues of Ukraine's 'federalisation', the creation of a 'South-Eastern Autonomy', and the granting of state status to the Russian language in Ukraine. The event was planned for 11 May, to coincide with the so-called 'referendums' scheduled in parts of the Donetsk and Luhansk oblasts controlled by pro-Russian forces. However, Kharkiv-based activists failed to coordinate the 'referendum' with their counterparts in Donetsk and Luhansk. Ultimately, on 9 May, one of the leaders of the Kharkiv pro-Russian movement, Yurii Aptukhin, announced the abandonment of plans to hold such a 'referendum' in Kharkiv.[18]

Between May and November 2014, pro-Russian activists repeatedly attempted to organise mass actions in Kharkiv in the form of rallies or marches through the city streets. These events were often timed to specific dates: the early presidential election in Ukraine (25 May), the anniversary of the outbreak of the German-Soviet war (22 June), the anniversary of the liberation of Kharkiv from German occupation (23 August), and the anniversary of the Bolshevik coup in Petrograd (7 November). However, such actions typically attracted only several dozen to two or three hundred participants. The decline in pro-Russian activity was largely the result of the determination demonstrated by the Ukrainian authorities in combating insurgent groups in certain areas of the Donetsk and Luhansk oblasts – indeed, the first significant successes of the ATO were achieved precisely in May–June. This was further compounded by the arrest of pro-Russian leaders or their departure from Kharkiv – either to the Russian Federation or to Ukrainian territories under Russian control.

In 2014, despite numerous attempts by pro-Russian forces to destabilise the situation in Kharkiv and the Kharkiv Oblast, the region remained under the full control of Ukraine's legitimate authorities. This effectively marked the collapse of the 'Novorossiya project', which, instead of encompassing a broad arc of eastern and southern Ukrainian regions, was reduced to isolated areas of the Donetsk and Luhansk oblasts.

2
THE KHARKIV DEFENSIVE OPERATION (24 FEBRUARY–14 MAY 2022)

At the beginning of 2022, the city of Kharkiv had a population of more than 1.4 million. At the same time, it was relatively densely populated: in terms of area (310km^2), Kharkiv is smaller not only than Kyiv but also, for example, than Kryvyi Rih or Zaporizhzhia, each of which has roughly half the population of Kharkiv (by area, Kharkiv ranks ninth among Ukrainian cities). Kharkiv was an exceptionally important industrial centre. For example, the plants Turboatom and Electrotyazhmash accounted for approximately 17 percent of the global production of generators and turbines for power plants. KhADO Technology was Ukraine's leading producer of automotive oils. The Kharkiv State Aviation Manufacturing Enterprise – one of only two aircraft manufacturing plants in Ukraine – was experiencing difficult times but nevertheless retained significant production potential. The city was also home to key enterprises of the defence-industrial complex, foremost among them Ukraine's sole tank manufacturer, the Malyshev Factory; the country's main armoured-vehicle design centre, the Kharkiv Morozov Machine Building Design Bureau; and a major repair facility, the Kharkiv Armoured Plant. In total, 380 industrial enterprises were located in Kharkiv. The city also constituted a major transportation and communications hub. Kharkiv was home to more than 20 institutions of higher education, including four military ones: the Ivan Kozhedub Kharkiv National Air Force University, the Kharkiv Institute of Tank Troops, the Military Law Institute of Yaroslav Mudryi National Law University, and the National Academy of the National Guard of Ukraine.

All of this underscores Kharkiv's exceptional importance for Ukraine – its economy, cultural and educational sphere, and national defence capability. At the same time, the city was (and remains) highly vulnerable to attack from the Russian Federation, given that the minimum distance from the Russian-Ukrainian border to Kharkiv is only 40 kilometres.

Having failed to establish control over Kharkiv and the Kharkiv Oblast through indirect means in 2014, the Russian military-political leadership attempted to do so by force in 2022. At the same time, captive to its own ideological myths, the Russian leadership believed that the majority of Kharkiv's population supported the ideas of the so-called 'Russian world' and would therefore welcome Russian troops.[1] The Armed Forces of Ukraine were regarded as having low combat effectiveness, being poorly organised and inadequately equipped.

The Kharkiv Defensive Operation, conducted by the Armed Forces of Ukraine with the active involvement of other components of the Defence Forces, lasted two and a half months – from the first day of Russia's full-scale invasion (24 February) until 14 May 2022. In presenting this operation, we employ the periodisation developed by the Centre for Military History Studies of the Armed Forces of Ukraine.[2] Its experts distinguish three stages of the operation: 1) thwarting of Russian plans to capture Kharkiv (24 February – 3 March 2022); 2) stabilisation of the line of combat engagement (4 March – 28 April 2022); 3) completion of the defence of Kharkiv (29 April – 14 May 2022).

Thwarting Russian plans to capture Kharkiv (24 February – 3 March 2022)

Prior to the launch of the full-scale invasion, the Russian command concentrated forces of the Western Military District – namely, the 1st Guards Tank Army, the 6th Combined Arms Army, and the 20th Combined Arms Army – along the Kharkiv, Okhtyrka, and Sumy axes (which, from the perspective of the Ukrainian command, constituted the Slobozhanska operational area).[3] In the Kharkiv direction, units of the 25th, 138th, and 200th Separate Motor Rifle Brigades (OMSBr) and a number of other units were operating under the command of the 6th Army's headquarters.[4]

In the strategic military plan prepared by Russian officers before the start of the full-scale armed conflict with Ukraine, operations in the Kharkiv operational axis were considered secondary. In this regard, the troop grouping in this direction was not large, approximately the equivalent of nine battalion tactical groups. Its main task was to secure the left flank of the 1st Guards Tank Army, which was to attack Kyiv along the Sumy – Romny – Pryluky and Hlukhiv – Ichnia axis, as well as the right flank of the 20th Guards Army, which was to conduct offensive operations along the Vovchansk – Kupiansk axis in the direction of Izium. Thus, the Russian group in the Kharkiv direction was to act as a classic connecting link between the aforementioned armies, which were performing the primary tasks defined by the strategic military plan.

The composition of the aforementioned grouping included:

- the 200th Separate Motor Rifle Brigade – a brigade trained for operations in Arctic conditions and equipped accordingly – numbering approximately 3,500 personnel, organised into three battalion tactical groups (BTGs), equipped with T-80BVM tanks (41 vehicles on establishment) and MT-LB armoured personnel carriers;
- the 138th Separate Motor Rifle Brigade, numbering approximately 2,000 personnel, organised into two BTGs, equipped with T-72B3 tanks (41 vehicles on establishment) and MT-LB armoured personnel carriers;
- the 2nd Special Purpose Brigade of the Main Directorate of Intelligence (Spetsnaz GRU), numbering approximately 800 personnel, equipped with Tigr-M armoured vehicles and KamAZ armoured trucks configured as armoured personnel carriers.

These brigades were additionally reinforced by:

- a BTG of the 25th Separate Motor Rifle Brigade, a tank battalion (equipped with T-72B3 tanks) from the 59th Tank Regiment of the 144th Motor Rifle Division, and a combat group of the 33rd Rosgvardia Brigade[5] with a strength of about 500 personnel, which was subordinated to the 138th Brigade;
- self-propelled and rocket artillery *divizions* (battalion-sized units) of the 9th and 26th Artillery Brigades, assigned to the 200th Brigade.

In total, the Russian group in the Kharkiv direction numbered about 9,000 servicemen and had 120 tanks.[6]

In the first days of the war, the Kharkiv grouping was tasked with encircling Kharkiv from the west and north using the forces of the 200th Brigade, and from the east using the 138th Brigade with its attached units. After isolating Kharkiv along these axes, both Russian brigades were to conduct active offensive operations within the city in order to fix as many Ukrainian forces in combat as possible. Given the limited size of the grouping, the Russian command did not expect it to be capable of fully encircling Kharkiv from all directions, including the south. Nevertheless, the grouping was to seek to cut the Kyiv–Kharkiv and Kharkiv–Chuhuiv–Izium highways (both being sections of the M03/E40), which was intended to facilitate the offensive operations of the Russian 1st Tank Army and 20th Army. In summary, the task of the Russian grouping operating in the Kharkiv Oblast was to encircle and isolate the city of Kharkiv, with a subsequent advance toward the cities of Poltava and Dnipro. At the same time, the left flank of this grouping was to form the northern face of an encirclement ring around the Ukrainian Joint Forces grouping with access to the barrier line of the Dnipro River.[7] The pace of the offensive operation was to be very high – all of the above tasks were to be completed within the first week, and then the fighting was to move to the right bank of Ukraine.[8]

For the defence of Kharkiv and the Kharkiv Oblast, the Ukrainian command formed the Operational Group of Forces (OGF) 'Sloboda'. The exact date of its formation has not yet been established on the

Principal directions of the Russian invasion of Ukraine. (Map by bbh.illustrations)

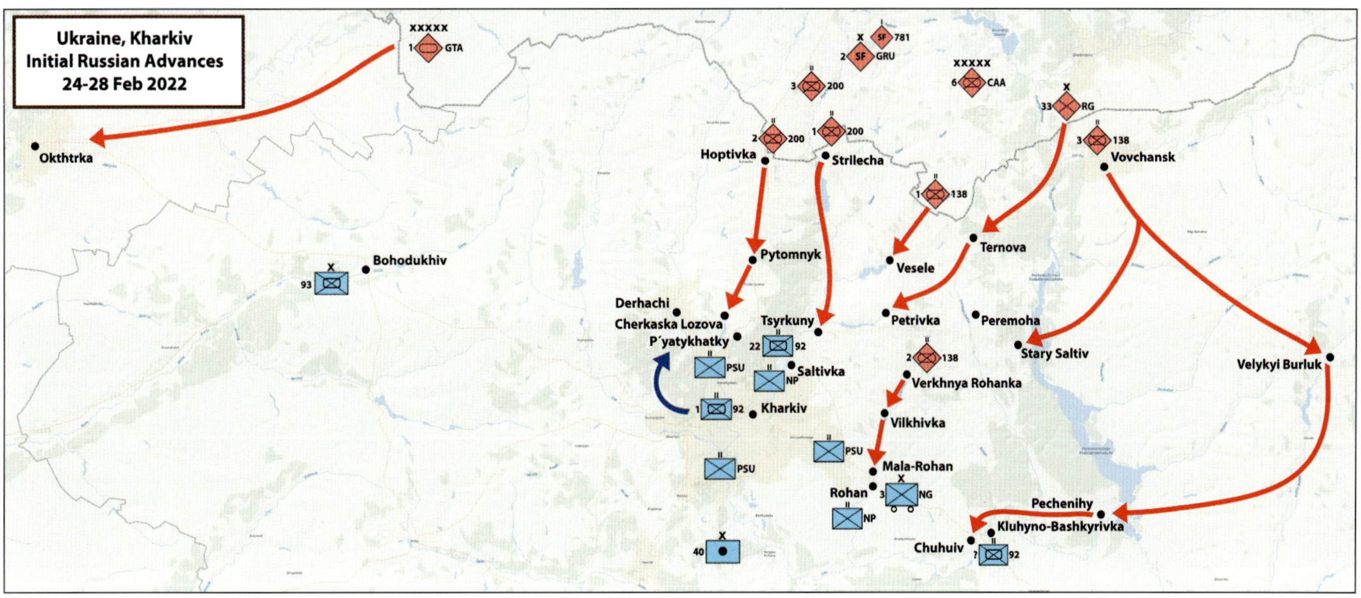

Armed Forces of Ukraine (ZSU) units and initial Russian advances into the northern Kharkiv Oblast, 24–28 February 2022. (Map by bbh.illustrations)

basis of open sources; however, the earliest reference to this OGF dates to 24 February 2022.[9] The OGF consisted of two separate mechanised brigades (92nd and 93rd OMBr), three territorial defence brigades (BrTrO), the 40th Artillery Brigade, the 27th Rocket Artillery Brigade, the 'Grim' tactical group and other units.[10] Parts of the National Guard of Ukraine (NGU) – the 3rd and 5th Brigades – were also located in Kharkiv.

The composition of these units was very uneven. The strongest brigade – the 92nd Mechanised Brigade – had about 4,000 servicemen and included a tank battalion (T-64BV), three mechanised battalions (mainly BTR-4) and a motorised infantry battalion.[11] In contrast, the 3rd Brigade of the National Guard underwent significant reductions in 2018–21 and numbered only about 800 fighters (most of whom were young conscripts). It had 11 T-64BV tanks, as well as armoured personnel carriers (BTR-3 and Varta). The territorial defence brigades were typical light infantry units, without any artillery or armoured vehicles, only with small arms and a minimal number of mortars.

Combat operations in the Kharkiv Oblast were organised by the enemy in the form of a combined air-ground offensive, in which the advance of the ground echelon was synchronised with aviation and missile strikes. The attack began at 04:50 on 24 February. Priority targets in the Kharkiv Oblast included the command post of the 302nd Anti-Aircraft Missile Regiment of the Air Force of Ukraine, the positions of its battalions, a radio-technical battalion in the village of Rohan', repair plants, as well as military educational institutions – the Ivan Kozhedub Kharkiv National Air Force University and the Kharkiv Institute of Tank Troops. Strikes were also carried out against residential districts of Kharkiv.[12] Other cities in the oblast were attacked as well. In particular, at dawn on 24 February, the airfield in the city of Chuhuiv was struck by missiles. The 203rd Training Aviation Brigade, subordinated to the Kharkiv National Air Force University, was stationed there. Most of its equipment – L-39C training aircraft, An-26 transport aircraft, and Mi-8 helicopters – was evacuated in time. However, five L-39C aircraft were destroyed or damaged at the airfield. In addition, as follows from materials of the Unified State Register of Court Decisions of Ukraine, after the missile strike at the Chuhuiv airfield two ground control stations and four Bayraktar TB2 unmanned aerial vehicles were destroyed – most likely to prevent their capture by the enemy.[13]

Covering the state border along the Kharkiv sector was the responsibility of the 4th Border Detachment of the State Border Guard Service of Ukraine, reinforced by units of the 92nd Separate Mechanised Brigade (permanent stationing point: the village of Kluhyno-Bashkyrivka, in the vicinity of Chuhuiv). The movement of 92nd Brigade units to their designated defensive areas began at 03:00 on 24 February, and the brigade's artillery took up firing positions. However, the length of the brigade's forward defensive line reached approximately 180 kilometres, making the establishment of a continuous positional defence under such conditions impossible. Together with units of the 4th Border Detachment, the 92nd Separate Mechanised Brigade conducted delaying actions, seeking to prevent the encirclement of its forces. In the course of this manoeuvre defence, ambushes were widely employed in order to inflict losses on the enemy.[14] The 93rd Mechanised Brigade was deployed on the left flank of the 92nd Brigade, approximately on the line Okhtyrka (Sumy Oblast) – Bohodukhiv (Kharkiv Oblast) – Kharkiv. Its main forces were located in the Okhtyrka area, with one battalion tactical group (on BMP-2 infantry fighting vehicles) operating in the Kharkiv Oblast.

The right wing of the 200th Separate Motor Rifle Brigade advanced into Ukrainian territory in two columns along the Hoptivka–Pytomnyk and Strilecha–Tsyrkuny axes. The vanguard of the 2nd Battalion Tactical Group advancing along the first axis engaged in a brief meeting engagement with elements of the reconnaissance company of the 92nd Separate Mechanised Brigade several kilometres south of Hoptivka on the E105 highway. As a result of the clash, a Tigr-M armoured vehicle of the 200th Motor

A BTR-4E from the last batch transferred to the 92nd Mechanised Brigade before the start of the full-scale Russian invasion. Anti-HEAT (high-explosive anti-tank) warhead grilles are installed only on the combat module. (TyskNIP)

Rifle Brigade was destroyed, while the 92nd Brigade lost a BTR-4 armoured personnel carrier. Subsequently, the column continued its movement that day without further contact with the enemy, and by midday its units had occupied the village of Pytomnyk. Ukrainian units deployed in the suburbs of Kharkiv, under pressure from Russian forces, withdrew toward the city's ring road, demolishing during their withdrawal the road bridge over the Lozovenka River in the settlement of Ruska Lozova.

At the same time, the 1st Battalion Tactical Group of the 200th Brigade, operating on its left wing, occupied the village of Tsyrkuny early in the morning without resistance. Exploiting the absence of a continuous defensive line by Ukrainian forces, Russian units reached the outskirts of Kharkiv already on the morning of 24 February. The village of Tsyrkuny, located on the north-eastern edge of the city, became a de facto forward base for subsequent assaults and shelling of Kharkiv. From 05:00 on 24 February, the city was subjected to artillery fire. In general, a defining feature of combat operations on the Kharkiv axis during the first days of the full-scale invasion was the extensive use by Russian forces of heavy artillery, including Smerch multiple launch rocket systems. On other axes, artillery employment was relatively limited, as Russian forces sought to seize cities and other key objectives rapidly through the actions of raiding groups.[15]

The regional capital was the key defensive point of Kharkiv Oblast and the principal objective of the Russian offensive on this axis. The aggressor's first attempt to seize the city on the move was repelled by the Ukrainian forces available at the time. However, there remained a real danger of increased pressure on Kharkiv through the commitment of second echelons and reserves. It was therefore necessary to reinforce the city's defences – and this reinforcement was provided by the 92nd Separate Mechanised Brigade. Conducting a manoeuvre defence, the brigade's units held back the enemy while gradually withdrawing toward Kharkiv

In the first days of Russia's full-scale invasion, the core of Kharkiv's defensive forces – alongside units of the 92nd Separate Mechanised Brigade and the National Guard of Ukraine – consisted of three officer battalions from the Ivan Kozhedub Kharkiv National Air Force University, reinforced by a small number of senior cadets. The defence of the city was led by Colonel Serhii Huzchenko, Head of the Department of Tactics and Combined Arms Disciplines at the university. In recognition of his merits, Colonel Huzchenko was awarded the title of Honorary Citizen of Kharkiv on 24 August 2022. On the same day, this title was also conferred on another leader of the defence of the Kharkiv Oblast – Major General Oleh Mikats, Commander of the Operational Command East of the Ground Forces of Ukraine.[16] Tasking of the battalion commanders of the Ivan Kozhedub Kharkiv National Air Force University was carried out at 02:00 on 24 February, with movement to assigned positions taking place in the morning. The engineering preparation of positions was conducted by the units themselves, after deployment.[17]

The first attack on the city began at approximately 08:30 on 24 February with a strike against Saltivka, a residential district in north-eastern Kharkiv. One of the battalions of the Ivan Kozhedub Kharkiv National Air Force University, commanded by Colonel Vitalii Kirpenko, was defending this sector, together with the 22nd Separate Motorised Infantry Battalion of the 92nd Separate Mechanised Brigade.[18] Two additional battalions belonging to the Kharkiv National Air Force University occupied positions along the Kharkiv Ring Road, on the eastern and south-eastern outskirts of the city. This attack was repelled, and the enemy retreated to the village of Tsyrkuny, losing a T-80BVM tank and three MT-LB armoured personnel carriers. A decisive role in repelling the attack was played by the support of the 22nd Separate Motorised Infantry Battalion – particularly its anti-tank guided missile (ATGM) teams – since the Kharkiv National Air Force University battalion was armed only with small arms. Soon, reinforcements arrived for the defenders of this section – three tanks from the Kharkiv Institute of Tank Troops. According to Colonel Ihor Budur, head of the philosophy department at the Kharkiv National Air Force University, who fought as an anti-tank grenadier, the Russians tried to attack again on 25 February. Both sides used tanks in the battle. This attack was also repelled, and the Russians lost up to half of their infantry company. The next day, the Russians used attack helicopters. The Kharkiv National University of Internal Affairs battalions had trained air defence specialists in their ranks, as one of the university's faculties trained such personnel for the Ground Forces. One of the Russian helicopters was shot down with a man-portable air-defence system (MANPADS) by Major Dmytro Rybalka.[19] A missile was launched at a second helicopter by a senior cadet, but missed. In these first battles, the city's defenders enriched their arsenal with trophies – for example, Colonel Kirpenko's battalion captured two ZU-23-2 anti-aircraft guns mounted on new KamAZ trucks. Their crews were manned by senior cadets and actively used the trophies in battle.[20]

Along with the officer battalions, the first to defend Kharkiv were the fighters of the National Guard of Ukraine, in particular, a unit of the 3rd Operational Brigade (BrOP), which took up positions in the area of the village of Rohan, on the south-eastern approaches to the city. It had to repel an enemy attack from Mala Rohan, north of its own positions. The advantage was that the fighters of the 3rd BrOP had BTR-4E armoured vehicles, whose cannon fire proved effective against enemy BMPs and cars. Lieutenant Yevhen Hromadskyi, who commanded one of the units in this direction, sent to assist the Kharkiv National Air Force University battalion, described the enemy's tactics as follows: 'Sabotage groups are probing our positions, and direct tank battles are taking place. First, they fire mortars, and then tanks shell our positions [...] We fire back with anti-tank guided missiles and conventional small arms. They abandon their tanks and scatter; there are always a lot of people'.[21] On 25 March 2022, Y. Hromadskyi was awarded the title of Hero of Ukraine for his defence of Kharkiv.[22]

The next point through which the Russians attempted to break through to Kharkiv on 24–25 February was Pyatykhatky, an area in the north of the city through which the Kharkivske Highway leads to the centre. According to the testimony of Andrii Platonov – at the time a senior staff officer of the rapid response unit of the 4th Border Detachment of the State Border Guard Service of Ukraine – the defence in this area was held by a mixed grouping formed from units of the 92nd Separate Mechanised Brigade, the National Guard of Ukraine, the National Police of Ukraine, border guards, and Territorial Defence Forces. In addition to a tank platoon of the 92nd Brigade, the defenders of Pyatykhatky had several BTR-4E armoured personnel carriers from the National Guard, 'Korsar' anti-tank guided missiles, and 82mm mortars at their disposal. Territorial Defence servicemen were dressed in civilian clothing, and some of them had no weapons other than hunting shotguns.[23] On the Russian side, the 3rd Battalion Tactical Group of the 200th Separate Motor Rifle Brigade was operating in this sector, advancing in the second echelon along the Hoptivka–Pytomnyk axis. In the afternoon of 24 February, it occupied without resistance a chain of low hills near the village of Bilashi, approximately three kilometres east of the city of Derhachi. Soon afterward, other elements of this battalion tactical group exploited this success, entered the village of Cherkaska Lozova, and crossed the Lozovenka River there. Late in the evening, the group's forward detachment bypassed Kharkiv via the ring road and occupied Pyatykhatky without a fight. In the following hours, additional elements of the brigade's 3rd BTG (including artillery) arrived in the settlement. Early in the morning of 25 February, following a counterattack by the 1st Battalion of the 92nd Brigade, Russian forces were pushed back to the right bank of the Lozovenka River. As a result of the engagement, Ukrainian forces destroyed a multiple launch rocket artillery battery – knocking out three BM-21 'Grad' launchers – and captured an R-149BMR command-and-staff vehicle.

The left flank of the 138th Separate Motor Rifle Brigade crossed the Ukrainian-Russian border early on the morning of 24 February in the Zelene–Ternova sector. Advancing along the Vesele–Petrivka and Ternova–Peremoha axes, its columns reached the Staryi Saltiv–Kharkiv road, occupying without resistance the villages of Fedorivka, Shestakove, and Kutuzivka located along it. In the afternoon of the same day, the 2nd Battalion Tactical Group, encountering no enemy resistance, began an envelopment manoeuvre of Kharkiv from the east, advancing along the Verkhnia Rohan'ka–Vilkhivka–Mala Rohan' axis. In all of these villages, taken without a fight that day, Russian forces deployed units of the 138th Brigade and began establishing strongpoints, thereby forming a thin cordon isolating Kharkiv from the east. In the evening, the brigade's forward detachment reached the settlement of Rohan', thus cutting the M03/E40 Kharkiv–Chuhuiv–Izium highway. During the advance to this last objective, Russian forces abandoned a disabled Tunguska air defence system, which was subsequently captured by Ukrainian forces.

Over the following two days, the tempo of Russian operations in the Kharkiv area decreased noticeably. Russian forces focused primarily on consolidating their hold on occupied territory and bringing up rear-area services. Units of the second echelon – the 2nd Special Purpose Brigade and the 33rd Rosgvardia Brigade – were also introduced into the combat zone. Artillery shelling of Kharkiv commenced, concentrated on the city's peripheral districts. At the same time, these areas were subjected to intensive air strikes using Su-34 multirole aircraft. By the end of the day on 24 February, units of the 2nd Mechanised Battalion of the 92nd Separate Mechanised Brigade took up defensive positions along the northern edge of the Kharkiv Ring Road and to the east of the city. The 1st and 3rd Mechanised Battalions of the same brigade received orders to withdraw toward Nova Vodolaha (southwest of Kharkiv) for regrouping. However, at approximately 23:00, a new directive was received from the command of Operational Command East: the 1st and 3rd Mechanised Battalions were to establish a circular defence of Kharkiv by 05:00 on 25 February, in coordination with the 2nd Mechanised Battalion, along the northern and north-eastern outskirts of the city.[24] Thus, from the morning of 25 February, all major units of the 92nd Separate Mechanised Brigade were integrated into Kharkiv's system of circular defence. On 27 February, the first battery of the 40th Separate Artillery Brigade arrived in Kharkiv, significantly strengthening the city's defenders. The brigade was equipped with 152mm towed artillery systems, specifically the 2A36 'Hyacinth-B' and the 2A65 'Msta-B'.[25]

The specific features of how the defence was organised on the approaches to Kharkiv in the first days of the full-scale invasion can be illustrated by a combat episode described by the commander of

Two Russian Grad multiple launch rocket systems destroyed during the first attempt to break through to Kharkiv from the direction of Pyatykhatky. (Andriy Platonov)

the 2nd Mechanised Battalion of the 92nd Separate Mechanised Brigade.[26] On 25 February, the 6th Mechanised Company of the aforementioned battalion was holding a defensive line north-east of Kharkiv along the Staryi Saltiv–Shestakove–Kutuzivka highway. The length of this sector was approximately 25 kilometres. A battalion commander's reserve, which consisted of two tanks, was positioned in Kutuzivka, while two additional tanks were deployed farther west, at the entrance to Kharkiv. To replenish the fuel stocks of the combat vehicles of the 6th Company, the battalion commander dispatched a fuel tanker accompanied by the battalion deputy commander for logistics. On its return route, the tanker crew detected a vehicle column of the 33rd Rosgvardia Brigade, which had emerged from open fields onto the highway between Shestakove and Kutuzivka. The battalion commander committed his reserve (two tanks) to attack the column, while the 6th Mechanised Company struck the enemy from the rear. As a result, the column was destroyed, including one BTR-80 armoured personnel carrier, three Tigr-M armoured vehicles, 10 KamAZ trucks configured as police transport vehicles ('avtozak'), four Ural trucks in an armoured troop-carrier configuration ('Federal'), and seven other vehicles. In our view, several aspects of this episode merit particular attention. First, the absence of a continuous defensive line: a single company was physically incapable of controlling a 25-kilometre sector. Second, the underdevelopment of reconnaissance on both sides: the enemy column was discovered purely by chance by a logistics vehicle crew, while the adversary, for its part, failed to react in any way to the appearance of the fuel tanker, which passed the column unimpeded. Third, the employment by the enemy of a police formation rather than a combined-arms unit for an advance toward Kharkiv – a force lacking armoured vehicles and heavy weapons. This once again underscores the Russian military-political leadership's underestimation of the expected resistance of the Defence Forces of Ukraine and of Ukrainian society as a whole.

Russian forces also conducted limited, localised offensive actions, seeking to improve their positions and tighten the semi-encirclement around the city. Operating north-west of Kharkiv, the 200th Separate Motor Rifle Brigade occupied the village of Chaikivka without resistance on 25 February and then struck south toward Mala Danylivka, dislodging units of the 92nd Separate Mechanised Brigade and thereby cutting the Derhachi–Kharkiv road. During the night of 25–26 February, Ukrainian units briefly recaptured the settlement in a counterattack, but by late on 26 February it had again fallen under Russian control. On 26 February, a Russian tank detachment penetrated the Oleksiivka residential district (in the northern part of the city), but its tanks were quickly destroyed.[27] Russian sabotage groups, which had infiltrated the city before the start of the large-scale invasion, were active in the city itself. For example, on 26 February, one such group was neutralised while attempting to infiltrate a military unit. Among the group's equipment were specialised sniper weapons and a DJI Mavic drone.[28]

In many cases, the actions of Russian forces on the Kharkiv axis can hardly be described as well-planned. Perhaps the most striking example was the best-known raid carried out on 27 February. This was an attempt to break through to the centre of Kharkiv from the north-west by a detachment of the 2nd Special Purpose Brigade of the Main Directorate of Intelligence, specifically, the 2nd Company of the 781st Special Purpose Detachment.[29] It is possible that the group was reinforced by additional elements; its strength is estimated at approximately 150–170 personnel. The group included 12 Tigr-M light armoured vehicles and four KamAZ trucks in a special modification produced in small numbers exclusively for special purpose units. These were standard KamAZ-5350-379 trucks with a 6×6 wheel configuration, but fitted with a reinforced chassis capable of carrying an armoured cab with bullet-resistant windows and an armoured troop container (the so-called 'capsule') in the cargo bed. At the same time, the group was entirely devoid of tank or artillery support.

At dawn on 27 February, the Russian column advanced toward Kharkiv. After crossing the Lozovenka River in Chaikivka, the force turned onto the local Kyivska Street, using it to reach the vicinity of the Metro hypermarket located on the western edge of the Shevchenkivskyi District of Kharkiv. South of this point, the column crossed the Kharkiv Ring Road and proceeded into the city along Liudvika Svobody Avenue. Initially, Ukrainian resistance was minimal. Only after most of the column had passed through the intersection did Ukrainian BTR-4 armoured personnel carriers approach from the south and, following a brief engagement with the rear guard of the 2nd Brigade's company, re-establish control over this exit from the city. During this clash, Russian forces sustained their first losses: one Tigr-M armoured vehicle equipped with an AGS-30 automatic grenade launcher was destroyed.

Meanwhile, the main body of the Russian column was already moving toward Kharkiv's 338th microdistrict, a typical Soviet-era high-rise residential area built of prefabricated panel blocks. There, winding through narrow streets between apartment buildings and playgrounds, the Russian vehicles advanced without contact toward the Lisopark, a large forested area covering approximately 1,900 hectares. The park contained numerous pedestrian paths; in the first two decades of the twenty-first century, some of them were converted into bicycle lanes by widening and reinforcing them with gravel. It was precisely one such path that the Russians planned to use for further movement toward the centre of Kharkiv. At around 10:00 Kyiv time, the special forces vehicle column entered the park from the west. Its subsequent movement followed one of the bicycle paths that run across the entire Lisopark from west to east. After roughly 30 minutes of slow movement through the park, without encountering any Ukrainian forces, the column reached Kharkivske Highway near its intersection with Akademika Proskury Street.

Had the operation ended at this point, it would have been successful. However, the ease with which the column had advanced thus far prompted the Russian command to decide to push deeper into the centre of Kharkiv. To this end, the Russian company commander, Captain Aleksandr Zhykharev, detached a combat group from his company consisting of five Tigr-M vehicles and one armoured KamAZ truck (approximately 50 servicemen) and proceeded with it into the city. The remainder of his personnel stayed near the eastern edge of the Lisopark, continuing to hold a blocking position in this area along Kharkivske Highway.

Advancing deeper into the Kyivskyi District, which borders the Lisopark to the east, Zhykharev's group entered the city via Staroshyshkivska Street. The column then reached Saperna Street. Videos recorded that day by local residents show dismounted special forces personnel moving slowly and cautiously along the street, providing all-around security, with Tigr vehicles advancing immediately ahead of them. By contrast, the KamAZ truck, also empty, remained at the rear of the column. Soon, the entire group reached the area of the intersection with Shevchenka Street. There, contact with Ukrainian units finally occurred, and a firefight began. One disabled Tigr had to be abandoned on Saperna Street, as did the disabled KamAZ. The remaining four armoured vehicles and 27 servicemen reached School No. 134 on Shevchenka Street, near the centre of Kharkiv, where they barricaded themselves. The armoured vehicles, however, were subsequently captured by Ukrainian units.

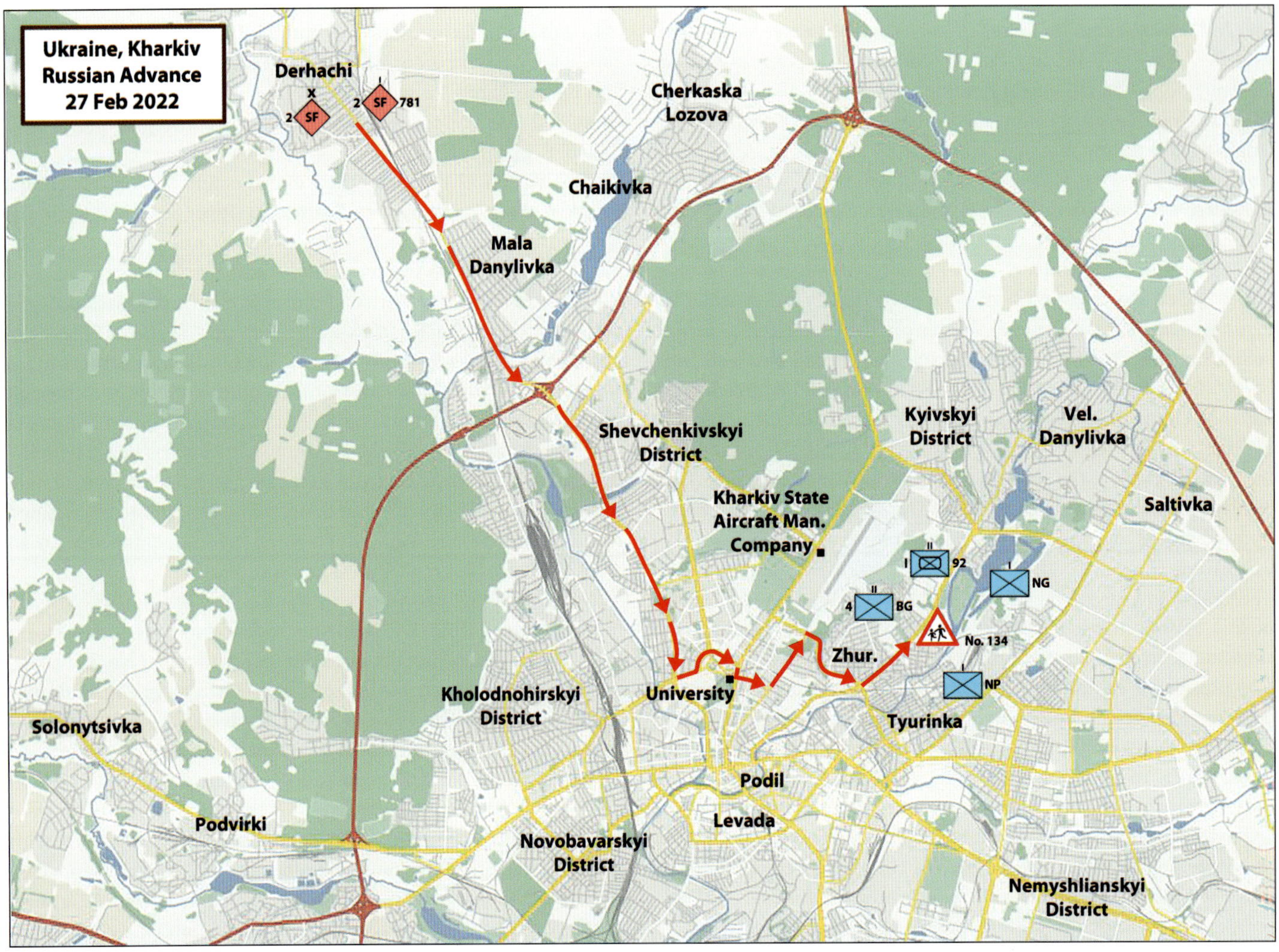

Route taken by a Russian reconnaissance and sabotage group during an attempt to break through to the centre of Kharkiv on 27 February 2022. (Map by bbh.illustrations)

By using the radios installed in the captured Tigr vehicles, Ukrainian servicemen were able to intercept the enemy's communications. Additional forces were brought up to School No. 134, including a BTR-4E armoured personnel carrier from the 92nd Separate Mechanised Brigade. However, the Russians managed to disable it with a grenade launcher. Overall, they acted in a highly professional and coordinated manner and rejected an offer to lay down their arms. Toward evening, a T-64BV tank from the tank battalion of the 92nd Brigade was deployed to the school. The battalion commander, Lieutenant Colonel Roman Zui, later recalled: 'After our losses, I stopped playing games with them. I had no desire to take them prisoner. They became simply the enemy – a target… When the Russians refused to surrender, I just opened fire on them with the tank.'[30]

On 27 February, Russian forces also attempted to break through to the centre of Kharkiv via Pyatykhatky, east of the location where the first group had previously penetrated the city. This attempted advance took place at around 10:00, as Andrii Platonov recalled:

> Strangely enough, mobile internet was working, and I was aware of the situation in the city, so I was worried that I might end up encircled – but this was avoided. The orcs [Russians] tried to move in after our tanks had pulled back to reload – at that point I had to act on my own [firing an anti-tank guided missile]. The officers of the 92nd Separate Mechanised Brigade drew the right conclusions from this, and later, whenever tanks were withdrawn for reloading, a BTR-4E was sent forward in their place, which restrained the orcs far more effectively than infantry squads armed with light anti-tank weapons could have done.[31]

The final act of this entire operation by the 2nd Special Purpose Brigade occurred late in the evening of 27 February on the eastern outskirts of the Lisopark, along Kharkivske Highway. As a result of a counterattack launched by units of the 92nd Separate Mechanised Brigade from the area of Kharkiv Airport, the remainder of the spetsnaz company holding a blocking position there was forced to withdraw toward Pyatykhatky. In the fighting, Russian forces lost two additional Tigr-M vehicles completely destroyed by fire, as well as an armoured KamAZ truck, which they abandoned. Ukrainian units thus restored control over the northern exit from Kharkiv and over the eastern entrances to the Lisopark from the side of Akademika Proskury Street.

The purpose of the Russian breakthrough remains unclear, as it would have been, at the very least, naïve to expect the capture of the city by such a small detachment. It may have constituted a form of reconnaissance in force. The Head of the Main Directorate of the National Police in Kharkiv Oblast, Volodymyr Tymoshko, offers the following interpretation:

> My personal view is that they were by no means idiots; they must have had some sort of coherent plan. I see only one explanation: most likely, their task was to enter one of the buildings in the so-called government quarter – the regional

Russian Tigr armoured vehicles destroyed near the entrances to School No. 134. In the background, a T-64BV tank of the Ukrainian 92nd Separate Mechanised Brigade can be seen, 27 February 2022. (armyinform.com.ua)

state administration, the Security Service, or the Main Directorate of the National Police – barricade themselves there, raise the tricolour, and thus create an image for everyone that the city had been captured.[32]

According to another version, this spetsnaz group served as the advance detachment of a larger formation composed of units of the 25th Separate Motor Rifle Brigade and Rosgvardia; however, its main forces were halted on the approaches to the city.

Units of the National Guard, the Territorial Defence Forces, the 92nd Separate Mechanised Brigade, the Security Service of Ukraine's 'Alpha' special forces unit, the KORD police special forces unit,[33] and the 'Freikorp' volunteer territorial community formation,[34] with a total of about 100 people, took part in this battle.[35] The list of these units alone clearly shows the specific nature of the defence organisation of both Kharkiv and Ukraine as a whole, which was carried out not only by the Armed Forces of Ukraine, but by a broad conglomerate – the Defence Forces of Ukraine.

Before continuing with the chronological account of events, it is worth dwelling a little more on the volunteer formations that participated in the defence of Kharkiv. The volunteer territorial community formation 'Freikorp' emerged as a right-wing military-patriotic organisation in May 2017. Its members participated in the ATO as volunteers. By 12 February 2022, 'Freikorp' had completed its preparations for possible combat operations, and with the start of the large-scale invasion, it became the first volunteer formation to support the Defence Forces of Ukraine in Kharkiv.

In an interview recorded in November 2022, the Chief of Staff of 'Freikorp', Bohdan Voitsehovskyi, characterised the formation's manpower and armament as follows:

> As for the number of fighters, I will reveal a secret: "Freikorp" is neither a battalion nor a company. It cannot be described, using standard categories, as either a battalion or a company. As for transport, we essentially perform the role of light infantry and remain a volunteer unit; that is, we did not become part of either the Armed Forces or the National Guard. Our fighters captured a significant amount of heavy equipment, but we exchanged it for other trophies with the Armed Forces of Ukraine. This was more practical, since maintaining heavy equipment is simply beyond our means [...] It is better for the Armed Forces to receive a 152-mm self-propelled artillery system, while for us a 120-mm mortar is more useful, because it is more practical for us to employ. We take all captured equipment and then try to exchange it for what is more useful and necessary for us. We employ the full range of infantry weapons.[36]

Another volunteer unit that played a significant role in the defence of Kharkiv and the Kharkiv Oblast was 'Kraken'. Its core was formed by former fighters of the 'Azov' Regiment, supported by officers of the Main Directorate of Intelligence of the Ministry of Defence of Ukraine. Preparations for future combat operations began approximately six months prior to the full-scale invasion. The

Soldiers of the Freikorp during the defence of Kharkiv. (057.ua)

'Kraken' unit operates under the command of the Main Directorate of Intelligence of the Ministry of Defence of Ukraine, carrying out special missions.[37] The commander of Kraken, with the callsign 'Vito', described the unit's role in the defence of the city as follows:

> We arrived in the city of Kharkiv on the orders of our commander. We organised resistance to this aggression. On 23 February, we were the first to issue weapons to our, let's say, partisans, and these people occupied a hemisphere around the city with units of the Armed Forces of Ukraine and were the first to take the brunt of the enemy's offensive.[38]

Another volunteer unit, 'Khartiia', was created in Kharkiv. It was organised by Vsevolod Kozhemyako, a businessman who ranked 88th on the Forbes Ukraine list in 2020. The 'Khartiia' volunteer battalion became part of the 127th Territorial Defence Brigade.[39] In March 2023, the 'Khartiia' unit was integrated into the National Guard of Ukraine and became the core of the 13th Operational Brigade of the National Guard of Ukraine 'Khartiia'.[40]

Not limiting themselves to attacks directly on Kharkiv, the Russians tried to surround the city. On 25 February, Chuhuiv, an important city located southeast of Kharkiv, was occupied. On 27 February, Russian troops occupied Kupiansk, the second largest (after Kharkiv) railway junction in the Kharkiv Oblast.[41] This was not prevented by the destruction of the railway bridge on the approaches to the city by Ukrainian troops on 24 February. Mayor Hennadiy Matsegora agreed to cooperate with the occupiers.[42] Unfortunately, this was not the only case of collaboration with the enemy among officials of such rank. In particular, Matsegora's example was followed by Ivan Stolbovyi, the mayor of Balakliia, which was occupied on 3 March.[43]

On the northern side of Kharkiv, Russian troops reached the town of Derhachi (12km from the Kharkiv Ring Road). Attempts to break through further to the south-west in order to cut off communications between Kharkiv and Poltava were blocked by units of the 93rd Separate Mechanised Brigade.

Attempts to seize Kharkiv on the move failed. The reason was obvious: the Russian military-political leadership underestimated the will of Ukrainians to resist aggression and, as a result, committed forces sufficient for a raiding or policing operation, but wholly inadequate for a full-scale assault on a major city. Instead, Russian artillery took up positions on the north-eastern outskirts of Kharkiv and began shelling the city in an effort to break the will of the Ukrainian population to resist. The North Saltivka district suffered the most: on 3 March alone, shelling set approximately 40 multi-storey residential buildings ablaze. As early as 26 February, the intensity of the bombardment in Kharkiv made it necessary to shut down gas supplies. Heavy civilian casualties also resulted from the shelling on 28 February of the airport area and adjacent residential neighbourhoods.[44]

By decision of Kharkiv Mayor Ihor Terekhov, the operation of the Kharkiv Metro was suspended, and its stations were used as shelters for civilians. Organised deliveries of medicines, water, and baby food were arranged there. From the first day of the invasion, evacuation trains began departing westward across the country.

A nine-storey residential building in Kharkiv, at 40a Buchmy Street, partially destroyed by Russian shelling on 26 February 2022. (State Emergency Service of Ukraine)

Metro stations in Kharkiv served as shelters for civilians. Seen here is Heroiv Praci station, (Saltivka), 24 February 2022. (Photo by Serhiy Petrov)

Also, from the first day of the war, the Kharkiv Regional Civil-Military Administration began operating in the city, headed by Oleh Syniehubov.

On 1 March, the city centre was hit by rocket fire. Two Kalibr cruise missiles hit Freedom Square and the Kharkiv Regional Military Administration building located there, killing 29 people.[45] On the same day, one of the city's hospitals was hit, and around midnight, strikes were recorded on the Kharkiv Institute of Tank Troops. At 00:55 on 2 March, the aggressor carried out an air strike against the barracks of the Ivan Kozhedub Kharkiv National Air Force University at 228 Klochkivska Street, causing a fire. Buildings of the nearby headquarters of the 4th Border Detachment of the State Border Guard Service of Ukraine were partially destroyed, and adjacent residential buildings sustained damage

Destroyed barracks of the Ivan Kozhedub Kharkiv National Air Force University. (Andriy Platonov)

For the first time since the Second World War, a European city with a population of over one million found itself on the front line. The enemy, despite all declarations about 'one people' and an alleged 'unity of Russians and Ukrainians', unleashed a campaign of terror against the civilian population of Kharkiv. Let us quote the impressions of a Kharkiv resident describing the first day of the Russian invasion:

> We were awakened not by explosions, but by a message from a colleague asking how we were supposed to work under these conditions. I immediately understood what had happened. And then a series of explosions followed, as confirmation. My husband had spent the night at my mother's place because she had developed serious health problems, so I called him. He already knew. I woke the children. Everyone turned to the media. The blasts were intense – we didn't yet understand how severe it really was. Friends who lived nearby called and advised us not to go outside; they said they had seen that the shelling was very close. My husband returned on foot sometime in the afternoon. Public transport wasn't running. That day it was too late to go to the military enlistment office because of the enormous queues. The next morning, he went there. He got in almost by a miracle – the line was many times longer than those at grocery stores. We didn't see each other again until October....[46]

The evacuation of the civilian population became an enormous challenge for the authorities. From the outset of the full-scale invasion, Ukrainian Railways (Ukrzaliznytsia) suspended regular passenger services; for a certain period, it operated exclusively in evacuation mode. Railway workers fully rose to this challenge. On 8 March 2022, the head of the Kharkiv Regional Civil-Military Administration, Oleh Syniehubov, noted: 'If we are talking about evacuation from Kharkiv, at this point more than 600,000 people have been transported by rail. As for road transport, both the Kyiv and Lviv directions remain overloaded'.[47]

Despite the campaign of terror directed against the civilian population, Russian forces failed to seize Kharkiv. Their units continued to sustain losses; for example, on 2 March, soldiers of the 93rd Separate Mechanised Brigade captured six T-80BVM tanks belonging to the 200th Separate Motor Rifle Brigade. As a result, by 3 March Russian forces in the vicinity of Kharkiv had transitioned to the defence. At that time, on the approaches to the city they fielded six battalion tactical groups drawn from the 6th Combined Arms Army and the coastal troops of the Northern Fleet.[48] In our view, the most fitting summary of the fighting for Kharkiv in the first days of the full-scale invasion is provided by the words of Colonel Pavlo Fedosenko, commander of the 92nd Separate Mechanised Brigade:

> They tried to enter Kharkiv on the first and second days of the full-scale invasion. But they were repelled by everyone. Because at that time, in our city of Kharkiv and in Kharkiv Oblast, everyone was fighting. Border guards were fighting, National Guard troops were fighting, the Armed Forces were fighting, the police were fighting, ordinary people were fighting – simply the residents of Kharkiv and the Kharkiv Oblast. That is why they failed to enter.[49]

Stabilisation of the line of combat (4 March – 28 April 2022)

In March 2022, the Defence Forces of Ukraine finally halted the Russian advance on Kharkiv. Russian troops began fortifying their positions on the northern and north-eastern outskirts of the city. Throughout March and April, they continued shelling Kharkiv. At the same time, they conducted combat operations aimed at bypassing Kharkiv from the southeast and advancing on the city of Izium. In March, additional units of naval infantry from the Baltic Fleet and the Northern Fleet were allocated to accomplish these tasks. An attempt by the vanguard of the 6th Combined Arms Army to bypass Kharkiv from the south, advancing from the Balakliia area, was blocked by the 25th Separate Airborne Brigade.[50]

One of the last attempts by Russian forces to break into Kharkiv was another raid carried out by the 2nd Special Purpose Brigade of the Main Directorate of Intelligence on 5 March 2022. It took place

Evacuation of civilians. Railway station in Kharkiv, 6 March 2022. (suspilne.media)

under a somewhat different operational situation for Russian troops in the Kharkiv area, at a moment when they were beginning to lose the initiative to the Ukrainian side. The raid formed part of a local offensive operation planned by the Russian command on the north-western outskirts of Kharkiv, aimed at seizing a key road junction on the ring road near Mala Danylivka. The main strike from the direction of this village was to be delivered by a battalion tactical group of the 200th Separate Motor Rifle Brigade. The company of the 2nd Special Purpose Brigade, meanwhile, was to move during the night of 4–5 March from the Pyatykhatky area (from the northern direction) into the rear of Ukrainian forces and block the possible approach of reserves. The raid plan was essentially a copy of the failed attempt of 27 February: a march along a bicycle path through the Lisopark, followed by the seizure of positions near the city centre. However, repeating the same manoeuvre with only a short interval in the very same area of operations proved to be a poor idea, something the Russian forces learned painfully that night. The company of the 2nd Brigade fell into an ambush by Ukrainian troops and, having lost three Tigr-M armoured vehicles and three KamAZ trucks, was forced to withdraw. Following this failure, the offensive operation of the 200th Separate Motor Rifle Brigade was cancelled. This marked the final attempt by Russian forces to regain the initiative and alter the course of the battle for Kharkiv.

Gradually, Ukrainian forces transitioned to counterattacks, initially on a limited scale. Of particular importance was the liberation of the city of Chuhuiv on 6 March by units of the 92nd Separate Mechanised Brigade. Chuhuiv was a key communications hub located on the M03/E40 highway (Kharkiv–Izium–Sloviansk). Russian forces defending this area suffered heavy losses; among those killed were the commanders of the 61st Separate Naval Infantry Brigade and the 31st Separate Air Assault Brigade.[51] Ukrainian forces also undertook efforts to push Russian positions away from the outskirts of Kharkiv. On 25 March, the village of Mala Rohan', located east of the city, was liberated. Two days later, Ukrainian troops liberated the village of Vilkhivka, situated further north. By the end of March, on the Kharkiv axis, two battalion tactical groups of the 200th Separate Motor Rifle Brigade, two battalion tactical groups of the 138th Separate Motor Rifle Brigade, and one battalion tactical group of the 59th Tank Regiment of the 144th Motor Rifle Division were defeated.[52] In the final days of March, units of the Armed Forces of Ukraine liberated the settlements of Husarivka, Nortsivka, and Zalyman. The large bridgehead thus created south of Balakliia enabled reconnaissance operations and later facilitated the liberation of the city itself, while also strengthening Ukrainian capabilities in the fighting for Izium, located further to the south. The Russians, however, continued to hold positions on the northern and north-eastern outskirts of Kharkiv.

Having realised the impracticality of capturing Kharkiv, the Russian command redirected its main effort toward the Izium axis. The seizure of the city of Izium would have created conditions for access to the operational rear of the Ukrainian grouping operating in Donbas, within the zone of the Joint Forces Operation. This axis also appeared promising to the Russian command because it lay along the junction of the combat dispositions of the Operational Group of Forces 'Sloboda' and the Ukrainian Joint Forces grouping.

An attempt to seize Izium on the move failed. Artillery shelling and aerial bombardment of the city began, and the fighting for Izium lasted nearly a month. Russian forces concentrated between 12 and 15 battalion tactical groups there, primarily from the 144th Motor Rifle Division, but also from the 47th Tank Division, the 106th Airborne Division, and the 61st Separate Naval Infantry Brigade. On the Ukrainian side, the city was defended by various units, including a battalion tactical group of the 81st Separate Airmobile Brigade, later reinforced by units of the 95th Separate Air Assault Brigade and the Territorial Defence Forces.[53] From mid-March, the northern part of the city was occupied, while the southern part was blockaded by Russian forces, creating serious obstacles to the delivery of humanitarian aid and the evacuation of civilians. Local supporters of the so-called 'Russian world' also became more

The 200th Separate Motor Rifle Brigade, equipped with specialised equipment for operations in the Arctic (including DT-10PM Vityaz transporters, one of which is visible here), suffered heavy losses in battles in the Kharkiv Oblast. (suspilne.media)

Fighters of the Kraken volunteer unit in liberated Vilkhivka against the backdrop of a captured MT-LB transporter. (x.com/kraken_ab3/)

active, conducting agitation even during the fighting for Izium. In a video address recorded on 25 March 2022, Izium's mayor, Valerii Marchenko, noted:

> They [the collaborators] go from bomb shelters to basements where people are hiding, telling them that Kyiv has fallen, Kharkiv has fallen, Izium has fallen, and that it is necessary to cooperate with the Russian occupiers. Under the pretext of humanitarian aid, they collect personal data of those who remained in the city. They pass on lists of civic activists and Territorial Defence members.[54]

As a result of their significant superiority in forces, after heavy fighting, the Russians were able to seize Izium on 1 April.[55] In the occupied city, a strict police regime was imposed, for the enforcement of which representatives of the so-called Donetsk People's Republic were brought in, performing the functions of local police.[56]

On approximately 2 April (the exact date has not been established), that is, already after the occupation of Izium, the dam of the Oskil Reservoir, an artificial body of water 85km in length and covering an area of 122km^2, located on the Oskil River, was destroyed. Responsibility for the explosion has not been definitively established. Initially, a version was put forward that the dam had been destroyed by Ukrainian forces in order to slow the enemy's advance downstream along the Oskil River and the Siverskyi Donets, into which the Oskil flows.[57] However, at that time, the dam was already under Russian control: Russian forces had reached it as early as 11 March, advancing from the direction of the village of Komarivka. Subsequent investigation demonstrated that the destruction of the dam was the work of the occupying forces and was carried out in several stages; at the beginning of March, at the end of March, and between the first and second 10-day periods of September 2022.[58]

In the immediate approaches to Kharkiv, Russian forces continued combat operations; however, their objective was no longer the seizure of the city but rather the fixation of Ukrainian forces in order to prevent their redeployment to other operational directions. Through uncontrolled sections of the state border, the adversary continued to move additional units into the territory of Kharkiv Oblast – via the settlements of Kozacha Lopan, Lyptsi, Velykyi Burluk, and Dvorichna. By early April, seven Russian battalion tactical groups were positioned in the vicinity of Kharkiv. Shelling by tube and rocket artillery continued. The areas affected included the districts and localities of Saltivka, North Saltivka, Kholodna Hora, Pyatykhatky, Derhachi, and Oleksiivka.[59]

Having seized Izium and regrouped its forces, the adversary resumed offensive operations on 9 April toward Barvinkove, advancing in a south-westerly direction along the administrative boundary between the Kharkiv and Donetsk oblasts. The enemy achieved limited success, capturing Brazhkivka (approximately 7km from Izium); however, an attempt to break through toward Sulyhivka (east of Brazhkivka) by the forces of a single battalion tactical group from a tank regiment failed.[60]

The blown-up dam of the Oskil Reservoir. (Artem Listopad)

Overall, combat operations in the Kharkiv Oblast in April 2022 were conducted by the adversary under the overarching objective of preparing for the battle for the Donbas. The Russian command planned to encircle the Joint Forces grouping by delivering two converging blows: in the north, along the boundary between the Kharkiv and Donetsk oblasts, and in the south, along the boundary between the Donetsk and Zaporizhzhia oblasts. As a result of the effective actions of the Defence Forces of Ukraine, Russian troops were forced to withdraw from the northern regions of Ukraine. After regrouping, these forces were redeployed to the Donbas. A Ukrainian operational situation report as of 06:30 on 11 April stated: 'The conduct of the enemy's offensive operation in the Eastern Operational Zone is planned for 12–19 April 2022'.[61]

In early April 2022, Russian forces operating within the Kharkiv Oblast were divided between two axes: the Kharkiv and Izium directions. According to information published on 14 April, on the Kharkiv axis, under the command of the 6th Combined Arms Army, the enemy deployed the 26th Tank Regiment of the 47th Tank Division, the 437th Training Tank-Motor Rifle Regiment, and one motor rifle battalion tactical group each from the 25th, 138th, and 200th Separate Motor Rifle Brigades. Altogether, these forces comprised approximately 4,100 personnel, 145 tanks, up to 70 infantry fighting vehicles, more than 120 MT-LB armoured personnel carriers, and over 100 artillery and multiple launch rocket systems. On the Izium axis, the headquarters of the 1st Tank Army, the 20th Combined Arms Army, and the 35th Combined Arms Army were engaged, exercising command over 10 regiments (five tank, three motor rifle, and two airborne) drawn from the 4th Tank Division; the 2nd, 3rd, and 144th Motor Rifle Divisions; the 98th and 106th Airborne Divisions; as well as one battalion tactical group of the 38th Separate Motor Rifle Brigade. This grouping numbered more than 18,200 personnel and fielded 570 tanks, up to 520 infantry fighting vehicles and 220 airborne combat vehicles, and approximately 100 artillery and multiple launch rocket systems.[62] The grouping formed on the Izium axis was the most powerful of all seven Russian force groupings operating along the front at that time. The adversary concentrated its strongest armoured fist there, along with a substantial number of armoured vehicles. In the forthcoming battle for the Donbas, the Izium grouping was tasked with the decisive mission: to strike southward and attempt to encircle the Donetsk grouping of the Armed Forces of Ukraine by linking up with the southwestern grouping of Russian occupation forces. The axis of this advance ran along the southern boundary of the Kharkiv Oblast and onward into the Donetsk Oblast. Across the remainder of Kharkiv Oblast, Russian forces were assigned no tasks other than blocking a potential counteroffensive by the Defence Forces of Ukraine. This was reflected in the composition of the Kharkiv-axis grouping, which was numerically limited and equipped with relatively small quantities of weapons and military equipment.

The relatively limited strength of Russian forces in the central and northern Kharkiv Oblast was expected by the adversary to be offset by the active employment of its air power, which had both quantitative and qualitative superiority over Ukrainian aviation. Kharkiv and its surrounding areas were subjected to systematic air strikes, with the most severe attacks occurring during the first two weeks of the full-scale invasion. Subsequently, the intensity of air raids decreased, owing in no small measure to the effective actions of Ukrainian air defence. One of the most widely known episodes was the shootdown on 6 March of a Su-34 bomber from the 47th Composite Aviation Regiment by a Buk-M1 surface-to-air missile system; the aircraft crashed into an urban area of Kharkiv. The pilot, Lieutenant Colonel Maksym Kryshtop, deputy commander of the regiment, was captured, while the navigator was killed.[63]

The Russian Air Force also suffered significant losses during the battles for Izium. On 13 and 15 March, two Su-30SM fighters from the 14th Fighter Aviation Regiment were shot down near this city.[64] In the first case, one of the crew members, Lieutenant Colonel Sergei Kosik, managed to eject and was taken prisoner,

Su-34 bomber (tail number RF-95070), shot down on 6 March 2022, which crashed into a civilian building. (militarnyi.com)

while in the second case, both crew members were killed. On 3 April, a Su-35S from the 159th Fighter Aviation Regiment was shot down by Ukrainian air defence forces near the village of Pisky-Radkivski (north-east of Izium).[65] Its pilot, Lieutenant Colonel Serhii Malov, was captured. On 2 May 2023, he – together with the aforementioned Maksym Kryshtop and Sergei Kosik – was exchanged for 45 fighters of the Azov Regiment who had been taken prisoner in May 2022 in Mariupol. On the Kharkiv axis, the confirmed loss of two additional Su-34 aircraft from the 47th Regiment was recorded; they were shot down on 21 and 25 April. The first was destroyed by air defence units of the 93rd Separate Mechanised Brigade near the village of Zavody (west of Izium), while the second was downed in the vicinity of Balakliia. In both cases, the crews survived. Overall, during the first two months of fighting in Kharkiv Oblast, Ukrainian air defence forces destroyed approximately 50 enemy aircraft, helicopters, and UAVs, although not all of these claims were fully confirmed.[66]

Another means used to deter Ukrainian counterattacks was the extensive employment of remote area-mining systems. Notably, it was in the Kharkiv Oblast that the occupying forces, for the first time since the outset of the full-scale invasion of Ukraine, employed the newly introduced Zemledelie remote mining system using POM-3 anti-personnel mines. The first confirmed appearance of such mines was recorded on 27 March.[67] These minefields not only impeded the manoeuvre of military units but also posed a serious threat to the civilian population.

Su-35S fighter jet (tail number RF-81752), shot down on 3 April 2022. (General Staff of the Armed Forces of Ukraine)

One of the Russian POM-3 anti-personnel mines found in the spring of 2022 in the Kharkiv Oblast. (armamentresearch.com)

While relative calm prevailed in the outskirts of Kharkiv and in the northern part of the region, combat operations related to the battle for the Donbas unfolded in the south. A detailed account of that battle lies beyond the scope of this study; nevertheless, several episodes directly connected to the Kharkiv Oblast merit attention. The Russian offensive began on 18 April with simultaneous attacks along multiple axes. In the Izium area, on 18 April, the enemy conducted a reconnaissance in force along the line Dmytrivka–Brazhkivka–Sulyhivka–Dibrivne. On 19 April, the presence of three battalion tactical groups from the 51st and 137th Airborne Regiments of the 106th Airborne Division, as well as the 331st Airborne Regiment of the 98th Airborne Division, was recorded in this sector.[68] Over the following week, Russian forces continued offensive operations along the Izium–Barvinkove axis, concentrating up to 10 battalion tactical groups south of Izium: three tank, five motor rifle, and two airborne. In order to reduce flight time and extend the effective combat radius of army aviation, the occupying forces established a helicopter landing site approximately 6km southeast of Izium.[69] Ukrainian forces sought to slow the enemy's advance, inflicting losses in numerous combat engagements. For example, on 25 April, Ukrainian sources reported the repulse of a Russian attack on the village of Zavody in Izium District, an advanced frontline position under Ukrainian control, during which an enemy BMP-2 infantry fighting vehicle was destroyed.[70] In general, this settlement, located on the right bank of the Siverskyi Donets River, west of Izium, was a constant hotbed of fierce fighting; the enemy tried to attack Zavody on 22 April, but was equally unsuccessful.[71]

The second phase of the Kharkiv Defensive Operation was thus marked by a shift of the main area of combat operations toward the southern part of the region. This, in turn, created favourable conditions for the subsequent Ukrainian counteroffensive in the vicinity of Kharkiv, which constituted the third and final phase of the Kharkiv Defensive Operation.

Completion of the defence of Kharkiv (29 April – 14 May 2022)

By late April 2022, 22 of the 56 territorial communities of Kharkiv Oblast – that is, approximately 40 percent – remained under Russian occupation. The occupying forces imposed a harsh regime, resorting to repression and intimidation of the local population. Personnel of the Federal Security Service of Russia and the Rosgvardia conducted so-called 'filtration measures' in settlements temporarily beyond the control of the Ukrainian authorities. The most frequent victims of these actions were men of conscription age, veterans of the Anti-Terrorist Operation/Joint Forces Operation (ATO/JFO), former servicemen and law enforcement officers, and pro-Ukrainian activists. Civilian vehicles and hunting firearms were confiscated. The enemy sought to coerce representatives of local authorities into cooperation and participation in occupation administrations; in some cases, this effort met with success. Detachments intended to uphold the 'new order' began to form, drawing on former law enforcement personnel disaffected with the Ukrainian authorities as well as criminal elements.[72] Under these circumstances, the earliest possible liberation of the occupied territories was highly desirable. Even aside from strategic considerations, such a development would have had a positive effect on the population of the areas that remained under occupation, offering hope for liberation. At the turn of April–May 2022, the most favourable conditions for a localised counteroffensive emerged in the Kharkiv Oblast. This counteroffensive, conducted under the command of Colonel General Oleksandr Syrskyi, Commander of the Ground Forces of the Armed Forces of Ukraine, was a logical consequence of the successful defence of Kharkiv.

The primary objective of the counteroffensive was to relieve the city and push enemy forces back toward the Russian-Ukrainian border to the north and north-east of Kharkiv; a secondary objective was to threaten the supply lines of the enemy grouping near Izium, thereby preventing a Russian advance on Kramatorsk and Sloviansk.

The counteroffensive was conducted by the forces of Operational Grouping 'Sloboda', including the 92nd and 93rd Separate Mechanised Brigades, the 4th Separate Tank Brigade, the 81st Separate Airmobile Brigade, separate artillery and rocket artillery brigades, the 113th and 127th Territorial Defence Brigades, the 3rd Operational Brigade of the National Guard of Ukraine, units of the State Border Guard Service of Ukraine, and other formations. Opposing them on the Russian side were units from two combined arms armies – the 6th Army of the Western Military District and the 41st Army of the Central Military District – as well as coastal troops of the Northern and Baltic Fleets, including in particular the 25th, 27th, 138th, and 200th Separate Motor Rifle Brigades and the 61st Separate Naval Infantry Brigade.[73] By late April, only five battalion tactical groups were deployed directly in the vicinity of Kharkiv.[74] Given that the length of the front there was approximately 100km, each battalion tactical group was responsible for roughly 20km of frontage. By comparison, on the Izium axis at the same time, 22 Russian battalion tactical groups were deployed along a 60km front.[75] Thus, the Ukrainian command's choice of the Kharkiv direction for a counterattack was entirely justified.

During the counteroffensive, Ukrainian forces delivered several successive strikes. Between 28 and 30 April, units of the 92nd Separate Mechanised Brigade and the 127th Territorial Defence Brigade, in the course of a rapid offensive, pushed the enemy back some 40km eastward from the north-eastern outskirts of Kharkiv. On 2 May, the urban-type settlement of Staryi Saltiv, located on the right (eastern) bank of the Pechenihy Reservoir (on the Siverskyi Donets River), was liberated, along with the villages of Kutuzivka, Verkhniia Rohanka, and Slobidske situated between it and Kharkiv. By 6 May, most of the villages along the T2104 road – Shestakove, Fedorivka, Oleksandrivka, Peremoha, and Molodova – had been liberated.[76]

On 29–30 April, units of the 93rd Separate Mechanised Brigade, advancing northward from the town of Derhachi along the T2117 road, drove the occupiers out of the urban-type settlements of Slatyne

A school in Staryi Saltiv was used to house Russian military personnel during the occupation. (commongoal.org.ua)

and Prudianka. The Russians began constructing field fortifications on the outskirts of the settlement of Kozacha Lopan, located approximately 2km from the Russian-Ukrainian border. In May, active combat operations on the northern axis were largely absent. Only on 18 May did Ukrainian forces dislodge the enemy from the village of Dementiivka, situated east of Prudianka.[77]

On 29 April, the 113th Territorial Defence Brigade, in cooperation with the 3rd Operational Brigade of the National Guard of Ukraine, liberated the village of Ruska Lozova, located north of Kharkiv along the E105 highway (running parallel to the T2117). In the course of fierce fighting, these brigades expelled the occupiers from the village of Tsyrkuny by 7 May. In an attempt to slow the Ukrainian counteroffensive, the enemy demolished three road bridges in the areas of Tsyrkuny and Ruski Tyshky.[78] This, however, proved ineffective: on 10 May, a General Staff of the Armed Forces of Ukraine situation report stated that the villages of Ruski Tyshky and Cherkaski Tyshky, located north of Tsyrkuny, had been liberated. At the same time, it was reported that the Russian command had redeployed up to 500 personnel mobilised in the occupied areas of Donetsk and Luhansk oblasts to the territory of the Kharkiv Oblast.[79] This marked one of the first instances of personnel mobilised in the so-called Luhansk People's Republic (LPR) and Donetsk People's Republic (DPR) being committed to the Kharkiv axis. It should be recalled that at that time these quasi-state entities had not yet been formally incorporated into the Russian Federation.[80]

On 5 May, Russian forces attempted to regain lost positions by launching counterattacks in the Staryi Saltiv area. These attacks, however, were repelled by units of the 92nd Separate Mechanised Brigade. As a result of the losses sustained, the 138th Separate Motor Rifle Brigade was withdrawn for reconstitution to Belgorod. Meanwhile, Ukrainian forces continued advancing northward along the Siverskyi Donets. By 10 May, primarily through the efforts of units of the 127th Territorial Defence Brigade, the villages and settlements of Bairak, Zamulivka, Verkhnii Saltiv, and Rubizhne were liberated.[81] During the fighting east of Kharkiv, two Russian Mi-28N attack helicopters from the 549th Separate Helicopter Regiment were shot down on 6 and 12 May; respectively in the area of the village of Bobrivka, on the north-eastern outskirts of Kharkiv, and near the village of Elitne, located slightly farther south. In addition, on 19 May, air defence units of the 92nd Separate Mechanised Brigade shot down a Ka-52 helicopter near Lyptsi, north-east of Kharkiv.[82]

As a result of the counterblow delivered by the Defence Forces of Ukraine on this axis, the occupation troops were compelled to withdraw to the left (eastern) bank of the Siverskyi Donets. Russian forces were thus steadily pushed back from Kharkiv. Moreover, the town of Vovchansk, an important logistical hub for the Russian grouping operating on the Izium axis, fell within the effective range of Ukrainian artillery, including rocket artillery.

In order to prevent Ukrainian forces from crossing the Siverskyi Donets, Russian troops demolished bridges in the areas of Rubizhne and Staryi Saltiv. It should be emphasised that the Ukrainian counteroffensive was by no means easy. Units of Operational Grouping 'Sloboda' remained under constant Russian fire, and for a considerable time it proved impossible to push the enemy away from the northern outskirts of Kharkiv. Russian shelling of the city continued. This, however, in no way diminishes the significance of the Ukrainian counteroffensive.

The importance of the events unfolding in the Kharkiv Oblast in the first half of May was also noted by foreign experts. In its report of 13 May, analysts from the Institute for the Study of War stated:

> Russian forces have likely decided to fully withdraw from their positions around the city of Kharkiv due to Ukrainian counteroffensives and the limited availability of reinforcements [...] Ukraine has thus won the Battle of Kharkiv. Ukrainian forces prevented Russian troops from encircling Kharkiv, let alone capturing it, and then pushed them away from the city, as they had previously done to Russian forces attempting to seize Kyiv.[83]

Assessing the scale of the Ukrainian counteroffensive on the Kharkiv axis, one may conclude that it was local in nature and confined to the area north-east of Kharkiv. Its significance, however, extended far beyond the region, influencing the situation across the entire Eastern Operational Zone. The successful Ukrainian counterblow forced the Russian command to choose between repelling the Ukrainian advance and reinforcing its troop groupings to continue the offensive toward Sloviansk–Kramatorsk and Sievierodonetsk–Lysychansk. The Russian command opted to reinforce its forces on the Kharkiv axis, redeploying units of the Western Military District that had previously been withdrawn from Kyiv and Chernihiv regions. At the same time, 19 battalion tactical groups were tasked with guarding the Russian border in the Belgorod Region. In addition, part of the forces had to be redeployed to prevent Ukrainian units from advancing into the rear of the Russian grouping in the Izium area. The Russians began establishing a new defensive line on the left bank of the Siverskyi Donets and reinforced the defence of Kupiansk to a strength of four battalion tactical groups, which was deemed necessary to prevent the severing of supply routes from Belgorod and Valuyki.[84]

Soldiers of the 227th Battalion of the 127th Separate Territorial Defence Brigade on the border between Ukraine and Russia near the village of Ternova, 15 May 2022. (Ministry of Defence of Ukraine)

The regrouping of Russian forces did not prevent units of the Defence Forces of Ukraine from reaching the state border of Ukraine. The first to do so was the 227th Battalion of the 127th Territorial Defence Brigade, which reached the border on 15 May near the village of Ternova.[85] This created favourable conditions for a subsequent advance toward Vovchansk. Units of the 92nd Separate Mechanised Brigade succeeded in forcing the Siverskyi Donets in the Staryi Saltiv area and establishing a bridgehead on its left (eastern) bank, between the villages of Buhaiivka and Khotimlia. These actions threatened Russian supply lines in the eastern part of the Kharkiv Oblast.

The Kharkiv counteroffensive brought to an end an 80-day siege lasting from 24 February to 14 May 2022. Strictly speaking, this was not a siege in the classical sense of the term: Russian forces never managed to fully encircle Kharkiv or cut its lines of communication. The Russian command had anticipated a rapid seizure of the city by raiding groups, but the course of events demonstrated that Ukrainian forces and the will to resist had been gravely underestimated. Once it became clear that Kharkiv could not be taken quickly, the Russians simply lacked the forces to implement a Plan B, that is, a full blockade of the city. They failed not only to sever supply routes but even to pose a serious, sustained threat to them.

It is telling that publications in Russian military periodicals written in the wake of the first months of the full-scale invasion openly acknowledge the fallacy of expectations regarding broad support for the occupying forces among the population of eastern and southern Ukraine. One such article states:

> Given the rapid decision to conduct the SVO [as is well known, the Russians euphemistically refer to the full-scale invasion of Ukraine as a "special military operation" (Spetsyalnaia Vojennaia Opieratsia, SVO)—A. Kharuk], measures of military-political propaganda and agitation aimed at transitioning personnel from a peacetime to a wartime footing were not carried out […] the available assessments of the military-political situation in Ukraine did not fully correspond to reality. Local residents of Russian-speaking regions, instead of flowers and ceremonial bread as we expected, met the rear columns of our troops with civic resistance […] information regarding the moral and psychological state of the personnel of the Armed Forces of Ukraine proved to be inaccurate. Expectations of their unpreparedness for armed resistance and of mass surrender did not materialise.[86]

This admission confirms that the planning of the invasion of Ukraine was driven by ideological – indeed, even mythological – assumptions that often bore little relation to reality. Particularly illustrative in assessing the readiness of the city's residents and the oblast as a whole to resist Russian aggression is the assessment offered by a commander of the 'Kraken', callsign 'Vito': '… what surprised me in Kharkiv was that the moral and psychological state of the people, both the civilian population and those who took up arms, was generally better than had been suggested. Kharkiv is truly a Ukrainian city'.[87]

The breaking of the siege of Kharkiv by the Defence Forces of Ukraine had far-reaching consequences. In addition to the liberation of more than 20 settlements and the pushing back of the enemy by several dozen kilometres, it created a serious threat to the supply routes of the Russian grouping on the Izium axis. As a result, the Russian command failed to realise its intention to encircle and defeat Ukrainian forces in the Donbas. In the medium term, the counteroffensive near Kharkiv created favourable conditions for the successful offensive operation conducted in September 2022 to liberate the eastern districts of the Kharkiv Oblast.

It should be emphasised that the success of the Kharkiv counteroffensive in April–May 2022 was achieved without a significant share of Western-origin heavy weaponry; Western artillery and rocket systems had not yet reached frontline units. Nevertheless, from the first day of the war, Western infantry weapons were employed with great effectiveness: Javelin anti-tank guided missiles, NLAW and Carl Gustaf launchers, and MANPADS such as Stinger and Piorun, among others.[88]

Territorial Defence soldiers in Kharkiv Oblast learn how to use Western weapons. Seen here is a Carl Gustaf grenade launcher. (militarnyi.com)

The defence of Kharkiv became one of the most important components of the first strategic defensive operation conducted by the Defence Forces of Ukraine. Its successful execution not only prevented the enemy from capturing the city of Kharkiv, but also halted the further advance of Russian troops deep into Ukrainian territory and thwarted the encirclement of the Joint Forces grouping in the Donbas. At the same time, it created the necessary preconditions for the conduct of the Slobozhanska Offensive Operation in September 2022.

3
COMBAT OPERATIONS IN THE KHARKIV OBLAST IN THE SECOND HALF OF MAY – AUGUST 2022

Throughout May and the entire summer of 2022, the Defence Forces of Ukraine conducted the second strategic defensive operation. The aggressor's main efforts were concentrated in the Eastern Operational Zone, where attempts to isolate the Joint Forces grouping continued, particularly by seeking to penetrate into its rear along the Kupiansk–Balakliia–Izium–Sloviansk–Kramatorsk line. Accordingly, the principal area of combat operations in the Kharkiv Oblast remained the southern part of the area. For their part, the Defence Forces of Ukraine assigned primary importance to maintaining a resilient defence along the Balakliia–Izium–Kreminna (Luhansk Oblast) line and further south. To the north, the defence of Kharkiv was maintained, alongside limited counteroffensive actions aimed at improving the operational situation; this phase of the Kharkiv defensive operation having been discussed in the preceding chapter.

Occupation, Collaboration and Resistance

In late spring and throughout the summer of 2022, the Russians undertook active measures to establish an occupation administration system in the Kharkiv Oblast. The seat of this administration was located in Kupiansk. The occupiers appointed Vitalii Hanchev as head of the so-called temporary administration, a former deputy head of the Derhachi District Department of Internal Affairs. In 2014, he betrayed his oath of allegiance to the people of Ukraine and fled to the terrorists in the temporarily occupied territory of the Luhansk Oblast, where he served in the 'police' of the so-called Luhansk People's Republic. In the spring of 2022, Hanchev repeatedly appeared on Russian propaganda programmes about life in Kozacha Lopan and Lyptsi, where he was presented as the 'head of the temporary administrations of the liberated territories of Kharkiv Oblast'.[1] In June 2022, he was appointed head of the so-called 'military-civil administration of Kharkiv Oblast'. Hanchev's deputy was Volodymyr Demchenko, whose biography closely mirrors his own: a former Ukrainian police officer, a pro-Russian activist in the spring of 2014, and one of those who attempted to establish the 'Kharkiv People's Republic'. He was detained, but as a result of a prisoner exchange ended up in occupied Donetsk, where he became deputy head for armaments of the 'people's militia of the Donetsk People's Republic'.[2]

In late April 2022, the occupiers appointed Vladyslav Sokolov as head of the occupation administration of Izium; also a former police officer and, subsequently, head of security at a commercial bank.[3] However, there were insufficient collaborators to fill all posts, and the occupiers were compelled to 'import' administrators for certain positions. Thus, in Balakliia, after the lawfully elected head of the city council, Ivan Stolbovyi, left for Russia, no local residents were willing to cooperate with the occupiers. As a result, a Russian citizen, Yurii Shevchenko, was appointed head of the city's occupation administration. In the neighbouring settlement of Borova, this post was filled by a Belarusian citizen, Andrei Semashko (a former deputy head of the Baranavichy city executive committee).[4]

It should be emphasised that the activities of all local occupation administrators, whether collaborators or 'imported' appointees, were conducted under the close supervision of Russian military commandants. A Russian national was also appointed to the key resource-distribution post of 'chairman of the council of ministers and deputy head of the military-civil administration of Kharkiv Oblast'. On 19 August 2022, this position was assumed by Andrei Alekseenko. From October 2021 he had served as mayor of Krasnodar, but in December of the same year he was detained on charges of accepting a bribe on a particularly large scale. The case was ultimately shelved, and Alekseenko was dispatched to 'restore order' in the occupied territories.[5] It is noteworthy that Alekseenko remained alone in the 'government of the Kharkiv Oblast', the other 'ministers' were simply not appointed in time due to the start of the Ukrainian offensive in September 2022.

The Russian authorities sought to establish control over the occupied territories as rapidly and as efficiently as possible. During the occupation, which in some districts of the Kharkiv Oblast lasted for up to six months, the occupiers organised the removal of agricultural produce to the territory of the Russian Federation, as well as to the temporarily occupied Luhansk and Donetsk oblasts. In this context, Vitalii Hanchev claimed: 'Our task was simply to help people sell their grain. The Russian government assisted us very quickly. Kharkiv grain immediately entered the market'.[6] In advancing this narrative, Hanchev omitted the fact that the agricultural produce was, in reality, expropriated from grain storage facilities. For this purpose, a so-called 'State Enterprise "Food Resources"' was established in the temporarily occupied part of Kharkiv Oblast and subordinated to structures under Hanchev's control. This enterprise was created on the basis of the Kupiansk Bread Factory company, whose owners refused to cooperate with the occupying authorities. One of the company's employees was forcibly appointed as director, after which the enterprise began exporting agricultural products to the Russian Federation.[7]

During the period of occupation, Russian authorities managed to organise the removal of agricultural produce to Russia, as well as to the temporarily occupied areas of Luhansk and Donetsk oblasts. Schools issued Russian-style certificates, Ukrainian curricula were replaced with Russian ones, and libraries were supplied with Russian books in place of confiscated Ukrainian titles. A Russian mobile network operator began operating in the occupied areas, and in a number of towns, most notably Kupiansk and Vovchansk, centres were opened for obtaining Russian passports.[8]

The overwhelming majority of the population in the occupied districts of the Kharkiv Oblast, however, did not accept the occupation. Some residents engaged in passive or active resistance, to which the Russians responded with terror. On 1 March 2022, about a thousand residents of Kupiansk took part in a peaceful rally against the Russian army, which had already seized the city. The protest was organised by the city council deputy and Anti-Terrorist Operation veteran Mykola Maslii. That same day he was abducted, and his whereabouts remain unknown. His relatives and human rights defenders have been trying to establish his fate and have filed a case against Russia with the European Court of Human Rights.[9] A similar fate befell the blogger Serhii Stroiev. After the start of the Russian occupation in the settlement of Kivsharivka near Kupiansk, he participated in the civic

Rally in occupied Kupiansk, 1 March 2022. (suspilne.media)

'Anti-Marauder' initiative (its members, taking shifts day and night, guarded abandoned homes against looting). On 1 March Stroiev was filming the rally in Kupiansk, and on 28 April FSB officers seized him near his home and took him away, telling his mother that he had been taken 'to Belgorod for re-education'. Nothing has been heard of Stroiev since; he is considered missing.[10]

These and many other examples of terror by the occupiers did not break the will of Ukrainians to resist. Despite the constant threat of repression, in most settlements there were activists who, risking their lives, found ways to pass crucial information about the enemy to the Armed Forces of Ukraine and security services, carried out acts of sabotage by damaging enemy equipment, and engaged in other forms of resistance. Indeed, the issue of the resistance movement in the occupied territories is so complex and significant that, in our view, it deserves a separate, dedicated study. For illustrative purposes, we will cite just one example. Residents of the village of Pisky-Radkivski in Izium District, Olena and Viacheslav Kuzmenko, using hidden mobile phones, established contact with the Armed Forces of Ukraine and transmitted information about the coordinates of enemy targets. Viacheslav also carried out acts of sabotage, like stuffing cotton wool into the fuel tanks of Russian vehicles. Although their activities were not exposed by the occupiers, Viacheslav was brutally beaten for his pro-Ukrainian views, which he did not conceal. As a result of the injuries he sustained, he died on 24 December 2022.[11]

An important element of resistance to the occupation was the partisan movement. However, information about this movement in the Kharkiv Oblast is much more limited than in southern Ukraine. Reports mentioned the activity of partisans in temporarily occupied Kupiansk, where they distributed leaflets with patriotic slogans such as: 'Kupiansk, hold on – the Armed Forces of Ukraine will come soon!', 'The occupiers will be punished! Nothing is forgotten, nothing is forgiven!', and 'Death to traitors, death to occupiers – Kupiansk is Ukraine!'.

The most coherent and systematic information about the partisan movement concerns the city of Derhachi, located north of Kharkiv. Its mayor, Viacheslav Zadorenko, already on 24 February, the first day of Russia's full-scale invasion of Ukraine, formed a partisan unit from local residents. It consisted of 15 volunteers, including former participants of the ATO. The unit carried out missions in areas of the Kharkiv Oblast occupied by Russian forces.

The partisans conducted reconnaissance in occupied settlements, disguising themselves as homeless people to avoid detection by Russian occupiers. Another task they performed was the evacuation of civilians from occupied territories. The Derhachi partisans were the first to enter the town of Kozacha Lopan on 11 September 2022 during the Slobozhanska offensive of the Armed Forces of Ukraine. In Kozacha Lopan, Russian forces had been holding the mother of the leader of the Derhachi partisan unit, Viacheslav Zadorenko, in captivity.[12]

Ukrainian reconnaissance and sabotage groups also operated in the occupied territories. Due to the specific nature of their work, the results of their activities largely remain classified. However, some actions, such as the elimination of collaborators, cannot be concealed. For example, on 10 July 2022 it was reported that Yevhenii Yunakov, the head of the occupation administration of the settlement of Velykyi Burluk (an important railway hub for the occupiers), was killed when his car was blown up. As might be expected, the occupiers failed to capture either the organisers or the perpetrators of the attack.[13]

Course of Hostilities

Thanks to the success of the Ukrainian counteroffensive near Kharkiv, the situation in the northern part of the Kharkiv Oblast was stabilised. The Russians lacked sufficient forces to counter the Ukrainian counterblow and, more broadly, to conduct any active operations on the Kharkiv axis. Their main focus was redirected to the Donbas. At the same time, the Ukrainian command clearly understood that the principal threat lay in enemy strikes within the area of the Joint Forces Operation. It was there that the reserves of the Defence Forces of Ukraine were redeployed. In the Slobozhanska operational area, forces sufficient to contain the enemy remained, but they were insufficient to conduct active offensive operations. Daily situation reports of the General Staff of the Armed Forces of Ukraine consistently noted the absence of enemy activity, for example, in the report of 11 July: 'In the Slobozhanska direction, enemy units continue to focus their efforts on holding the occupied lines on the Kharkiv axis and preventing the advance of our troops. The enemy is taking measures to ensure the logistical support of its units'.[14]

In early June 2022, the actions of the Izium grouping of Russian occupation forces intensified. At that time, this grouping consisted of units from the 20th, 29th, and 35th Armies, reinforced by a battalion tactical group of the Wagner private military company. However, the vector of its efforts was directed not toward Kharkiv, but in the opposite direction – southward. The Russians were preparing for the widely announced 'battle for Sloviansk', the start of which was scheduled for 10 June.[15] Nevertheless, until the end of the month, Russian efforts on this axis produced no tangible results. On 6 July, the UK Ministry of Defence, citing intelligence data, noted that over the previous week Russian forces had likely advanced a further 5km down the main M03/E40 road from Izium, encountering extremely determined Ukrainian resistance, but had managed to close to within 16km of Sloviansk. It was predicted that 'the battle for Sloviansk will become the next key event in the fight for the Donbas'.[16] With great difficulty, the Russians managed to capture the village of Dovhenke (located on the M03/E40 road at the boundary between the Kharkiv and Donetsk oblasts), but they were halted on the approaches to Krasnopillia (already in Donetsk Oblast), failed to overcome the resistance of the defenders, and were unable to break through Ukrainian mine and engineering barriers.[17]

The futility of attempts to break through the Ukrainian defence became clear to the Russian command in early July. It was forced to take an operational pause. On 7 July, the spokesperson of the Russian Ministry of Defence announced that 'units carrying out combat missions during the special military operation are undergoing measures to restore combat capability. Servicemen have been given the opportunity to rest and to receive letters and parcels from home'.[18] These statements were an attempt to put a brave face on a bad situation, since the Russians simply lacked the physical capacity to continue the offensive. The reason lay in a shortage of manpower caused by enormous losses during the war against Ukraine. In effect, the Russian Federation had launched and waged the war with a peacetime army; an outcome of the Russian military-political leadership's underestimation of the Ukrainians' will to fight and of the combat effectiveness of the Defence Forces of Ukraine. Situations arose on the battlefield in which Russian artillery inflicted fire damage on Ukrainian positions, but there were insufficient infantry forces available to conduct an assault. At least for some Russian military specialists, this problem had been evident long before the start of the full-scale invasion of Ukraine. One way to mitigate its severity was the use of the Russian Airborne Forces (VDV) units as mechanised infantry. Reforms aimed at increasing the share of VDV formations oriented not toward airlift, but toward employment as mechanised units exclusively in the ground echelon, had been carried out in the Russian Airborne Forces as early as 2009–13. This was manifested, among other things, in the introduction of tank battalions into the tables of organisation of VDV divisions and brigades, as well as the acquisition of some other heavy equipment.[19] However, the core equipment of VDV units and formations continued to consist of airborne combat vehicles, which are less well protected and have lower troop-carrying capacity compared to infantry fighting vehicles. As a result, VDV units had lower manpower strength and firepower than Motor Rifle units. Their use in the role of 'ersatz infantry' led to significant losses.

As early as the spring of 2022, analysts were arguing that in order to continue the fighting the Russian government would have to declare mobilisation. There was even speculation that, given Vladimir Putin's penchant for symbolism, this might be done on 9 May.[20] However, this did not happen, for political and ideological reasons. Declaring mobilisation would have meant acknowledging the fact that Russia was waging a real war against Ukraine, rather than a 'special military operation'. The only exception was the temporarily occupied areas of the Donetsk and Luhansk oblasts, where general mobilisation had been declared as early as 19 February 2022, before the start of the full-scale invasion by Russian forces.[21] Instead of mobilisation, in the summer of 2022 the Russian regions began forming volunteer units, so-called 'named' battalions. In this way, the military-political leadership sought to compensate for massive personnel losses without formally announcing mobilisation. Another source of manpower replacement was the recruitment of prisoners, a process carried out by the private military company Wagner starting in July 2022.[22] Finally, measures of covert mobilisation – calling up reservists to military enlistment offices and subsequently persuading them to sign contract service – made it possible to form the 3rd Army Corps. However, the process of manning this formation proceeded rather slowly: it began as early as late March, and by the time the first units of the 3rd Corps started arriving at the front in late August 2022, its strength did not exceed 70 percent of its authorised manpower.[23]

The operational pause declared by the Russian command, of course, did not mean complete calm on the front. Clashes continued, although they did not reach a large scale. For example, on 7 July the General Staff of the Armed Forces of Ukraine reported in its daily briefing an unsuccessful attempt by the enemy to assault the village of Sosnivka.[24] Its location (in the north of Kharkiv Oblast, close to the Russian-Ukrainian border and slightly west of Kozacha Lopan) and its very small size allow one to assume that the Russians were attempting to conduct a reconnaissance in force, to probe the Ukrainian defences in this area.

The second 10-day period of July was marked by unsuccessful Russian attempts to carry out local offensive actions on the northern and southern sectors of the Kharkiv Oblast (respectively, north of Kharkiv and north of Sloviansk). Instead, throughout July and August Russian forces systematically shelled settlements near the line of contact using various types of weapons. For instance, even a single morning briefing of the General Staff of the Armed Forces of Ukraine noted that on the Kharkiv axis the enemy shelled, with tanks and rocket artillery, the areas of the settlements of Svitlychne, Shapovalivka, Prudianka, Dementiivka, Pytomnyk, Velyki Prokhody, Ruski Tyshky, Peremoha, Verkhnii Saltiv, Husarivka, Bazaliivka, Stara Hnylytsia, and Protopopivka, and also carried out air strikes near Rtyshchivka and Verkhnii Saltiv.[25]

From the first 10 days of August, the redeployment of units of the Eastern Military District was observed: formations that had previously conducted offensive operations toward Sloviansk were moved south, to defend the occupied territories in the western parts of the Zaporizhzhia and Kherson oblasts.[26] However, local attempts at offensive action continued. For example, on 15 August an enemy attempt to break through the defences of Ukrainian forces on the Kozacha Lopan–Udy axis was repelled.[27] Seeking to constrain the movement of Ukrainian troops and complicate the transfer of manoeuvre units to threatened sectors, the Russians intensified the use of remote mining systems. In particular, on 16 August the use of such systems was recorded in the areas of the settlements of Peremoha and Ukrainka.[28]

During July–August 2022, Ukrainian forces in the Kharkiv Oblast did not conduct active combat operations. Instead, in the second half of August the redeployment of additional forces to Kharkiv Oblast began, as preparations were underway for the Slobozhanska offensive. On 19 August, after a short pause to restore combat capability in the south-western part of the Kharkiv Oblast, the 14th Separate Mechanised Brigade arrived; it had previously operated in Donetsk Oblast. The brigade was deployed in the north of the Kharkiv Oblast, from Lyptsi to Slobidske.[29]

Almost continuously, without any 'operational pause', the Russians carried out shelling of Ukrainian cities, while steadily expanding its scale and adapting their tactics to new conditions. Significant losses of operational-tactical aviation, above all Su-34 bombers, at the beginning of the full-scale invasion led the Russian command to virtually cease the use of this aircraft in airspace controlled by Ukrainian air defence. Instead, from July onward in Kharkiv Oblast the enemy began using S-300 surface-to-air missile systems in a surface-to-surface mode, launching missiles on a ballistic trajectory. Such targets proved extremely difficult for Ukrainian air defence to intercept. The short flight time (no more than a few minutes) meant that in cities targeted by Russian strikes there was often not even enough time to announce an air-raid warning.

The capability of S-300 system missiles (in particular the 5V55 and 48N6) to strike ground targets had been incorporated into the system from the outset, but their effective aimed range in this role was limited to about 40km (the radar-horizon distance). The Russians, however, launched these missiles from much greater distances, effectively in an unguided mode. Because of their low accuracy, such launches were suitable only for striking large-area targets, that is, for terrorising Ukrainian cities.[30]

The first instances of such use of S-300 system missiles were recorded from 18 June in the Donetsk Oblast; from 8 July the Russians began using them to shell Mykolaiv. On the night of 12–13 July, the Kharkiv Oblast was shelled for the first time with 5V55 missiles; according to official reports, one of these missiles was shot down by Ukrainian air defence.[31] The next night, the shelling was repeated and 5V55 missiles fired at Kharkiv partially destroyed the metro depot in the Saltivsky district. Nearby industrial enterprises were also damaged.[32] The metro depot did not fall under the category of military facilities, but this did not stop the Russians.

By the end of August 2022, the Kharkiv Oblast had been shelled by S-300 system missiles at least 17 more times. The vast majority of these strikes targeted the regional capital, but other cities were hit as well, including Chuhuiv. As a result of a Russian missile strike on 25 July, the local house of culture in that city was virtually destroyed while civilians were sheltering in its basement; residential buildings and a school were also damaged.[33]

In addition to missiles, Russian forces continued to use tube and rocket artillery to shell towns and villages in the Kharkiv Oblast. For example, on the same day as the missile strike on Chuhuiv, reports also mentioned shelling of residential areas in the village of Korobochkyne and the urban-type settlement of Pechenihy, as well as a farming enterprise in the Bohodukhiv District.[34]

Such shelling was repeated day after day. I will mention only one more instance; the shelling of Kharkiv on the morning of 30 August 2022. On that day, the Russians used not missiles but 2S7 'Pion' 203mm self-propelled guns, which fired nine shells at the city. They exploded in the central part of Kharkiv, causing casualties.[35] Among those killed on Kultury Street, near the military hospital, was my son, Taras Kharuk.

House of Culture in Chuhuiv, destroyed by Russian rocket fire, 25 July 2022. (State Emergency Service of Ukraine)

The summer months of 2022 in the Kharkiv Oblast became a kind of pause between the Battle of Kharkiv – the defensive operation that lasted from 24 February to mid-May – and the Slobozhanska offensive in September. This relative lull was caused by the shift of the main combat operations further south, to the Donbas. However, fighting continued, as did the shelling of towns and villages. At the same time, the successful defensive battles in the southern Kharkiv Oblast and in the adjacent areas of the Donetsk Oblast played an extremely important role in thwarting the enemy's plans to encircle the Joint Forces grouping in the Donbas.

The aftermath of a 203mm shell hitting during shelling on 30 August 2022. Kharkiv, Kultury Street. (suspilne.media)

4

SLOBOZHANSKA OFFENSIVE OPERATION (SEPTEMBER–DECEMBER 2022)

In late summer and autumn 2022, the Defence Forces of Ukraine carried out a series of offensive operations, united by a common concept into the first strategic offensive operation.[1] One of its key parts was the Slobozhanska Offensive Operation.

A few words should be said about the terminology we will be using. The fact is that many media reports (especially those published during the operation) use the term 'Kharkiv counteroffensive' or 'counteroffensive in the Kharkiv Oblast'.[2] This term has also found its way into scholarly military-historical studies.[3] In our view, however, it is not entirely accurate. First of all, was it an offensive operation or a counteroffensive?

The official Dictionary of Military Terms and Abbreviations issued by the Military Scientific Directorate of the General Staff of the Armed Forces of Ukraine provides the following definition:

> An offensive (counteroffensive) operation is a set of coordinated and interrelated, in terms of purpose, tasks, place, and time, simultaneous or sequential offensive (counteroffensive) and defensive combat actions, strikes, and manoeuvres [...] conducted according to a single concept and plan under the command of a commander with the aim of defeating an enemy grouping of troops (forces) that is on the defensive, seizing important areas of terrain (lines, objectives), and creating favourable conditions for further actions.[4]

Thus, in this definition, there is in fact no clear distinction between the terms 'offensive' and 'counteroffensive'. By contrast, the dictionary of terms and abbreviations of the U.S. Department of Defense provides a very specific definition of a counteroffensive: 'A counteroffensive is a large-scale offensive undertaken by defending forces to regain the initiative from the attacking side'.[5] Soviet military terminology used a similar definition: 'A counteroffensive is a special type of offensive launched by defending forces during or after repelling an enemy offensive'.[6]

The designation 'Kharkiv operation' or 'operation in the Kharkiv Oblast' is also not entirely precise, since, developing their success, the Defence Forces of Ukraine moved beyond the boundaries of the Kharkiv Oblast, operating within the broader historical-geographical region of Slobozhanska Ukraine. In its modern boundaries, Slobozhanska (Sloboda Ukraine) encompasses the central-southern part of the Sumy Oblast, Kharkiv Oblast, the northern part of the Luhansk Oblast, and the north-eastern part of Donetsk Oblast of Ukraine, as well as the western, eastern, and southern parts of the Belgorod Oblast, the southern part of the Voronezh Oblast, and the western part of the Kursk Oblast of the Russian Federation.[7] Based on these definitions, we believe that the term Slobozhanska Offensive Operation is the most appropriate, since at the time it began the Russian forces in Slobozhanska Ukraine had already lost the initiative after the Defence Forces of Ukraine had won the Battle of Kharkiv and were no longer conducting offensive actions, remaining instead on the defensive.

Preconditions for the Operation

At the beginning of September 2022, the front line in the Kharkiv Oblast ran roughly from the settlement of Udy (in the north of the oblast, near the Ukrainian-Russian border) to Ternova in a south-easterly arc (at some distance from the state border of Ukraine), and then descended almost due south as far as Izium and the border with the Donetsk Oblast (with a salient at the level of Kupiansk).[8] The terrain here is forest-steppe, and in the east and south of the region predominantly steppe. The relief is an undulating plain with a slight slope in the south-western and south-eastern directions.[9] The area in which the Slobozhanska offensive unfolded is characterised by a relatively small forested area and the presence of significant water obstacles, in particular the Siverskyi Donets and the Oskil rivers (with the Oskil Reservoir, whose water level dropped markedly after the dam was blown up in the spring of 2022). These rivers flow from north to south and form a convenient line for the organisation of defensive positions.

The eastern Kharkiv Oblast was one of the most obvious areas where a Ukrainian offensive was expected during the autumn campaign (alongside the right bank of the Kherson Oblast). In addition to liberating occupied territory, an important argument in favour of conducting an offensive operation in the Kharkiv Oblast was the opportunity to seriously disrupt the occupiers' logistics by cutting the Valuyki–Kupiansk main railway line. This line is a double-track, electrified mainline with high carrying capacity and a well-equipped, powerful depot at Kupiansk.[10] Control over the Valuyki–Kupiansk line (including its continuation toward Lyman, Horlivka, and Ilovaisk) allowed the Russians to supply their occupation forces in the Donbas by the shortest route and, if necessary, to manoeuvre forces between different sectors of the front. The Kupiansk–Vovchansk line (with continuation toward Belgorod) was of lesser importance, as it is single-track and non-electrified.[11] Returning these lines, together with the Kupiansk junction station, to Ukrainian control would have significantly complicated the Russian command's ability to solve logistical tasks and created favourable conditions for the further liberation of occupied territories.

Analysing the Ukrainian side's preparations for the Slobozhanska Offensive Operation, it is worth highlighting a carefully planned and effective campaign of disinformation aimed at misleading the enemy. As early as 11 July 2022, Minister of Defence Oleksii Reznikov informed the media of an order by the President of Ukraine to 'liberate the occupied areas along the Black Sea coast that are important for Ukraine's economy'.[12] The Minister emphasised that, in order to carry out this directive, he had appealed to partners in a number of countries with a request for modern weapons. It is telling that Western analysts immediately noted the demonstrative nature of this announcement: 'If Russia takes the threat of a Ukrainian counteroffensive in the south seriously, this could affect the actions of Russian forces in eastern Ukraine and divert them from further active advances in that direction'.[13] However, the main addressee – the Russian military-political leadership – took these statements entirely seriously. The true plans, by contrast, were known in the Kharkiv Oblast to only a handful of people, and nationwide to only the highest military and political leadership.

The head of the Kharkiv Regional Civil-Military Administration, Oleh Syniehubov, recalled that one of the disinformation tools was the spread of rumours about an alleged planned withdrawal of the 92nd Separate Mechanised Brigade from the Kharkiv Oblast. Syniehubov even raised this issue in a conversation with Valerii Zaluzhnyi:

> I had a conversation then with Commander-in-Chief Zaluzhnyi, and I told him that this could not be done – this is our main combat 'organism'. Not even from a military point of view, but from a political one, it would be wrong, because people believe in it, they hold on, and this would only weaken their faith. To which he replied: "Oleh, let's do it this way – don't call me about this. Just for two days, don't bother me. I understand everything, but just don't bother me for two days. I promise you that everything will be fine".[14]

The 92nd Separate Mechanised Brigade, which had been fighting in the Kharkiv Oblast from the very first minutes of Russia's full-scale invasion, became a true symbol for the people of Kharkiv. The spread of rumours about its possible redeployment to another sector of the front was intended to convince the enemy that the Ukrainian command had no plans to launch offensive operations precisely in the Kharkiv Oblast.

An additional argument in favour of the assumption that the Defence Forces of Ukraine were preparing a large-scale offensive in the south was provided by attacks on enemy positions in the Kherson Oblast, which began on 29 August (in addition to the systematic strikes on supply lines carried out by Ukrainian forces since late May). The offensive in the Kherson Oblast began simultaneously in three sectors: in the area of the settlement of Vysokopillia, along the line of the settlements of Davydiv Brid and Snihurivka, and near the settlement of Ternovi Pody. By 5 September, units of the Defence Forces of Ukraine had liberated about a dozen settlements and had also seized and expanded a bridgehead on the eastern bank of the Inhulets River along the Bilohirka–Andriivka line.[15]

Reacting to this threat, the Russians began redeploying some units of the 1st Guards Tank Army, which had previously been operating in the Kharkiv Oblast, to the Kherson axis. In particular, this concerned the 147th Self-Propelled Artillery Regiment of the 2nd Motor Rifle Division.[16]

The main forces of the 1st Guards Tank Army remained in Slobozhanska, in the Izium area. These consisted of battalion tactical groups from the 2nd Motor Rifle Division, the 4th and 47th Tank Divisions, and the 27th Separate Motor Rifle Brigade, reinforced by artillery from the 288th Artillery Brigade and other units. However, these BTGs were to a large extent bled white: in many cases their actual strength did not exceed that of a company, morale among the personnel was low, and a significant proportion of equipment was unserviceable.[17] A similar condition characterised the formations of the 20th Combined Arms Army; the 3rd and 144th Motor Rifle Divisions. Units of the 18th Motor Rifle Division and the 7th Separate Motor Rifle Regiment were also present in Kharkiv Oblast; they were subordinated to the 11th Army Corps, which was home-based in the Kaliningrad Oblast of the Russian Federation.[18] The units redeployed as reinforcements from the 2nd Army Corps were marked by even lower combat morale, as they were staffed with forcibly mobilised reservists from the occupied areas of the Luhansk Oblast.[19] Among these servicemen, there were open riots with demands to 'let them go home' and accusations of looting against their commanders.[20] In addition, in a number of sectors Rosgvardia units were pushed forward to frontline positions, formations that, by definition, were not intended for combat against regular armed forces and were virtually devoid of heavy weaponry. As aptly noted by M. Strembski, the outcome of the Ukrainian disinformation campaign was the strengthening of Russian defences in the Kherson Region through the 'drain' of manpower and equipment from other sectors of the front, including the Kharkiv Oblast.[21]

Thus, in early September 2022, favourable conditions had taken shape in Slobozhanska Ukraine for the Ukrainian Armed Forces to carry out an offensive operation. According to the assessments of P. Batacchi and A. Mottola, its objectives were to be: 1) reducing the Russian threat to Kharkiv; 2) creating a threat to Russian forces in the Lyman–Yampil area, which in turn was to ease enemy pressure on Ukrainian troops in the Sloviansk and Kramatorsk area; 3) creating the preconditions for the liberation of the north-western part of the Luhansk Oblast; 4) exerting a demoralising effect on the enemy; 5) further disorganising Russian command, which was forced to address the problem of optimally employing insufficient resources.[22]

The tasks defined by the Ukrainian command for the forces operating in the Eastern Operational Zone envisaged breaking through the enemy's defences by decisive offensive actions and defeating the enemy grouping in the areas of Balakliia, Izium, Shevchenkove, and Kupiansk, as well as creating favourable conditions for a further advance into the Luhansk Oblast and pushing the enemy away from Kharkiv toward the state border. At the same time, farther south, in the Donetsk Oblast (the Sloviansk, Kramatorsk, Bakhmut, Avdiivka, and Novopavlivka operational directions), the plan called for holding the line of contact through a firm defence, preventing the operational encirclement and destruction of units and subunits of the Defence Forces of Ukraine.[23] Thus, the plan for Ukrainian forces in the Eastern Operational Zone for the autumn campaign envisaged active offensive operations in the Kharkiv Oblast and northern Luhansk Oblast, combined with defensive fighting in the Donetsk Oblast.

The forces allocated by the Ukrainian command to participate in the operation included the 92nd and 14th Separate Mechanised Brigades, the 25th Separate Airborne Brigade, the 80th Separate Air Assault Brigade, and battalion tactical groups of the 3rd and 4th Separate Tank Brigades.[24] Most of these units were 'old' formations, created long before the start of the full-scale invasion, with experienced personnel. The exception were the two separate tank brigades, which had previously belonged to the reserve corps; however, even they had acquired substantial combat experience since the spring of 2022. At the same time, the level of manning and equipment in these brigades varied considerably. Andrii Platonov recalls:

> The 3rd Tank Brigade was one of the main combat units in 2022 near Balakliia. I called it the "3rd Tankless Brigade" because its tank availability was at the level of just a few percent, in contrast to 104 percent in the 4th Tank Brigade, which was operating generally farther south, opposite Izium. But before the autumn offensive it [the 3rd Separate Tank Brigade] was finally re-equipped, and some forces were also transferred from the 4th Tank Brigade.[25]

MT-LB tracked transporter modernised in Ukraine with a Turkish-made Serdar combat module. (militarnyi.com)

These units were reinforced by battalion tactical groups of the 4th Operational Brigade, the 5th Separate Brigade, and the 15th Separate Regiment of the National Guard of Ukraine, as well as by a number of special operations units: tactical groups of the Separate Special Operations Centre 'Skhid' and the Separate Special Operations Centre 'Zakhid', the 'Kraken' unit of the Main Intelligence Directorate, the 518th Battalion 'Dyke Pole' of the 1st Separate Special Operations Brigade, and the Special Operations Centre 'A' of the Security Service of Ukraine.[26] The rapid response border command (roughly equivalent to a battalion) of the 4th Border Guard Detachment was also active here.

A characteristic feature of the Slobozhanska Offensive Operation was the extensive use of weapons and military equipment supplied by Ukraine's allies. In particular, the operation employed T-72M1 tanks and modernised T-72M1R tanks transferred by Poland; M113G4DK and M113AS4 tracked armoured personnel carriers (APCs) from Denmark and Australia, respectively; French VAB wheeled APCs; Turkish Kirpi vehicles; as well as modernised tracked MT-LB carriers fitted with Turkish-made Serdar combat modules. Mobile raiding groups, alongside HMMWV vehicles and various types of pickup trucks, also used Bushmaster wheeled armoured vehicles (Australian) and MaxxPro vehicles (American), and more rarely British light tracked APCs of the Spartan type.[27]

It was precisely during the Slobozhanska Offensive Operation that the Gepard self-propelled anti-aircraft guns supplied by Germany made their combat debut. While providing air defence cover for advancing troops, they operated in cooperation with mobile short-range Osa-AKM air defence missile systems.[28] For the Gepard, the battles in the Kharkiv Oblast were the first combat use since their production began in 1976.

Artillery support groups employed AHS Krab (of Polish manufacture), PzH 2000 (supplied by Germany and the Netherlands), and M109A3GN (formerly Norwegian) 155mm self-propelled artillery systems (SPGs), as well as M142 HIMARS and M270 MLRS multiple launch rocket systems (MLRS).[29]

The First Stage of the Slobozhanska Offensive Operation (6–12 September 2022)

The Slobozhanska Offensive Operation was relatively prolonged in time. At the same time, its first phase can be identified quite clearly: it lasted from 6–12 September and consisted of the liberation of Balakliia, Izium, Vovchansk, and Kupiansk, with Ukrainian forces reaching the line of the Oskil River. This stage is called the Balakliia Operation,[30] or the Balakliia–Kupiansk Offensive.[31]

The primary objective of the offensive that began on 6 September 2022 was defined by the Ukrainian command as the city of Balakliia, an important communications hub in the southern part of the Kharkiv Oblast, located on the left bank of the Siverskyi Donets River. Its liberation would create favourable conditions for the further development of the offensive toward Kupiansk. At the same time, it would eliminate the possibility of the enemy using Balakliia as a springboard for an advance and an envelopment of Kharkiv from the south. On the eve of the offensive, on 5 September, explosions were reported on the territory of artillery depots (the 65th Arsenal) in the village of Verbivka (on the northern approaches to Balakliia).[32] On 6 September, local residents reported accurate strikes on the deployment points of occupying forces in a number of surrounding villages: 'All the hits were very precise. After that, information spread through the villages that it was forbidden to go outside. It was prohibited to take photographs or go out to make

HIMARS multiple launch rocket systems played a significant role in the preparation and conduct of the Slobozhanska Offensive. (militarnyi.com)

Gepard self-propelled anti-aircraft guns, supplied by Germany, made their combat debut during the Slobozhanska Offensive. (Joint Forces Command)

phone calls under the threat of physical destruction. They said the ban was for three days for now, but it could be extended'.[33]

The main strike on Balakliia was delivered by Ukrainian forces north of the city, in the area of the village of Verbivka, where the 'Kraken' unit took control of the territory of the 65th Arsenal. Assault groups, supported by armoured vehicles, bypassed the city, successively capturing small villages around Balakliia.[34] Ukrainian troops pushed the enemy back to the left (northern) bank of the Siverskyi Donets and Serednia Balakliika rivers and on the same day entered Verbivka. The Russians began transferring reserves to the area, and their media outlets, cited in an ISW report, expressed concern that the attack aimed to cut Russian forces off from Izium and to drive a wedge into the territory of the Luhansk Oblast.[35]

Artillery support groups used, in particular, Polish-made AHS Krab 155mm self-propelled howitzers. (Land Forces Command of the Armed Forces of Ukraine)

By the end of 7 September, Ukrainian forces had advanced 20km into enemy-controlled territory and liberated an area of 400 square kilometres. The situation as described in the ISW report of 7 September was as follows: Ukrainian troops were advancing southeast along the M03/E40 and H26 highways toward Izium and Kupiansk respectively, as well as north-east along the T2110 road from Balakliia through Verbivka, Yakovenkove, and Volokhiv Yar (at the junction of the T2110 and M03/E40 roads), and further toward Shevchenkove (at the junction of the T2110 and H26 roads).[36]

Soldiers of the Territorial Defence Forces of Ukraine near the newly repainted (from the colours of the Russian flag to those of Ukraine) sign at the entrance to the village of Shevchenkove (Kharkiv Oblast), liberated from the Russian army. (militarnyi.com)

On 7 September, frontline reports began to outline a picture of the operational encirclement of Balakliia, with enemy forces still located inside the city. Whereas the previous day Russian military bloggers had insisted that there was 'no panic whatsoever' in Balakliia and that there was 'no talk of a deep breakthrough', by the next morning the tone of their posts had changed radically: 'do not expect good news'.[37] Among the final elements defending the city were not army units, but Rosgvardia units, specifically SOBR detachments[38] from the Volga region (Samara and Ufa).[39] Small in number (overall roughly equivalent to a company) and lacking heavy weapons and armoured vehicles, they were unable to effectively contain the pressure exerted by Ukrainian forces. The establishment of control by the Ukrainian Defence Forces over the T2110, M03/E40, and H26 highways created conditions for further advances to the south (toward Izium) and to the east (toward Kupiansk).

In the very first days of the operation, the distinctive features of how Ukrainian offensive actions were organised became apparent. In the Balakliia area, making use of firepower superiority and high operational tempo, Ukrainian tank and mechanised units broke through the enemy's overstretched defences, after which light mobile groups were introduced into the breach. One participant in the raid, Senior Lieutenant Maksym Buhel of the 80th Air Assault Brigade, described these events as follows:

> After the 25th and 92nd Brigades broke through the corridor on 6 September, we went on a raid. In two days we covered more than 150km in the enemy rear. Along the route of advance we set up ambushes, destroying enemy personnel and equipment, and by the morning of 8 September we reached the village of Senkove. After that, we continued the successful execution of the assigned tasks.[40]

The commander of the 80th Air Assault Brigade, Colonel Ihor Skybiuk, noted that the brigade had been assigned two tasks: the

Bushmaster armoured vehicles were widely used by mobile groups of Ukrainian paratroopers during the offensive in the Kharkiv Oblast. (militarnyi.com)

primary one was the liberation of the city of Izium, and the secondary one was to form (together with other units) an encirclement ring around the enemy grouping in the Izium area.[41]

Comparable successes were achieved on the right flank of the advance on Balakliia, where coordinated actions by units of the Armed Forces of Ukraine and border guards led to the liberation of the villages of Bairak, Nova Husarivka, and Shchurivka. This made it possible to force the Siverskyi Donets River in this sector and to enter Balakliia from the southern direction.

It was precisely in the Balakliia area that Ukrainian forces successfully employed infiltration as a form of offensive manoeuvre. Exploiting gaps in the enemy's positions, disrupting the enemy rear, and providing precise target designation for their own artillery, units of the Armed Forces of Ukraine during the first day of the offensive broke through the Russian defences in the Balakliia area, seizing three company-level strongpoints of the enemy.[42] The successful use of infiltration was made possible by a number of factors, not least among them the redeployment of several enemy units to other sectors of the front and, as a consequence, the thinning of the density of the enemy line. This once again underscores the importance of the information and psychological operation conducted prior to the offensive, which misled the enemy as to the location of the main strike by the Defence Forces of Ukraine.

It is worth emphasising that during the first days of the offensive Ukrainian officials maintained an information blackout, refraining from reporting on the successes of Ukrainian forces. Only in the evening of 8 September, during a briefing by representatives of Ukraine's security and defence sector, did the Deputy Chief of the Main Operational Directorate of the General Staff of the Armed Forces of Ukraine, Brigadier General Oleksii Hromov, announce that on the Kharkiv axis units of the Armed Forces of Ukraine had penetrated the enemy's defences to a depth of up to 50km. More than 20 settlements had been liberated, where filtration measures were ongoing. Notably, in his statement Hromov indicated that the actions of the Armed Forces of Ukraine on the Kharkiv axis were taking place 'within the framework of a defensive operation'.[43] The relevant information also appeared in the morning operational report of the General Staff of the Armed Forces of Ukraine on 9 September.[44]

Let us make a brief digression to explain that this approach – releasing official information with a certain delay, most often of several days – became standard practice during the Slobozhanska offensive. This reflected the application by the Ukrainian command of the principles of operational security (OPSEC), defined as a set of measures aimed at preventing (or reducing the risks of) the leakage

A billboard in liberated Balakliia. Underneath a torn Russian propaganda slogan is a portrait of Taras Shevchenko and a quote from his poem *Caucasus*. (militarnyi.com)

of critical information useful to enemy intelligence.[45] Although Ukrainian public opinion was eager for news about the liberation of new towns and villages, the delay in releasing this information was entirely justified in order to ensure the success of further actions by the Defence Forces of Ukraine.

It can be argued that a turning point in the fighting occurred on 8 September. Ukrainian troops liberated Balakliia, as officially confirmed by President V. Zelensky.[46] The 80th Air Assault Brigade advanced in a south-easterly direction toward Izium, while other units pushed eastward toward Kupiansk. Ukrainian troops approached to within 15km of the city, enabling them to shell enemy targets in the Kupiansk area with artillery.[47] The head of the occupation administration of the Kharkiv Oblast called on all residents of the occupied areas to evacuate to the Russian Federation.[48] The occupation administration, which had been based in Kupiansk, evacuated to Vovchansk (in the north of the Kharkiv Oblast, near the border with the Russian Federation).[49] More precisely, an order was given to evacuate to this city, but, it was not carried out (in the opinion of the authors) due to the rapid pace of the Ukrainian offensive and the liberation of Vovchansk.

As of 9 September, a critical situation for the Russians had developed near Izium. The Russian grouping there was squeezed between Ukrainian positions to the west and south and the Oskil Reservoir to the east. When Ukrainian units advancing from the Balakliia area approached Izium from the north, the enemy grouping found itself under threat of encirclement. Russian command attempted to transfer reserves to the area, including by using heavy Mi-26 transport helicopters (which carried not only personnel but also armoured vehicles).[50] However, these measures were largely demonstrative and, in our view, aimed at reassuring the Russian public that the command was doing everything possible to save the garrisons of Izium and Kupiansk. In reality, the Russians did not have sufficient reserves in the area of the Ukrainian offensive.

On 9 September, Ukrainian units reached the western shore of the Oskil Reservoir near the village of Senkove (25km south of Kupiansk). Offensive actions toward Vovchansk intensified, with Ukrainian forces advancing through Velykyi Burluk (42km north-west of Kupiansk). At the same time, Ukrainian forces stepped up attacks near Lyman (south of Izium, in the Donetsk Oblast).[51] Through these actions, the Ukrainian command sought to prevent the transfer of reinforcements from that area to Izium, and this objective was fully achieved.

To block the movement of Russian troops in the near rear (in particular in the Lyman area), remote mining with AT-2 anti-tank mines was employed using MARS multiple launch rocket systems (the German variant of the M270 MLRS). On the other hand, the Ukrainian manoeuvre was facilitated by well-planned engineer support using all available means; for example, a captured TMM-3M2 heavy mechanised bridge, seized from the enemy several weeks earlier, was used to establish a crossing over the Oskil River near Izium.[52]

According to the General Staff of the Armed Forces of Ukraine, as of 06:00 on 10 September more than 1,000 square kilometres of territory had been liberated from occupation. In certain sectors, units of the Defence Forces penetrated the enemy's defences to a depth of up to 50km. More than 30 settlements that had been temporarily seized by Russian occupying forces in the Kharkiv Oblast were liberated or brought under Ukrainian control.[53] That same day, units of the 92nd Separate Mechanised Brigade, together with the 1st Mechanised Battalion of the 14th Separate Mechanised Brigade and assault groups of the 'Kraken' unit, entered Kupiansk,

The Russians demonstratively used Mi-26 heavy transport helicopters to transfer reinforcements to the Izium area, but the overall significance of such actions was little more than of propaganda value. The photo shows the delivery of a UR-77 remote demining machine, which was useful during an offensive but completely unnecessary in defence. (militarnyi.com)

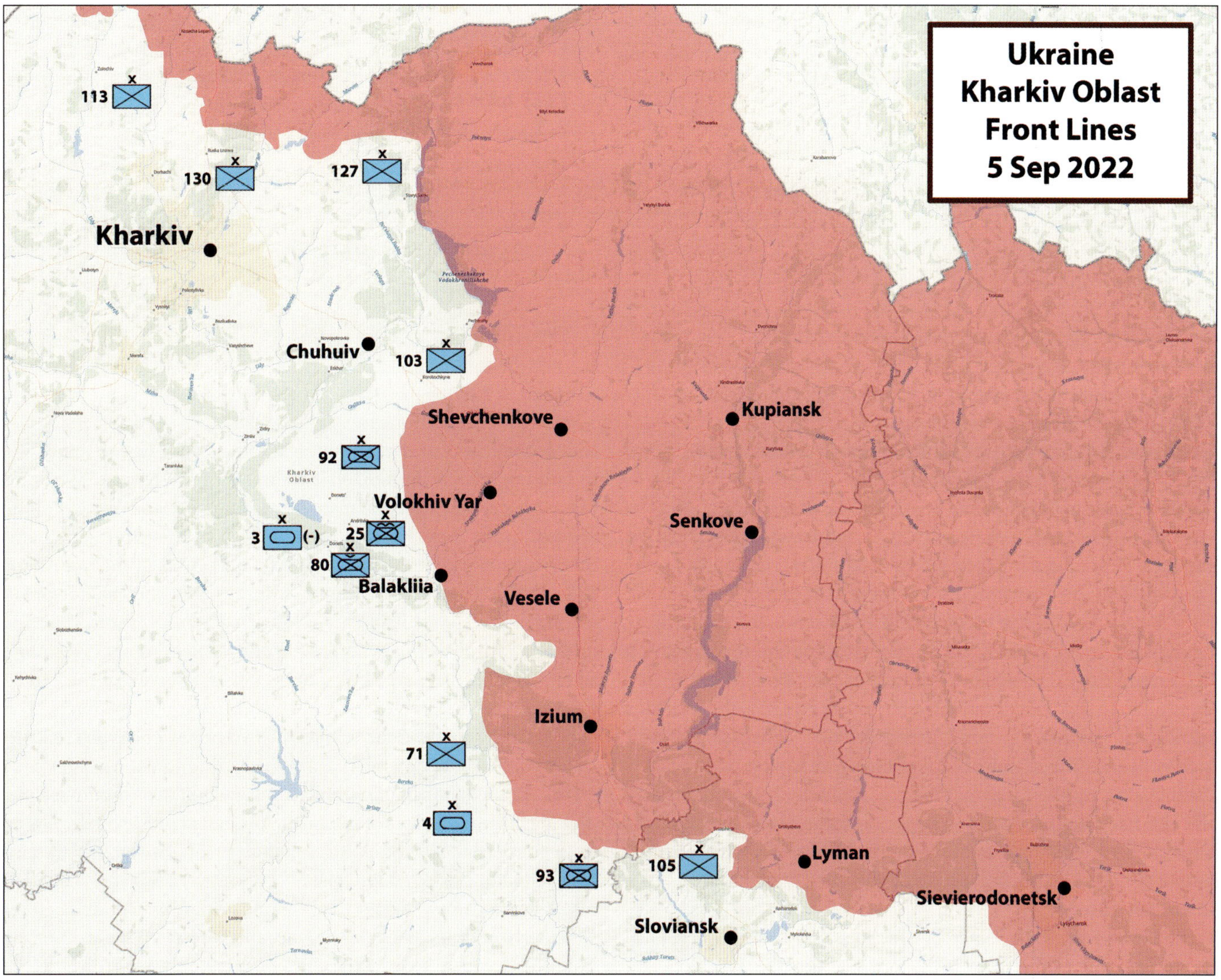

The frontline in the Kharkiv Oblast as of 5 September 2022. (Map by bbh.illustrations)

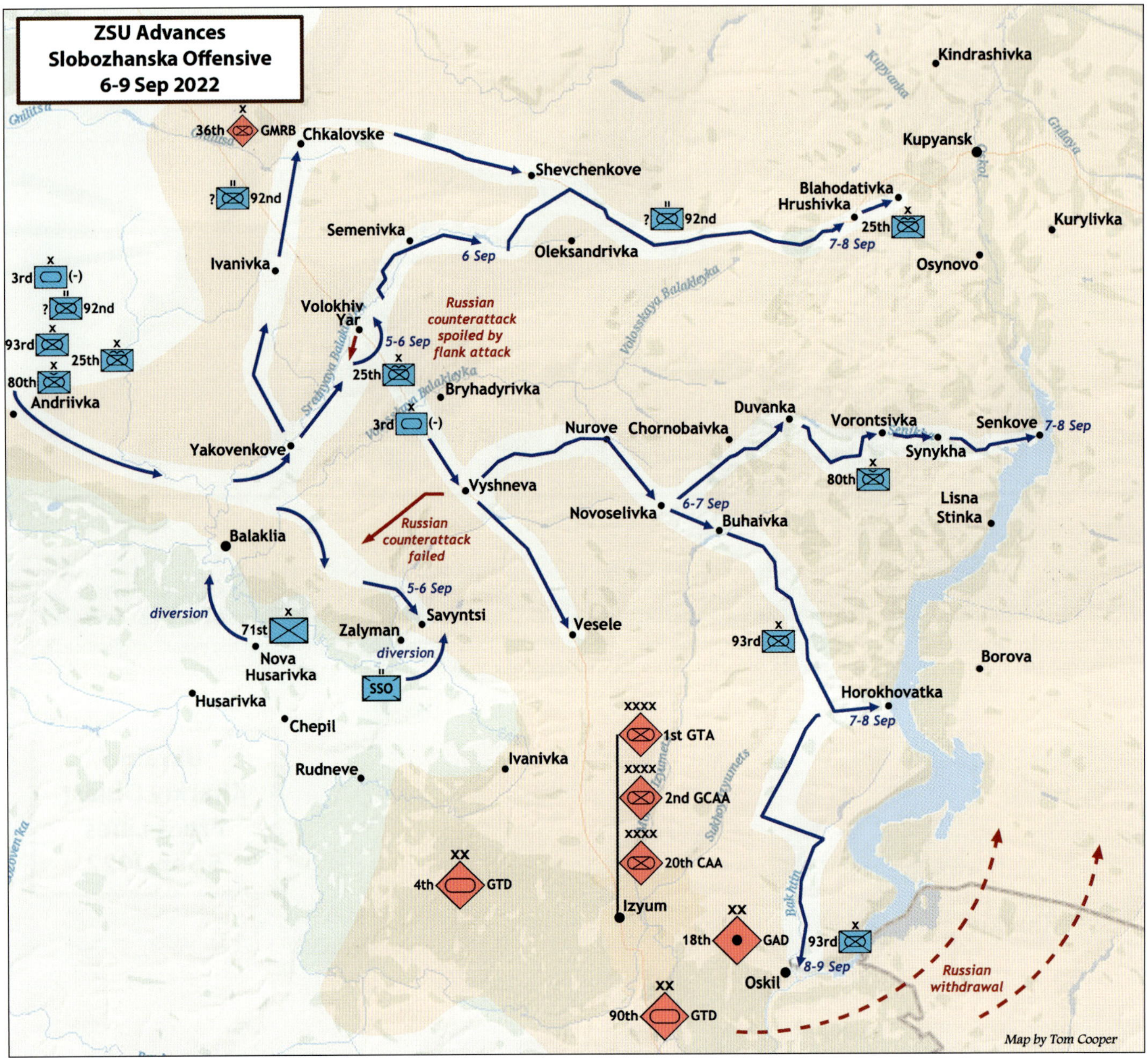

A detailed reconstruction of the initial stage of the Slobozhanska Offensive Operation, 6–9 September 2022. (Map by bbh.illustrations)

which had been under occupation since 27 February 2022, and raised the Ukrainian flag over the city.[54]

The liberation of Kupiansk was complicated by the fact that the city is divided into two parts by the Oskil River, whose bridges the Russians blew up during their retreat. Ukrainian mechanised units fairly quickly took control of the western, larger part of Kupiansk on the west bank of the Oskil. While engineers were establishing crossings over the river, Kraken infantry, using the remnants of a destroyed bridge, managed to infiltrate the eastern part of the city, Zaoskillia. In this area, dominated by private housing, the Russians managed to organise a fairly strong defence. Exhausting assault battles began. The actions of Ukrainian forces were significantly complicated by the large number of civilians who remained in the city itself and in nearby villages. In some cases, the Russians attempted to use them as human shields. However, the enemy's attempts to establish a new defensive line beyond the Oskil ultimately failed.[55]

By the evening of 10 September, the Russian Ministry of Defence announced the withdrawal of its troops from the Balakliia and Izium areas. As Russian propagandists typically do in such cases, this decision was presented not as a retreat but as a 'regrouping… to build up efforts in the Donetsk direction'.[56] Given the successful offensive actions of Ukrainian forces, the decision to withdraw proved to be belated, and a number of Russian units found themselves in a dire situation. In particular, units of the 3rd Motor Rifle Division were left without supply routes, and panic spread among the personnel.[57] Situations occurred such as the one reflected in the report of the General Staff of the Armed Forces of Ukraine as of 18:00 on 11 September: 'about 150 servicemen of the armed forces of the Russian Federation left in a convoy from Borshchova and Artemivka in Kharkiv Oblast in two buses, one truck, and 19 stolen passenger cars'.[58]

On 12 September, the morning report noted that 'over the past day, the occupiers have taken property and vehicles looted from local residents from the settlements of Velykyi Burluk and Dvorichna in the Kharkiv Oblast'.[59] Looting by Russian occupation forces has become widespread and rampant. Infrastructure facilities were destroyed. In particular, the occupiers blew up the dam of the Oskil Reservoir, which had already been partially destroyed in the spring. This was not about creating areas of flooding (the water level

Soldiers of the 14th Separate Mechanised Brigade at the entrance to the liberated Kupiansk. (14ombr)

in the reservoir after the spring explosion was insufficient for this), but about making it impossible for Ukrainian troops to cross this dam to the left bank of the Oskil River.[60]

The claim of an organised 'regrouping' contradicted the huge number of trophies captured by Ukrainian troops. According to various estimates, between 6 and 12 September, more than 100 and up to 300 armoured vehicles (most of them in working condition) were captured in the Kharkiv Oblast, not to mention other trophies. Particularly valuable acquisitions were a Zoopark-1M counter-battery radar, captured in perfect condition, and a complete set of the Orlan-10 unmanned aerial vehicle system, including a ground control station and technical documentation.[61]

A complete set of Orlan-10 unmanned aerial vehicles captured by Ukrainian troops, September 2022. (militarnyi.com)

The capture as a trophy of a complete and undamaged Orlan-10 system made it possible to improve methods of countering these aerial reconnaissance systems. In addition, a detailed analysis of the UAV's design and its ground control station revealed manufacturers and suppliers of Western-made components that were reaching the Russian Federation in circumvention of sanctions. The 1L261 radar station of the Zoopark-1M counter-battery radar system was captured in perfect condition, the enemy did not even attempt to disable it. The value of this trophy lay in the opportunity it provided to realistically assess the system's capabilities for detecting artillery, its operating modes and frequencies, and to create a precise 'fingerprint' of its emission signature.

Alongside the newest equipment, trophies captured during the offensive in the Kharkiv Oblast also included obsolete hardware; for example, T-62M tanks, which had been withdrawn from service in the Russian army long before the start of the full-scale invasion of Ukraine. Their return to service testified to the aggressor's heavy losses in Ukraine and the inability of its industry to compensate for them. In total, between 29 August and 12 September 2022, the loss of 442 pieces of Russian equipment in the Kharkiv Oblast was visually confirmed. Of these, 237 units (54 percent) became Ukrainian trophies.[62]

The seriousness of the problem posed by trophies left to the Defence Forces of Ukraine during the first stage of the Slobozhanska Offensive Operation is evidenced by the fact that it was discussed even in Russian military periodicals. Russian researchers noted that a large amount of equipment captured by advancing Ukrainian forces in September 2022 near Balakliia and Izium was primarily located in repair facilities or at damaged-vehicle collection points. The personnel of repair units were unable to repel an attack by superior enemy forces, as they lacked the necessary weapons and training. In such a situation, the repair crews had only one option; to withdraw. However, this meant abandoning damaged equipment to the enemy. The conclusions drawn from this were rather telling: it was deemed necessary to conduct special research to determine optimal methods for destroying or disabling one's own equipment so that it would not fall into enemy hands, and to conduct appropriate training for repair units, among other measures.[63]

Russian T-62M tank captured by Ukrainian troops. (t.me/Tsaplienko)

Representatives of the Ukrainian authorities accompanied the military to the liberated towns and villages. In this photo, taken in the village of Kozacha Lopan on 11 September, the head of the local administration, Viacheslav Zadorenko, stands in the centre. (suspilne.media)

The principal short-range ballistic missile deployed by Russia's ground forces in Ukraine was the 9M723 of the 9K720 Iskander-M (ASCC/NATO-reporting name 'SS-26 Stone') weapons complex. This was a single-stage, solid-fuel weapon, with a 480–700 kilogram warhead, launched from a 9P78-1 road-mobile transporter-erector-launcher (TEL). Shown here is an example of the 26th Rocket Brigade (6th Combined Arms Army), partially covered by a camouflage tarpaulin. With bad weather significantly hampering Russian Air Force (or more correctly Aerospace Forces) operations in the Kharkiv Oblast early during the invasion of late February 2022, Iskanders were deployed – often in salvos of three or four – against the most important targets in the area, such as major air defence nodes and air bases, local headquarters, assembly points, storage- and equipment sites. (Artwork by David Bocquelet)

The second most important long-range weapon in Russian Ground Forces service early during the invasion of Ukraine was the BM-27 Uragan: a self-propelled multiple rocket launcher. Consisting of a ZIL-135 8x8 chassis, carrying 16 launch tubes, the weapon is aimed with use of a PG-1 panoramic telescope. It deploys 220mm rockets, weighing 280kg, that can use HE-FRAG, explosive, and PTM-3 or PMF-1 scatterable mine submunitions detonated by electric timing fuses, over the maximum firing range of 35–70km. Together with the similar BM-30 Smerch (12 tubes of 300mm calibre), BM-27s of the 9th Artillery Brigade (6th Combined Arms Army) were deployed for striking both known Armed Forces of Ukraine positions along the border, and then the front lines, headquarters and assembly points in the rear and, quite early during the invasion, also various objects around the city. (Artwork by David Bocquelet)

Starting with the major Russian offensive from Izium in the direction of Sloviansk, in April 2022 the Russian Ground Forces began deploying TOS-1 Buratino multiple rocket launchers in the Kharkiv Oblast. Mounted on a T-72/T-90 tank chassis, the system comprised 30 220mm tubes for rockets equipped with thermobaric warheads. Because they rapidly became primary targets for the Ukrainians, and a number were knocked out as a consequence, the Russians began deploying TOS-1As individually, or in very small groups, to strike Ukrainian fortifications or assembly areas immediately behind the front line. (Artwork by David Bocquelet)

Developed as a successor to the T-64 in the late 1960s and early 1970s, the turbine-powered T-80 was once the most powerful main battle tank in the Soviet Army. Outwardly similar to the T-72 in many respects – especially because it incorporated similar suspension and a 125mm smoothbore main gun – it was slightly larger, mechanically different, and more expensive to manufacture. However, it also proved more mobile and better protected. The example here, showing overpainted water-soluble white camouflage, was assigned to either the 138th Motor Rifle Brigade or the 144th Motor Rifle Division as of late February 2022 while advancing in the direction of Poltava, an objective the Russians have never reached. (Artwork by David Bocquelet)

Following the complete failure to quickly seize Kharkiv, in early March 2022 the Russians redirected their main effort to the eastern Kharkiv Oblast. Correspondingly, elements of the 144th Motor Rifle Division – which were initially struck in the Kupiansk area – launched a new advance. After bypassing Shevchenkove, they drove on Balakliia, and then reached Izium, with the task of converting the town to a main springboard for an advance on Sloviansk. This T-72B3 – an upgraded variant of old T-72Bs through the installation of the 2A46M-2 gun, Sosna-U gunner's sight, digital VHF radio, improved autoloader, and other improvements, and equipped with the mine-clearing plough – was sighted in the Izium area, while decorated with the 'obligatory' Z quick-identification insignia. (Artwork by David Bocquelet)

Many Russian Ground Forces units deployed in the Kharkiv Oblast were still equipped with older T-72Bs, like this example probably assigned to the 138th Motor Rifle Brigade, sighted in April 2022. Originally pressed into service in 1985, this sub-variant included a new gun stabiliser, sights and fire control system (enabling the deployment of the 9K120 Svir guided missile system), upgraded composite armour for the hull, and an improved 840hp engine. As typical for the majority of main battle tanks in the 6th Combined Arms Army, the vehicle was painted in dark olive green overall, and wore no markings other than the white 'V' as a means of quick visual identification. (Artwork by David Bocquelet)

Because of massive tank losses during the first two months of the invasion, starting in April, the Russian Ground Forces rushed many old T-72s and T-80s recovered from storage to Ukraine. This T-80BV thus reached the battlefield still wearing its original olive green overall livery, and equipped with Kontakt-1 explosive reactive armour (ERA) on the turret and hull. The white inscription 'NT 2200' denoted an oversized load for the Russian railways, while '2SB' and '124' indicated the unit quickly equipped with such tanks and then rushed into ad-hoc counterattacks in the Kucherivka area (launched to stop the Ukrainian advance on Svatove), where large numbers of T-80BVs were knocked out or captured by the Armed Forces of Ukraine. (Artwork by David Bocquelet)

Mechanised formations of the self-proclaimed 'Donetsk People's Republic' were originally equipped with a miscellany of T-64s and T-72s. However, by September 2022, both their losses and those of the Russian Ground Forces incurred during the first months of the all-out invasion of Ukraine had reached such proportions that they had to be re-equipped with obsolete T-62Ms. This example was sighted in June 2022, when several assets of the DPR were redeployed to the Kharkiv Oblast, to replace Russian Ground Forces units needed for the offensive on Sloviansk. During the Slobozhanska Offensive of the Armed Forces of Ukraine, this was to prove a very bad decision. (Artwork by David Bocquelet)

As with main battle tanks, there were extensive losses of BMP-2 infantry fighting vehicles of the Russian motorised infantry formations in the first two months of the war. By the late summer of 2022, surviving examples sighted in the Kupiansk area often wore a mix of quick-identification insignia, such as this one, colloquially known as 'ZOV' (call). In addition to standard BMP-2s, as shown in the main artwork, the Russian Ground Forces also had a small number of upgraded BMP-1AMs – recognisable by the installation of the 30mm 2A72 autocannon turret as used in the BTR-80A and BTR-82, as shown in the inset. (Artwork by David Bocquelet)

The 2S19 Msta-S 152mm self-propelled howitzer was the primary weapon of this type in artillery brigades assigned to army-level units – like the 9th Artillery Brigade based in Luga (St. Petersburg Oblast) – originally assigned to the 6th Combined Arms Army. Due to heavy losses during the first months of the war, many such units were either disestablished, or reorganised into elements of the 18th Guards Artillery Division. Deployed in the Oskil area, this unit was subordinated to the HQs of the 1st Guards Tank Army and the 2nd and 20th Combined Arms Armies – all based in Izium at the time of the Armed Forces of Ukraine's Slobozhanska Offensive – and almost fell apart during the hurried withdrawal to the eastern bank of the Oskil. As a result, this example, equipped with a so-called 'cope cage' atop its turret for protection from top-attack anti-tank guided missiles and early attack UAVs, was captured by the Ukrainians. (Artwork by David Bocquelet)

The 2S5 Giatsint-S is a Soviet-designed 152mm self-propelled gun. Originally envisaged to replace the towed M-46 130mm field gun, and supplement the 2S3 Akatsiya 152mm self-propelled howitzer, but be longer-ranged, it comprised a chassis modified from the 2K11 Krug (ASCC/NATO-reporting name 'SA-4 Ganef') surface-to-air missile system, mounting the 2A36 Giatsint-B gun, carrying 30 rounds of 152mm ammunition. Never upgraded nor available in bigger numbers, by 2022, the 2S5 was a rare sight in the Russian Ground Forces: this example was sighted during the summer of that year, somewhere in the eastern Kharkiv Oblast. (Artwork by David Bocquelet)

The ill-fated 4th Guards Tank Division of the 1st Guards Tank Army was not supposed to fight in the Kharkiv area, but was originally ordered to drive via Okhtyrka all the way to Kyiv. The division encountered unexpected Ukrainian resistance and in early March lost this MT-LBu – a bigger, unarmed variant of the MT-LB armoured personnel carrier, used as basis for many specialised sub-variants – including several for artillery observation and command – in the Okhtyrka area. Unusually, the vehicle wore a camouflage pattern in dark sand applied atop its dark olive-green overall livery. (Artwork by David Bocquelet)

Indicating the rather poor overall standard of equipment for the units assigned to the 6th Combined Arms Army was the widespread deployment of old 9K35 Strela-10 mobile, short-range surface-to-air missiles (ASCC/NATO-reporting name 'SA-13 Gopher') – instead of more-modern systems like the 2K22 Tunguska ('SA-19 Grison'). This example – nick-named 'Kristina', and probably assigned to the 138th Motor Rifle Brigade – was sighted in the northern Kharkiv Oblast in late spring of 2022. (Artwork by David Bocquelet)

The GAZ Tigr was a Russian 4x4 multipurpose all-terrain infantry mobility vehicle. Manufactured by the Military Industrial Company, the first examples were delivered in 2006 and widely exported. Some 2,000 Tigrs were heavily used early during the Russian all-out invasion of Ukraine, frequently equipped with the Arbalet-DM remote weapons station – sometimes including a Kord 12.7mm machine gun, but more often with the PKTM 7.62mm machine gun. This example is shown in the configuration operated by the 2nd Spetsnaz Brigade during its foray into downtown Kharkiv on 27 February 2022. It was knocked out, abandoned and subsequently captured by the Armed Forces of Ukraine. (Artwork by David Bocquelet)

Developed in the early 2000s in cooperation between Ukraine and the United Arab Emirates, the BTR-3 was based on the Soviet BTR-80, but represented an all-new vehicle, rather than an upgrade of the existing design. It received the ZTM-1 or ZTM-2 dual-feed 30mm autocannon, mounted in a one-person turret, together with 350 rounds of ready-use ammunition. While widely exported, only relatively few were acquired by the Armed Forces of Ukraine: this example had then the misfortune of being captured by the units of the self-proclaimed 'Luhansk People's Republic' and pressed into service against its former owners in March–April 2022. (Artwork by David Bocquelet)

The BTR-4 Butsefal/Bucephalus was another development of the BTR-80 concept, but was supported by the Armed Forces of Ukraine that acquired around 160 by 2022. Unlike the BTR-3, it had its internal layout entirely re-arranged – with the driver and commander in the front of the hull, engine and transmission compartment in the middle, and the passenger compartment at the rear – and significantly improved armour protection. Moreover, Ukrainian BTR-4/4Es received the 2A72 30mm autocannon and coaxially installed 7.62mm machine gun in a large turret that was also able to support two or four anti-tank guided missiles. While operated by mechanised battalions of the Armed Forces of Ukraine's 92nd Brigade, the type proved its clear superiority in firepower, precision, and mobility to comparable vehicles of Russian design. (Artwork by David Bocquelet)

The 25th 'Sicheslav' Airborne Brigade, Armed Forces of Ukraine, came into being after the dissolution of the USSR, when the 98th Guards Airborne Division was split between Ukraine and the Russian Federation. Initially during the all-out invasion of late February 2022, the brigade fought in the Balakliia area, before one of its battalions took part in the Slobozhanska Offensive. By then, the unit included a company of BMP-1TS infantry fighting vehicles: these were old BMP-1s re-equipped with ZTM-1 30mm autocannon, 30mm automatic grenade launcher, and the ability to carry anti-tank guided missiles, a combination that proved superior to older BMP-2s. (Artwork by David Bocquelet)

The lack of firepower was one of the biggest problems of the Armed Forces of Ukraine during the first year of Russia's all-out invasion. Unsurprisingly, different units and enterprises made numerous attempts to find solutions. One of these resulted in an old BTR-60PB armoured personnel carrier being equipped with the turret of the BMP-2, including its 2A42 30mm autocannon and coaxially installed PKT 7.62mm machine gun. As far as is known, this vehicle survived not only the Slobozhanska Offensive, but was still in operational service as of two years later. (Artwork by David Bocquelet)

Except for the Bushmaster mine-resistant, ambush protected (MRAP) vehicles, the most important mounts of the Armed Forces of Ukraine during the Slobozhanska offensive were two indigenous light armoured vehicles. One was the Novator (left): in production since 2017, it was designed for traversing long distances while offering protection against small arms and shell splinters. Significantly heavier was the Ukrainian Armor Varta infantry mobility vehicle (right): manufactured since 2015, this was originally designed for use by both the National Guard and the Rapid Operational Response units. By 2022, small numbers (a few dozens) of both types had found their way into several Armed Forces of Ukraine units. (Artwork by David Bocquelet)

Another 'new acquisition' for the Armed Forces of Ukraine as of September 2022 was the AHS Krab: a self-propelled gun-howitzer of Polish origin, installed in a British BAE Systems AS-90M Braveheart turret, mounted on a modified South Korean K9 Thunder chassis. In late May 2022, the Polish government donated 18 Krabs to the Armed Forces of Ukraine, before Warsaw and Kyiv signed a deal for 60 additional guns, which made Ukraine the first export customer. The first Ukrainian Krabs reached the frontlines just in time to take part in the Slobozhanska Offensive. (Artwork by David Bocquelet)

Also available by September 2022 were 16 M142 High Mobility Artillery Rocket Systems (HIMARS) delivered to the 27th Rocket Artillery Brigade, Armed Forces of Ukraine. Mounted on a standard Family of Medium Tactical Vehicles (FMTV) body from the M1140 series, the HIMARS included the launcher of the Multiple Launch Rocket System (MLRS) with six tubes. Initially using M30A1 GMLRS (Guided MRLS) ammunition with the maximum range of 92km, during the summer of 2022 the Ukrainian HIMARS conducted a campaign of destroying Russian command nodes, artillery pieces, and every single ammunition dump within 77km from the frontline, greatly hampering Russian Ground Forces' operations. While painted in green overall, this example received a 'wide grin' across the front and the sides of its armoured cab. (Artwork by David Bocquelet)

This artwork shows a captured Tigr-M armoured car, seized by Ukrainian forces in the first days of the Russian invasion and, following repairs, transferred to the Kharkiv city police. It was first publicly displayed on 23 August 2022, the anniversary of the liberation of Kharkiv from German occupation in 1943. The armoured car is painted overall dark green, with white ПОЛІЦІЯ (POLICE) markings on both sides and Ukrainian flags depicted on the side and rear doors. On the right side there is a white inscription reading ДОБРОГО ВЕЧОРА МИ З ХАРКОВА (Good evening, we are from Kharkiv). The vehicle is armed with a PKM machine gun mounted on the roof. (Artwork by David Bocquelet)

A 57mm S-60 automatic anti-aircraft gun mounted on the chassis of a KrAZ-6510 civilian truck. At the beginning of the Russian invasion, a number of long-retired guns of this type were transferred to Territorial Defence brigades. This measure allowed for the strengthening of the Territorial Defence, as some of its units had no artillery whatsoever. In the 127th (Kharkiv) Territorial Defence Brigade, one such anti-aircraft gun was mounted on a truck chassis. It was seen in public for the first time in May 2022. (Artwork by David Bocquelet)

A BTR-4E armoured personnel carrier of the 92nd Separate Mechanised Brigade, from the batch delivered to the unit on 6 December 2021. The vehicle is finished in a pixel camouflage scheme. Slat (anti-HEAT) armour is fitted only to the combat module. At the start of the Russian invasion, the 92nd Brigade was the only mechanised formation of the Armed Forces of Ukraine operating the BTR-4E. In addition, such armoured personnel carriers were also in service with the National Guard of Ukraine. (Artwork by David Bocquelet)

The 5th National Guard Brigade employed a prototype of the modernised BTR-4MV1 armoured personnel carrier in combat operations in the Kharkiv region. It wore this camouflage scheme during the liberation of the city of Izium in September 2022. The vehicle carried rapid identification markings in the form of white crosses. Such crosses were a distinctive feature of Ukrainian equipment that participated in the Slobozhanska offensive operation. (Artwork by David Bocquelet)

During the fighting near Kharkiv in late February–March 2022, Ukrainian forces captured several T-80BVM tanks that had been used by the 200th Separate Motor Rifle Brigade. This particular vehicle was subsequently employed in May 2022 by Ukraine's 93rd Separate Mechanised Brigade as a training tank. The turret bore rapid identification markings in the form of Ukrainian flag emblems. The hull carried the inscription "УЧБОВИЙ" ("TRAINING"), whilst the gun bore evacuator was marked with the word "FURY" – a reference to the popular Hollywood film. (Artwork by David Bocquelet)

The T-72B3 was the main type of Russian tank used in combat in the Kharkiv region in the spring of 2022. This particular vehicle, photographed in April 2022, belongs to the T-72B3 model 2011 or 2014 variant. It carries rapid identification markings in the form of large white letters "Z". Additionally, the crew painted a motivational slogan on the tank: СЧАСТЬЕ НЕ ЗА ГОРАМИ (HAPPINESS IS JUST AROUND THE CORNER). A photograph of this tank after its destruction by Ukrainian forces was published on 13 April 2022. (Artwork by David Bocquelet)

The primary fighter-bomber unit of the Russian Aerospace Forces active in the Kharkiv area during the first seven months of the war was the Voronezh-based 47th Composite Aviation Regiment. Comprising two squadrons of Sukhoi Su-34s, the unit became heavily involved in air strikes on the city of Kharkiv early during the Russian all-out invasion, and then served as a 'fire-brigade' during the collapse of the frontlines caused by the Slobozhanska Offensive. With its jets being limited to low-altitude strikes with unguided bombs (like FAB-500M-62s, shown here), the type suffered significant losses. This Su-34 (RF-95004, a 'veteran' of the deployment to Syria in 2015–16) was shot down over the Izium area, on 10 September 2022, while trying to slow down the advance of the Armed Forces of Ukraine. (Artwork by Tom Cooper)

Since 20 February 2022, Valuyki Airbase in Belgorod Oblast, served as a home-base for an unknown Russian Aerospace Forces regiment equipped with a total of 22 Mil Mi-24 and Kamov Ka-52 attack helicopters. Amongst its mounts was this anonymised Ka-52, which had both its two-digit Bort number (usually applied on the engine nacelle) and the serial number crudely overpainted. While grounded by bad weather early during the Russian all-out invasion, attack helicopters saw intensive deployment in support of the Russian Ground Forces' offensive from Izium to the south, but suffered extensive losses at the hands of the 92nd and 93rd Mechanised Brigades. The helicopter is shown armed with Kolomna 9M120 Ataka (ASCC/NATO-reporting name 'AT-9 Spiral-2') anti-tank guided missiles. (Artwork by Luca Canossa)

A veteran of the War in Afghanistan in the 1980s – as shown by the corresponding insignia applied on the nose – and Donbas operations in 2014, this Ukrainian Su-25 was in storage as of February 2022. Quickly overhauled and repainted in grey overall, it was observed in action in May of the same year. Due to bad experiences with friendly fire, by June 2022, it had the lower section of the left engine nacelle painted in yellow, and that of the right engine nacelle painted in blue, and the lower portion of the rudder painted in Ukrainian national colours, as means of quick identification. The jet is shown as of September 2022, when it also flew combat sorties in support of the Slobozhanska Offensive, armed with B-13 pods for 122mm unguided rockets. (Artwork by Luca Canossa)

Russian sources cited by analysts at the Institute for the Study of War already asserted on 10 September that the transfer of reinforcements to the area of the Ukrainian offensive was carried out solely to ensure the withdrawal of the Russian grouping from the Izium area to the left bank of the Oskil River. The same sources indicated that the advance of Ukrainian Armed Forces units toward Velykyi Burluk was facilitated by the absence of a continuous Russian defensive line.[64]

Ukrainian mobile groups infiltrated the gaps between enemy strongpoints, forcing their garrisons to withdraw under the threat of encirclement. On 10 September, Ukrainian forces liberated Velykyi Burluk, and the following day they liberated the settlement of Kozacha Lopan, located in the northern Kharkiv Oblast directly adjacent to the border with the Russian Federation.[65] Thus, the Slobozhanska Offensive Operation spread not only to the southern and eastern parts of the Kharkiv Oblast, but also to the northern parts.

Even propagandists from the Russian Ministry of Defence could no longer conceal the successes of the Defence Forces of Ukraine and the failure of Russian occupation troops in the Kharkiv Oblast. This is clearly demonstrated by two maps from official briefings of the Russian Ministry of Defence held on 10 and 11 September. The second map reflects the occupiers' loss of control over the entire northern part of the region and the Izium area, although just a day earlier this fact had not been acknowledged.

The offensive from Barvinkove toward Izium was conducted by the 72nd Separate Mechanised Brigade and the 95th Air Assault Brigade, with support from units of the 80th Air Assault Brigade and the 25th Airborne Brigade, as well as the 49th Separate Infantry Battalion 'Carpathian Sich'. Organised resistance was encountered only on the first defensive line. After the destruction of forward observation posts and platoon strongpoints of the enemy, Ukrainian forces entered the city on 10 September, divided it into sectors, and carried out clearance operations against the remnants of the Russian garrison.[66]

On 12 September, the Command of the Air Assault Forces of the Armed Forces of Ukraine reported that 'air assault troops have raised the State Flags in the settlements of Kamianka, Bohorodychne, Izium, Oskil, and others'.[67] Of particular importance is the mention of the village of Bohorodychne (south-east of Izium), as it is located not in the Kharkiv Oblast but in the Donetsk Oblast. The Slobozhanska Offensive Operation continued to develop successfully, and on 12 September the city of Sviatohirsk (also in the Donetsk Oblast) was liberated.[68]

It can be stated that the first stage of the Slobozhanska Offensive Operation concluded on 12 September 2022. As a result of seven days of fighting, Ukrainian forces liberated the entire occupied part of the Kharkiv Oblast west of the Oskil River. In addition, several bridgeheads were established on the eastern bank of the river, facilitating the further development of offensive operations. Key transportation hubs – Balakliia, Kupiansk, Izium, and Vovchansk –were liberated, and the principal supply routes of the enemy's Donetsk grouping were severed.

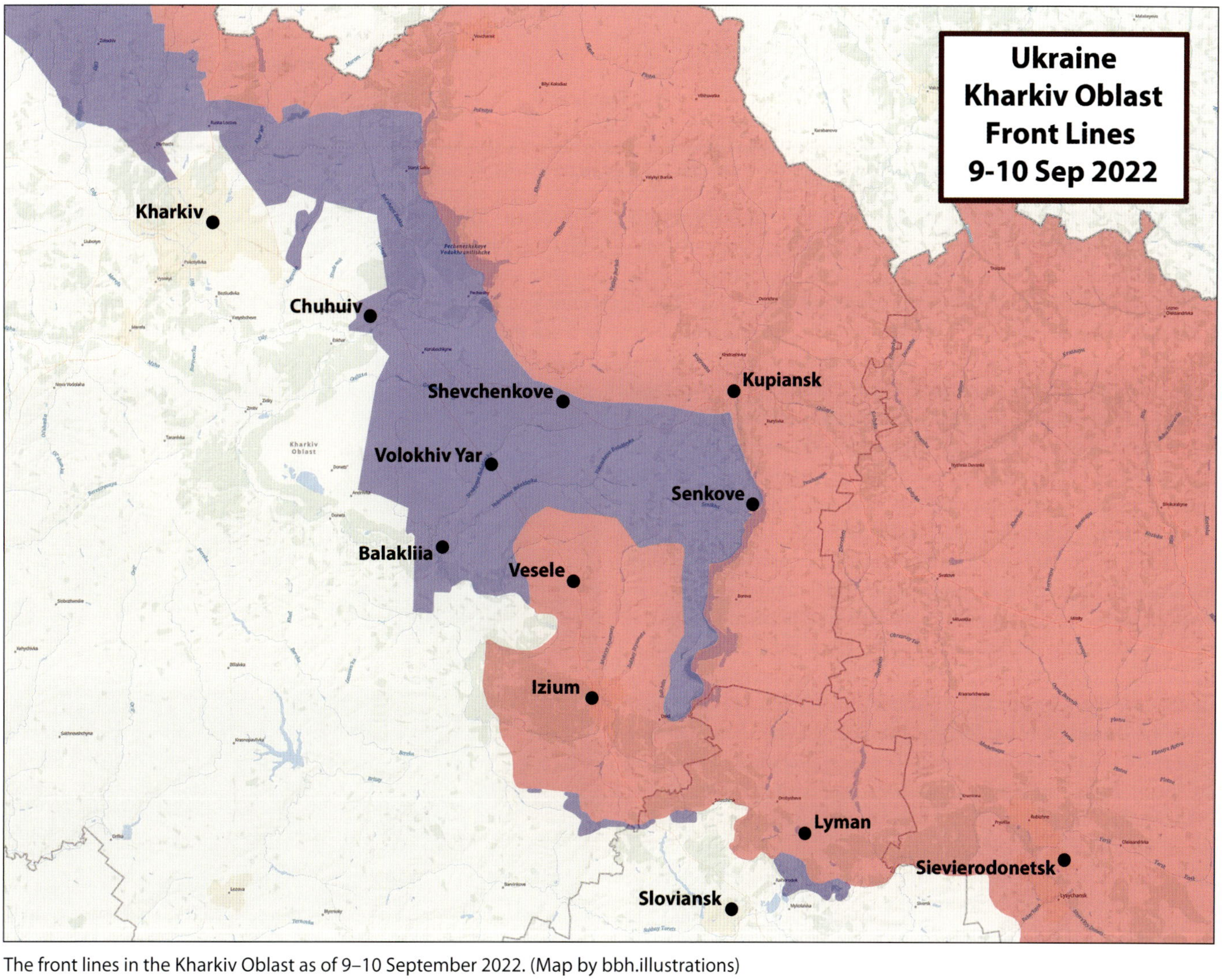

The front lines in the Kharkiv Oblast as of 9–10 September 2022. (Map by bbh.illustrations)

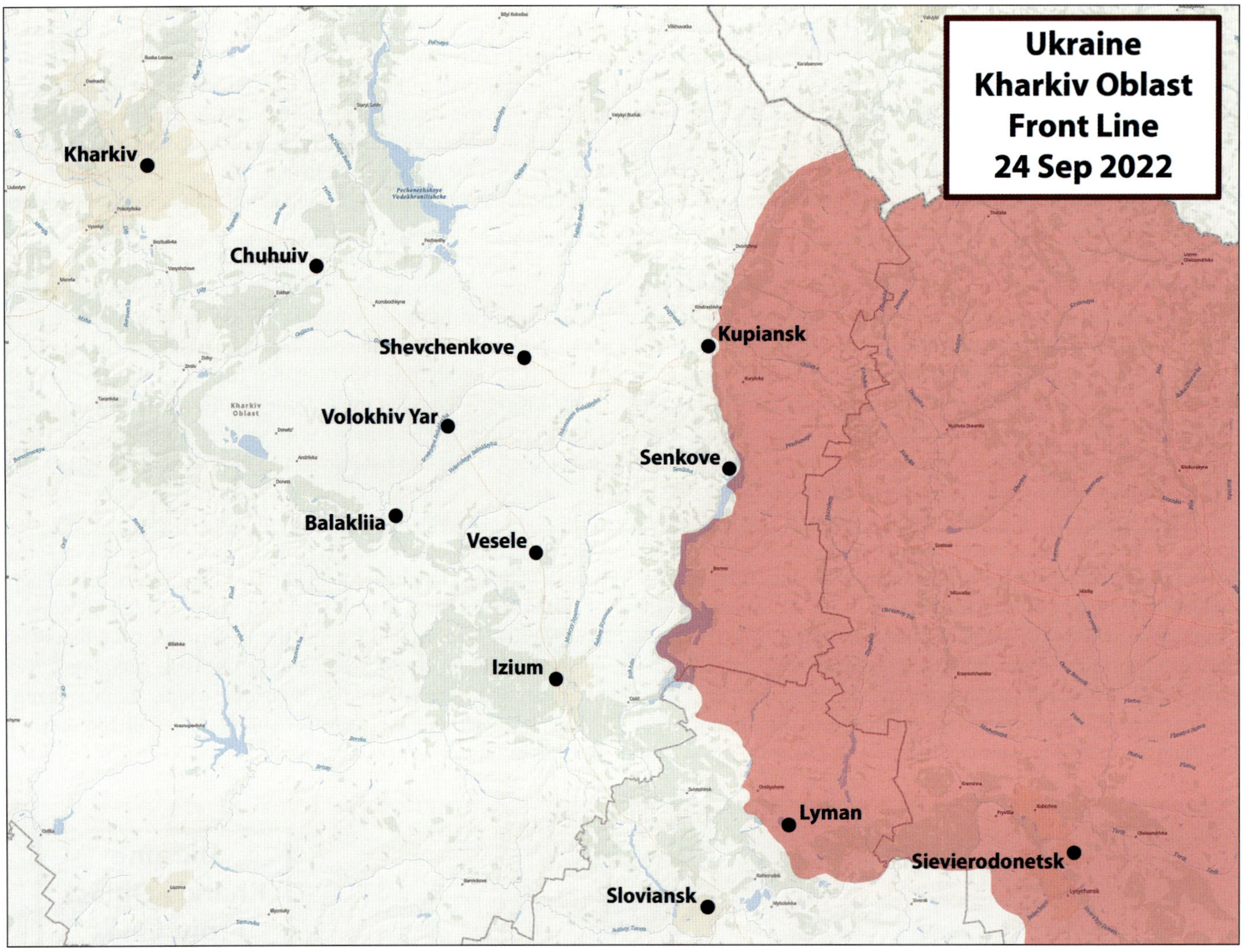

Situation on the front line in the Kharkiv Oblast as of 24 September 2022. (Map by bbh.illustrations)

P. Batacchi and A. Mottola identify the following main factors behind the success of the Ukrainian offensive: 1) long-range artillery; 2) the actions of mobile raiding groups; 3) air operations; 4) the actions of mechanised and tank units; 5) an air defence 'umbrella'; 6) coordination of all elements.[69] While generally agreeing with these conclusions, we nevertheless consider it necessary to make several clarifications. First of all, this concerns air operations. Assessing this factor is rather difficult, since the official reports of the General Staff of the Armed Forces of Ukraine contain only the overall number of strikes against enemy targets carried out by aviation on a given day, without a breakdown by operational direction. Therefore, we turn to an analysis of indirect data. To a certain extent, aviation losses may serve as an indicator of the intensity of combat operations. M. Strembski summarised information on Ukrainian and Russian aviation losses on the basis of an analysis of official and unofficial sources. According to Russian reports, from 6 to 12 September inclusive the occupiers shot down six Ukrainian aircraft (all in the south, over the Kherson and Mykolaiv oblasts) and one helicopter (over the Donetsk Oblast).[70] During this period, the Ukrainian side confirmed the loss of only one Su-25 attack aircraft, shot down by an enemy fighter on 7 September 2022 over Mykolaiv Oblast (the pilot, Major Vadym Blagovisniy, was killed).[71] Based on these data, it can be assumed that the activity of Ukrainian aviation on the Slobozhanska axis was limited, otherwise, reports from the Russian side would inevitably have included 'downed' Ukrainian aircraft and helicopters. At the same time, the assertion by Italian researchers regarding the effectiveness of Ukrainian air defence should be considered fully justified. In particular, on 7 September near Volokhiv Yar, a MANPADS crew of the 92nd Separate Mechanised Brigade shot down a Russian Su-25SM attack aircraft, which was confirmed by the recovery of its wreckage.[72] On the same day, air defence gunners of the 80th Air Assault Brigade also shot down an Mi-24 (or Mi-35M) attack helicopter.[73]

Ukrainian soldiers, in a Novator armoured vehicle, in liberated Izium. (pravda.com.ua)

A column of Ukrainian tanks led by a mine clearance vehicle converted from a T-64B tank. (militarnyi.com)

The first phase of the Slobozhanska Offensive Operation was flawlessly planned and executed. The Ukrainian command succeeded in misleading the enemy about its intentions, forcing it to redeploy part of its forces from the Kharkiv Oblast to the Kherson Oblast. The offensive itself was built on the interaction of heavy units (tank and mechanised) with light motorised raiding groups, supported actively by long-range artillery and multiple launch rocket systems. This combination of efforts enabled Ukrainian forces to achieve significant results in a very short time.

From the standpoint of traditional military science, this offensive should not have taken place at all, since it was conducted without fulfilling two seemingly mandatory conditions: numerical superiority of the attacking forces over the defending ones, and the establishment of air superiority. Nevertheless, the operation was successfully carried out, and the ratio of personnel losses was highly atypical for an offensive; approximately 1:9 or 1:10 in favour of Ukrainian forces.[74]

Another atypical feature of the Slobozhanska offensive was the significantly lower than expected expenditure of artillery ammunition. Major General Andrii Malinovskyi, Head of the Missile Forces and Artillery Directorate of the Training Command of the Ground Forces Command of the Armed Forces of Ukraine, believed that Ukrainian forces would require more than 100,000 rounds. In reality, during the first five days of the operation, which proved decisive, only 32,500 rounds were expended. This was facilitated by assistance from foreign partners: U.S. intelligence helped to allocate available resources rationally by precisely locating targets. According to the plan developed before the offensive, the Ukrainian side provided descriptions of targets anticipated in a given area, while the American side used geospatial intelligence to determine the exact coordinates of the objects. This significantly increased the effectiveness of Ukrainian artillery.[75]

The list of units mentioned by the President of Ukraine, Volodymyr Zelensky, in his address on 15 September is quite indicative:

> Today in Izium I honoured our heroes. It was an honour for me to present state awards on this very land to those who liberated it. I thank the soldiers of the 14th and 92nd Separate Mechanised Brigades, the 25th Separate Airborne Brigade, and the 80th Separate Air Assault Brigade – to all, all those who in just five days forced the enemy to retreat in panic, abandon equipment, ammunition, and numerous Russian flags. I thank the 107th Rocket Artillery Brigade, the 40th, 43rd, and 44th Separate Artillery Brigades, and I thank the 26th Artillery Brigade. I would like to thank the 15th Separate Artillery Reconnaissance Brigade – all the soldiers who ensured the timely destruction of enemy targets and the advance of our ground units. And, of course, I thank the fighters of the Main Intelligence Directorate, all those who skilfully turned the enemy's panic into real hysteria.[76]

Here, along with four combined arms brigades, six artillery brigades are mentioned, including such a specific one as the 15th Separate Artillery Reconnaissance Brigade. This emphasises the special role played by artillery in the Ukrainian offensive.

Certain statistical generalisations made by V. Landa and K. Hnennyi on 12 September, so to speak, in the immediate aftermath of events, make it possible to assess the success of the first phase of the Slobozhanska Offensive Operation in quantitative terms. Beginning on 6 September, the Russians were driven out of territories with a total area of nearly 9,000 square kilometres, which amounts to more than 28 percent of the Kharkiv Oblast. At the same time, the authors of the overview noted that the General Staff of the Armed Forces of Ukraine remained more cautious in its assessments: figures of 700, 1,000, and 2,500 square kilometres were reported, with the latest official figure at the time of publication being 3,000 square kilometres. This estimate did not include territories liberated on 11–12 September, nor those abandoned by Russian forces but whose liberation had not yet been officially confirmed by the Armed Forces of Ukraine. According to data from the General Staff of the Armed Forces of Ukraine, between 6 and 11 September 2,850 occupiers and 590 pieces of equipment were destroyed, the value of which, according to Forbes estimates, exceeded USD 670 million. Part of this equipment was destroyed during the counteroffensive in the Kharkiv Oblast (the specific items are difficult to establish with certainty). Enemy losses amounted to 86 tanks and 158 armoured combat vehicles, 106 artillery systems, 159 vehicles, and 46 units of other equipment.[77] Admittedly, these statistics refer to the entire line of contact. However, given that the most intense fighting – moreover, offensive operations – was conducted by Ukrainian forces precisely in the Kharkiv Oblast during this period, it can be assumed that the overwhelming majority of these losses were inflicted on the enemy during the Slobozhanska Offensive Operation.

The success of the offensive in the Kharkiv Oblast was of extraordinary importance for the population of the liberated areas. Soldiers of the 14th Separate Mechanised Brigade, whose units took part in the liberation of Kupiansk, described the attitude of local residents toward the liberators as follows: 'Seeing vehicles with Ukrainian flags and Ukrainian soldiers on the streets, locals warmly wave their hands, hurry to greet us with "Glory to Ukraine!" and say these words as if they were a long-forgotten prayer… Many openly cry, and these tears simply tear your soul apart…'[78]

The Second Stage of the Slobozhanska Offensive Operation (12 September – early October 2022)

The middle and second half of September 2022 was marked by the continuation of the Ukrainian offensive in Slobozhanska. Its tempo slowed compared to the first week of the operation. Russian forces withdrew to the left banks of the Oskil and Siverskyi Donets rivers, attempting to entrench themselves along new defensive lines. The main vector of effort of the Ukrainian grouping shifted to the south-east, toward the Lyman axis. At the same time, considerable attention was also devoted to the liberation of the settlement of Kupiansk-Vuzlovyi (with the railway station of the same name), located south of the city of Kupiansk on the left bank of the Oskil.

The small town of Lyman, situated in the north of the Donetsk Oblast, is an important communications hub that the Russians intended to defend stubbornly, concentrating reserves there. The key event of the second stage of the Slobozhanska Offensive Operation was the Second Battle of Lyman; the first had taken place in May 2022 and had been defensive in nature for the Ukrainian forces. The Russians redirected their efforts to this area after suffering a crushing defeat between 5 and 13 May during an attempt to seize a bridgehead on the right bank of the Siverskyi Donets near Bilohorivka (east of Lyman).[79]

On 23 May, fighting began on the northern approaches to the city. Lyman was defended primarily by units of the Air Assault Forces – subunits from the 79th, 80th, and 95th Separate Air Assault Brigades, as well as the 81st Separate Airmobile Brigade. They were supported by units of the 3rd (Luhansk) Border Detachment and the Consolidated Border Detachment 'Lviv' of the State Border Guard Service of Ukraine.

The Russians attacked with forces of the 15th Separate Motor Rifle Brigade, reinforced by a battalion tactical group of the 90th Tank Division, units of the 24th Special Purpose Brigade, as well as a battalion tactical group from the 2nd Army Corps. During 24–25 May, Russian forces intensively shelled Lyman with rocket and tube artillery, including the use of 240mm 2S4 Tyulpan self-propelled mortars. Strike aviation was also widely employed. Advancing behind a rolling barrage, Russian troops had occupied about 70 percent of the city by the evening of 25 May. In the second half of 26 May, Ukrainian units were forced to withdraw from Lyman, blowing up the bridge behind them.[80]

The first successes of the Defence Forces of Ukraine on the Lyman axis were achieved on the eve of the Slobozhanska Offensive Operation. The advance on Lyman began from the southern direction. On 3–4 September, photo and video materials appeared confirming that Ukrainian troops had crossed the Siverskyi Donets River and liberated the village of Ozerne, located south-east of Lyman. This operation involved the 63rd Battalion of the 103rd

Destroyed Russian pontoon bridge on the Donets River, Bilohorivka district, May 2022. (armyinform.com.ua)

Territorial Defence Brigade and units of the 15th Separate Regiment of the National Guard of Ukraine.[81] The official announcement of the liberation of Ozerne was published a few days later, on 8 September.

On 5 September 2022, social media reports confirmed that Ukrainian forces had liberated the small village of Staryi Karavan, located 13km southwest of Lyman and west of Ozerne.[82] This created a bridgehead on the left bank of the Siverskyi Donets from which an advance on Lyman could be conducted. Russian positions in the villages of Ozerne and Staryi Karavan blocked two roads leading to Lyman, and there were no remaining defensive lines between these villages and the city. Thus, the liberation of these settlements created the preconditions for the further development of the offensive toward Lyman.

The rapid crossing of the Siverskyi Donets by Ukrainian units in September 2022 stood in stark contrast to the bloody Russian attempt to force the same river in May, especially given that, in September, the Ukrainian forces involved included second-line units from the Territorial Defence Forces, and the National Guard.[83] On the morning of 10 September, one Russian military blogger wrote: 'South of Staryi Karavan, the enemy managed to establish a crossing over the river by laying a causeway. Heavy equipment – infantry fighting vehicles and tanks – is crossing it right now'.[84] Analysts from the Institute for the Study of War noted that on 10 September Ukrainian forces reached the southern and south-western outskirts of Lyman. This created a threat not only to the city's garrison but also to the Izium grouping, since the troops in Lyman were covering the withdrawal of that formation. It was noted that 'conflicting Russian reports claiming that Russian forces had withdrawn from Lyman are likely false, but they indicate a panicked and disoriented state of the Russian information space regarding the situation of Russian forces in this area'.[85]

The subsequent course of the Lyman operation consisted of the gradual encirclement of the city. On the southern sector, the liberation of the villages of Dibrova and Brusivka made it possible to link the two bridgeheads on the left bank of the Siverskyi Donets. On 17 September, Ukrainian troops liberated the village of Shchurove, located north of Staryi Karavan. One of the participants in the liberation of this settlement recalled: 'We were crossing, moving a very long distance, heavily loaded, waist-deep in water… We crossed a meadow that had been flooded because the dam had been blown up. We were walking through water, and accordingly the tripwires that had been set earlier were also underwater…'.[86]

The liberation of Bilohorivka on 19 September had not only tactical significance (the road connecting Lyman with Lysychansk passed through this village) but also symbolic importance; it was the first liberated settlement in the Luhansk Oblast. On that day, the head of the Luhansk Regional Military Administration, Serhii Haidai, stated: 'Luhansk Bilohorivka has been cleared and is fully under the control of the Armed Forces of Ukraine. We all need to be patient in anticipation of the large-scale de-occupation of the Luhansk Oblast. This process will be much more difficult than in the Kharkiv Oblast'.[87] Bilohorivka was liberated by units of the 8th Operational Regiment of the National Guard of Ukraine and servicemen of the Armed Forces of Ukraine. Evacuation of the remaining civilians had to be organised immediately, as Russian occupying forces launched intense shelling of the settlement.[88] Artillery bombardments, air strikes, and infantry assaults continued for months thereafter, but without success, as Ukrainian forces were well entrenched in the settlement, or rather, in what remained of it.[89]

From the western direction, the advance on Lyman was conducted from Sviatohirsk, liberated on 12 September. Approximately 20km remained to Lyman, but it proved impossible to take the city in a rapid push. On 15 September, Ukrainian forces drove the enemy out of the village of Sosnove (north of Sviatohirsk). After that, a small Russian garrison occupying the village of Studenok (north-west of Sosnove, already in Kharkiv Oblast rather than Donetsk Oblast) was forced to withdraw to avoid encirclement. Using these villages as jumping-off points, Ukrainian forces launched an advance along

Bilohorivka was completely destroyed as a result of shelling by Russian occupiers. (National Guard of Ukraine)

A column of Ukrainian troops approaches Lyman. In the foreground is a BTR-80 armoured personnel carrier, followed by a Varta armoured vehicle, September 2022. (armyinform.com.ua)

two axes. Advancing to the north-east, units of the Defence Forces of Ukraine had liberated Oleksandrivka, Krymky, Yatskivka, and a number of other settlements along the border between Donetsk and Kharkiv oblasts by 22 September. The second thrust was directed eastward, where intense fighting for the village of Yarova continued until 19 September.[90]

As Ukrainian forces approached Lyman, enemy resistance intensified. Between 21 and 24 September, the 81st Separate Airmobile Brigade, supported by a battalion tactical group of the 4th Rapid Reaction Brigade of the National Guard, fought the enemy for the settlements of Novoselivka and Drobysheve, which adjoin Lyman from the north-west. Ukrainian troops managed to liberate Novoselivka only on 25–26 September. Drobysheve was blocked by units of the 81st Brigade from three sides, the exception being the eastern one. The village was finally liberated only on 30 September.[91]

To the left of the 81st Brigade, the 25th Separate Airborne Brigade and the 95th Separate Air Assault Brigade were advancing. On 22 September, the former, together with the 1st Battalion of the 95th Brigade, attacked from the Krymky–Oleksandrivka area and liberated the settlements of Korovii Yar, Karpivka, and Ridkodub. On 23 September, Russian forces attempted a counterattack near Lypove, but were stopped and contained; on 25 September they were driven out of the settlement. Advancing south toward Lyman, Ukrainian paratroopers cleared Lypove and Nove of enemy forces and blocked them in Zelena Dolyna.

On 27 September, the spokesperson for the Eastern Group of Forces, Serhii Cherevatyi, reported that the Defence Forces of Ukraine had liberated the settlements of Drobysheve, Novoselivka, Shandryholove, and Serednie (all located north of Lyman), as well as Yampil (southeast of the city). The Russian grouping, numbering about 5,500 personnel, found itself in an operational encirclement; only a narrow corridor to the east remained, toward Zarichne–Torske and further on to Kreminna.[92]

The core of the enemy grouping around Lyman consisted of the 752nd Motor Rifle Regiment of the 3rd Motor Rifle Division and the BARS-13 volunteer detachment.[93] The latter was roughly equivalent in size to a battalion. It belonged to the system of BARS volunteer formations ('Combat Army Reserve of the Country') and was one of three such detachments (around 20 BARS units were formed in total in the Russian Federation) created by the 'Union of Donbas Volunteers'.[94] In addition to its numerical designation, BARS-13 also had the names 'Rurik' and 'Russian Legion'. The BARS-16 'Kuban' detachment also operated near Lyman.

In addition to these units, the Lyman grouping of Russian occupation forces included elements of the 509th Motor Rifle Regiment (from the 19th Motor Rifle Division), the 21st Separate Motor Rifle Brigade, as well as units from the LPR's 2nd Army Corps; the 2nd Separate Motor Rifle Brigade and the 208th 'Cossack' Rifle Regiment.[95]

To liberate Lyman and the adjacent territories, the Defence Forces of Ukraine, in addition to the already mentioned 25th, 81st, and 95th Air Assault Brigades and the 4th Brigade of the National Guard of Ukraine, also deployed units of the 66th and 93rd Separate Mechanised Brigades, as well as the 103rd and 125th Territorial Defence Brigades.[96]

The situation for Russian forces in the eastern Kharkiv Oblast and the adjacent parts of the Donetsk and Luhansk oblasts continued to deteriorate. The Russians attempted to establish a new defensive line stretching from the city of Svatove in the north through the valley to Kreminna, located 40 kilometres to the south. However, the valley – surrounded on all sides by higher ground – was not a particularly favourable terrain for defence. In an effort to support

Wreckage of a Su-34 bomber (tail number RF-81852) found in Lyman on 2 October 2022. (General Staff of the Armed Forces of Ukraine)

the ground units that had been encircled, Russian aviation intensified its operations in late September. Nevertheless, Ukrainian air defence demonstrated its effectiveness. On 24 September, two Su-34 frontline bombers were shot down in Kharkiv Oblast.[97] The wreckage of another aircraft of this type was found by Ukrainian troops on 2 October 2022 in Lyman, after the liberation of the city.[98]

The situation of the Russian grouping in Lyman on 25 September was vividly characterised by Mike Martin, a research fellow in the Department of War Studies at King's College London: 'Lyman looks like an old mousetrap. First, you can press from the northern and eastern flanks of Lyman, forcing the Russians to reinforce the defence of this critical railway hub. And then you expand the encirclement to trap even more enemy forces'.[99]

Having assessed the situation, the Russian command decided not to continue holding Lyman, as this would inevitably have led to the encirclement and destruction of the Lyman grouping. Instead, it opted to withdraw its forces eastward. To facilitate this manoeuvre, the 503rd Motor Rifle Regiment of the 19th Motor Rifle Division, reinforced with newly mobilised personnel, was redeployed to the area of Torske.[100]

On 1 October, the Ministry of Defence of the Russian Federation announced: 'Due to the creation of a threat of encirclement, allied forces [meaning formations of the Armed Forces of the Russian Federation and the LPR – A. Kharuk] were withdrawn from the settlement of Krasnyi Lyman to more advantageous defensive lines'.[101] It should be noted that the Russians used the old name of the city – Krasnyi Lyman – without recognising the changes in the names of settlements in the Donetsk and Luhansk oblasts made after 2014.

The withdrawal of Russian troops took place through a corridor in the direction of Torske and further toward Kreminna. It occurred under constant Ukrainian artillery fire; additionally, the withdrawal route was remotely mined with AT-2 anti-tank mines using MARS II multiple rocket launchers supplied by Germany. As a result, the Russians were unable to extract their entire Lyman grouping from the encirclement – some of its forces remained in Lyman itself and in several small 'cauldrons' east of the city. Certain Russian units lost contact with the main forces and were forced to hide in the surrounding forests.

For some time, organised Russian defence in the Lyman area effectively ceased to exist. The city itself was cleared of the remnants of the Russian garrison on 2 October 2022 by forces of the 81st Separate Airmobile Brigade and the Operational Assignment Battalion of the National Guard of Ukraine named after Hero of Ukraine Major General Serhii Kulchytskyi. 'Vovk', a serviceman of the latter unit, recalls the Russian withdrawal from Lyman:

> It turned out that they had been preparing to withdraw throughout that entire day. The main part of their forces had already pulled back, and those remnants that stayed behind were withdrawing during our assault. Some fled, some remained and changed into civilian clothes. These were people without documents, who could not orient themselves – didn't know which street was which, who was born where, who had relatives where, and so on. Their cover stories kept changing. We realised that these were most likely soldiers disguised as civilians and handed them over....[102]

On 2 October, Ukrainian President Volodymyr Zelensky confirmed the liberation of Lyman: 'As of 12:30, Lyman has been completely cleared'.[103]

Advancing on the heels of the retreating enemy, Ukrainian forces liberated the villages of Terny, Yampilivka, and Torske. This was reported on 2 October by the spokesperson of the Eastern Grouping of the Armed Forces of Ukraine, Serhii Cherevatyi: 'Our troops have taken the village of Torske, which lies on the route to Kreminna, and are striking with artillery fire the enemy units that are attempting to entrench themselves in Kreminna and establish

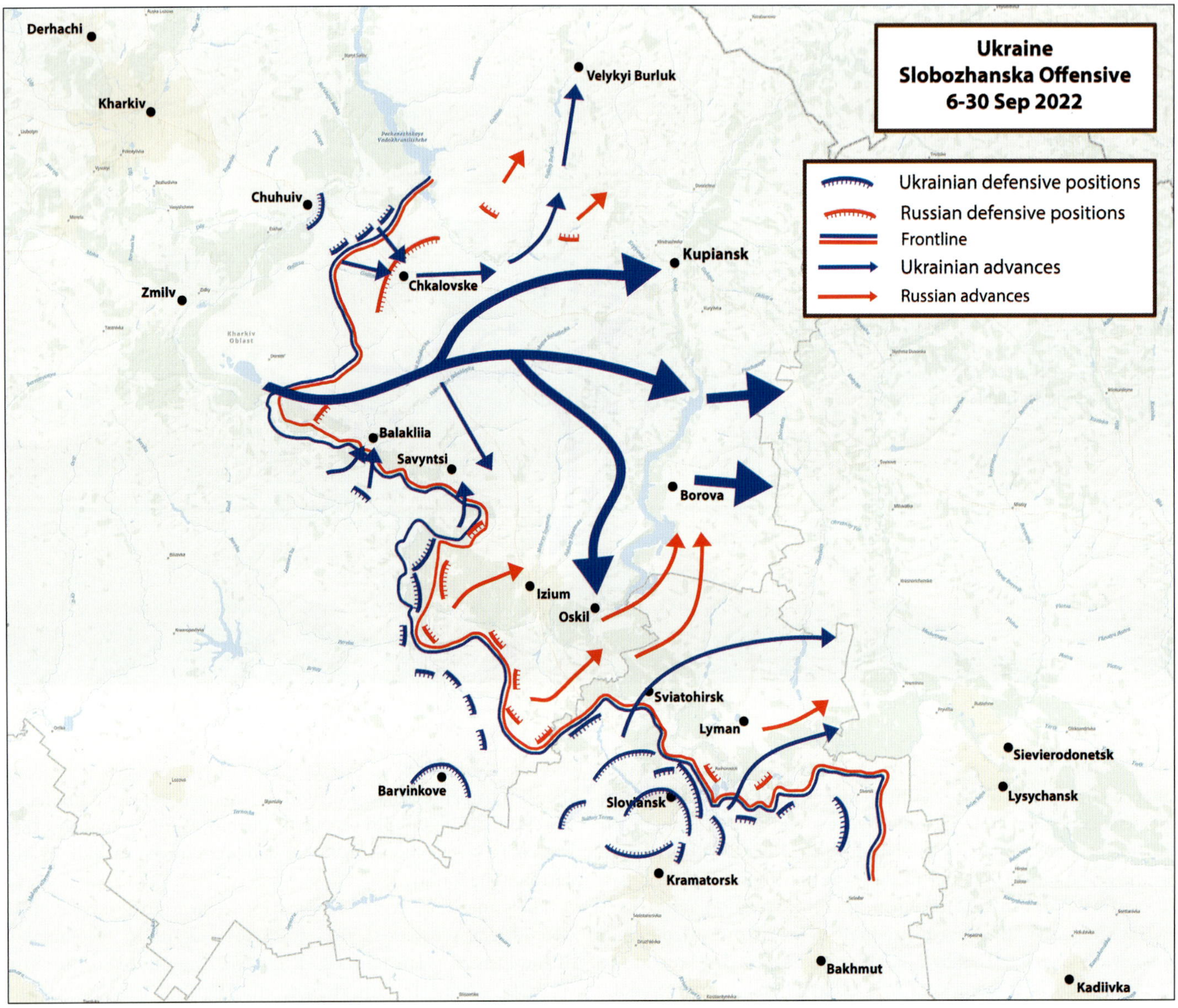

A zoomed-out presentation of the first phase of the Slobozhanska Offensive. Notable is the principal direction of the initial advances in the direction of the Oskil River and Kupiansk. Also shown are supporting attacks in the Sviatohirsk and Lyman areas, first crossings of the Oskil River and the exploitation in the direction of Velykyi Burluk. Combined, these led to a wholesale collapse of the Russian frontlines in this part of Ukraine – resulting in a crisis the Russian Ground Forces' commanders managed to solve only late the same month. (Map by bbh.illustrations)

Ukrainian military near the city council building in liberated Lyman. (militarnyi.com)

defences'.[104] These villages are located on the eastern bank of a chain of reservoirs stretching from north to southeast of Lyman. Holding them would have allowed Russian forces to organise a new defensive line anchored on water obstacles. However, the Russians lacked sufficient forces to do so.

In parallel with the operation to liberate Lyman, Ukrainian troops expanded their offensive farther north, aiming to complete the liberation of the Kharkiv Oblast by driving the enemy out of the left bank (relative to the Oskil River) part of the region. The clearing of the left bank part of Kupiansk was completed by 18 September. On 21 September, units of the Defence Forces of Ukraine began crossing the Oskil River at several locations north of Kupiansk. The 1st and 2nd Mechanised Battalions of the 14th Separate Mechanised Brigade crossed near the settlement of Holubivka, while the 3rd Battalion crossed near Dvorichna, located farther north. The villages of Hrianykivka and Dvorichne, situated opposite the settlement of Dvorichna on the left bank of the Oskil, were liberated.

Units of the 92nd Separate Mechanised Brigade crossed the river between Holubivka and Kupiansk. Between 22 and 24 September, gradually pushing the enemy away from Kupiansk, they drove Russian forces out of Kivsharivka and Podoly, and reached the western outskirts of Petropavlivka. Farther north, the 14th Separate Mechanised Brigade liberated the settlements of Lyman Pershyi, Masiutivka, and Horobiivka, and began fighting for Tavilzhanka. The enemy offered fierce resistance and in some places even attempted counterattacks, which is why the tempo of the Ukrainian advance was relatively slow compared to the first stage of the Slobozhanska Offensive Operation.

A significant success was achieved on 26 September with the liberation of Kupiansk-Vuzlovyi, which hosts an extremely important railway station. Notably, confirmation of this was indirect: in the evening report of the General Staff of the Armed Forces of Ukraine for 26 September, Kupiansk-Vuzlovyi was listed among the settlements shelled by Russian forces.[105] The following day, this was confirmed by the head of the Kharkiv Regional Civil-Military Administration, Oleh Syniehubov. At that point, 454 settlements in the Kharkiv Oblast had already been de-occupied, and six percent of the region's territory remained under Russian occupation.[106]

During the fighting in the second half of September 2022, the participation of new Russian volunteer formations – regional 'named' battalions – was noted. In particular, the 'Baikal' Battalion, formed in July–August in Buryatia, operated in the Kupiansk area.[107] On 28 September, in the battle for the village of Petropavlivka, it was almost destroyed: 180–200 fighters were killed and another 170 were wounded.[108]

Between 27 and 30 September, the 92nd Separate Mechanised Brigade liberated Synkivka and Novoosynove. Combat engagements with Russian forces took place near Krokhmalne and Stelmakhivka. By 7 October, the brigade had liberated these villages as well as Berestove, and transitioned to the defence in the areas of Stelmakhivka, Novoselivske, and Kotliarivka (on the administrative border between the Kharkiv and Luhansk oblasts). Later, along this line, the 92nd Brigade was replaced by the 103rd Territorial Defence Brigade.

After liberating Lyman Pershyi on 25 September, the 14th Separate Mechanised Brigade began operations to liberate Lyman Druhyi. By the end of the month, the brigade's units had reached the line Mykolaivka (of the Dvorichna territorial community) – Orlianka–Vilshana, where fierce fighting was underway. Together with units of the 92nd Separate Mechanised Brigade, on 7 October

Occupiers reduced Kupiansk-Vuzlovyi to ruins. (armyinform.com.ua)

Destroyed Russian tank in the village of Oskil. (Artem Listopad)

they succeeded in forcing the enemy out of Ivanivka and transitioned to the defence along the line Shaparivka halt–Yahidne–Mykolaivka (of the Petropavlivka territorial community), effectively along the border between the Kharkiv and Luhansk oblasts.

In the southern part of Kharkiv Oblast, the 80th Air Assault Brigade conducted offensive operations. It crossed the Oskil River near the village of the same name, downstream from the Oskil Reservoir. Advancing northward along the left (eastern) bank of the reservoir, the brigade's units liberated the villages of Rubtsi and Lozove from Russian occupation. On 24 September, Pisky-Radkivski was liberated.[109]

The commander of the 3rd Battalion of the 80th Brigade, Colonel Pavlo Rozlach, recalled the fighting for this village as follows:

> We did not have sufficient forces to take full control of Pisky-Radkivski, so I made a decision. Pisky-Radkivski is divided by a railway. We could gradually clear and hold one half. The plan, therefore, was this: we move out, block all railway crossings, and then – toward the river – we block the area, take it under fire control, set up ambushes, and in this way clear and drive the enemy out of the right side of Pisky-Radkivski. The left side we block, because the railway embankment prevents them from crossing. We take the crossing and leave them one last route through which they could escape – but under fire control. We chased them methodically from left to right through these Pisky… A proper slap in the face for the Russian Federation. We broke them psychologically and physically. We captured a lot of equipment that will serve us.[110]

In the following days, the 80th Air Assault Brigade drove the occupiers out of the villages located further to the north and north-east: Nyzhche Solone, Vyshche Solone, Iziumske, and Maliivka. On 3 October, the settlement of Borova, located even further north near the Oskil Reservoir, was liberated.[111]

On 5 October, the 80th Air Assault Brigade liberated the village of Andriivka (south of Iziumske, near the administrative border with the Luhansk Oblast). The bridgehead secured by the 80th Brigade was linked with the territory de-occupied by the 14th and 92nd Separate Mechanised Brigades to the north, and with the forces of the Lyman grouping to the south. The new line of contact ran along the line Yampil–Torske–the Zherebets River–Andriivka–Dvorichne.

The stabilisation of the line of contact roughly along the eastern administrative border of the Kharkiv Oblast can be regarded as the completion of the second stage of the Slobozhanska Offensive Operation. This stage was characterised by significantly slower tempos compared to the first stage, due to stronger enemy resistance. The Defence Forces of Ukraine implemented their main objectives in two sectors: the Lyman area (southern Kharkiv Oblast and northern Donetsk Oblast) and the left bank of the Oskil River (from the river to the administrative border between the Kharkiv and Luhansk oblasts). It was not possible to fully liberate the territory of the Kharkiv Oblast; 29 settlements, accounting for 1.6 percent of the oblast's territory, remained under occupation. The head of the Kharkiv Regional Civil-Military Administration, Oleh Syniehubov, explained why the liberation of the oblast could not be completed: 'The military had to make balanced decisions […] the risk must be a healthy one. The military explained that the operational situation on the battlefield was such that we stopped where we stopped. There was already a concentration of enemy forces there, fortified positions, minefields, and everything else'.[112]

A distinctive feature of the second stage of the Slobozhanska Offensive Operation was that, in the northern sector, the Defence Forces of Ukraine employed 'heavy' formations; mechanised brigades. Further south (in the Lyman area and between Lyman and the Oskil Reservoir), operations were conducted primarily by the brigades of the Air Assault Forces. On the Russian side, this period saw a marked intensification of aviation activity, as well as the widespread use of volunteer formations (BARS units and regional 'named' battalions).

The success of the two stages of the Slobozhanska Offensive Operation had a number of far-reaching consequences. In purely military terms, the Defence Forces of Ukraine seized the strategic initiative, which made it possible to consolidate positions, occupy lines advantageous for further offensive actions, and push the line of contact farther away from the densely populated cities of eastern Ukraine, thus avoiding, thanks to the element of surprise, even greater destruction and costly urban fighting in the cities of the Kharkiv Oblast.[113]

Successes on the battlefield were translated into political gains. The effective Ukrainian offensive in the Slobozhanska region encouraged Ukraine's partner countries to believe in the state's ability not only to withstand the Russian onslaught but also to conduct systematic and effective offensive operations.[114] This subsequently had a positive impact on the volume of military-technological and macro-financial assistance provided to Ukraine.

From a strategic perspective, a direct consequence of the aggressor's defeat in the Kharkiv Oblast was the declaration of a 'partial mobilisation' by decree of the President of the Russian Federation on 21 September 2022.[115] Notably, this occurred on the International Day of Peace, established by the UN General Assembly. The stated requirement was 300,000 mobilised personnel, despite the fact that the Russian Federation had launched its full-scale invasion of Ukraine with forces numbering approximately 150,000–170,000 people.[116] According to statements by Russian officials, this mobilisation plan was completed by 31 October 2022, i.e. in 40 days.[117] Such a pace of mobilisation indicates an extremely acute shortage of manpower. This is further confirmed by numerous instances in which mobilised personnel were sent into combat without even minimal training; the Russian command attempted to halt the Ukrainian advance through the mass use of what was effectively 'cannon fodder'.

Another consequence of the success of the Defence Forces of Ukraine in the Kharkiv Oblast was the impossibility for Russia to organise the incorporation of the Kharkiv Oblast into the Russian Federation. The idea of holding so-called 'referendums' in the occupied territories had been circulated in the information space by collaborators and Russian officials since approximately July 2022. Preparations for these events were fairly intensive: Russian political technologists were active in the Donetsk, Luhansk, Zaporizhzhia, Kherson, and Kharkiv oblasts (naturally, in their occupied parts). However, on 11 September, reports emerged that the Russian authorities had 'put on hold' the holding of these 'referendums', with the successful Ukrainian offensive in Kharkiv Oblast explicitly cited as the reason.[118] Ultimately, between 23 and 27 September 2022, these 'referendums' were conducted, but only in the occupied territories of Donetsk, Luhansk, Zaporizhzhia, and Kherson oblasts. In the small part of the Kharkiv Oblast that still remained under Russian occupation, even Russian propagandists did not dare to organise such an event. The other four regions were then hastily incorporated into the Russian Federation (it should be emphasised that these acts, just like the 'referendums' themselves, are legally null and void under both Ukrainian and international law). This was intended, on the one hand, to exert a propaganda effect on the domestic population against the backdrop of defeats at the front and the mobilisation of conscripts, and on the other hand, to legally formalise the occupation of these regions, at least from the standpoint of Russian law, or rather, Russia's purported 'law'.

The Third Stage of the Slobozhanska Offensive (second half of October – December 2022)

The Slobozhanska Offensive Operation subsequently evolved into fighting for Svatove and Rubizhne, aimed at the liberation of northern Luhansk Oblast and at pushing the enemy away from Kupiansk and Lyman. After the breakthrough of the Russian defensive lines on the left bank of the Oskil River, Ukrainian forces compelled the Russian occupiers to retreat to the Svatove–Kreminna line. General Sergey Surovikin, appointed on 8 October 2022 as commander of the Joint Grouping of Russian Forces in Ukraine, initiated the deployment of an extensive network of minefields and defensive fortifications in the Luhansk Oblast. His defensive concept envisaged the implementation of the principle of echeloned defence, with several defensive lines in depth, the creation of an extensive system of protective engineering works, and dense mining of the terrain. In addition, Russian units that had suffered heavy losses were rapidly reinforced with mobilised personnel conscripted in late September 2022. All of this significantly complicated the further implementation of the offensive strategy of the Defence Forces of Ukraine.

The Ukrainian command was therefore forced to take a short operational pause in order to reconstitute combat units. On 21 October, Ukrainian forces resumed the offensive with the objective of reaching the Svatove–Kreminna line. Achieving this goal would have created the possibility of encircling the Russian grouping in Sievierodonetsk and Lysychansk, and of subsequently liberating the entirety of the Luhansk Oblast. As of 24 October, Ukrainian forces had liberated the settlements of Miasozharivka, Nevske, and Karmazynivka in Luhansk Oblast, as well as Novosadove in Donetsk Oblast, thereby bringing the entire northern section of the R66 highway on the Svatove–Kreminna stretch under Ukrainian fire control.

Building on this success, Ukrainian troops in early November crossed the Zherebets River and established positions near Stelmakhivka, north-west of Svatove. On 14 November, as a result of assault and offensive actions, units of the 81st Separate Airmobile Brigade and the 198th Separate Territorial Defence Battalion (part of the 111th Luhansk Territorial Defence Brigade) advanced on the Lyman axis by 2km east of Makiivka. By 21 November, they had liberated territories east of the settlement of Stepova Novoselivka on the Kupiansk axis.[119]

Further offensive actions were complicated by the construction of new Russian defensive positions. This enabled Russian forces to conduct limited counterattacks, attempting to regain positions previously lost on the Kupiansk direction. Advancing toward the Svatove–Kreminna line, Ukrainian forces on several axes approached to within 4–8km of the R66 highway connecting these towns. However, prolonged heavy rains made further offensive operations outside populated areas impossible. These circumstances forced both sides to take an operational pause in order to build up the capabilities of their groupings and to prepare defensive positions. By the end of November, the frontline on the northern sector of the Eastern Operational Zone had stabilised and changed little, even after Ukrainian successes in the areas of Stelmakhivka, Makiivka, and Stepova Novoselivka.

The beginning of December on the Kupiansk and Lyman axes was characterised by localised offensive actions by both sides. In particular, Ukrainian units conducted offensive operations toward Chervonopopivka and in the forested area near Dibrova, with the intention of blocking Kreminna from the north and south, respectively. At the same time, fighters of the 'Kraken' unit liberated

Kyslivka and Kotliarivka in the Kharkiv Oblast, pushing enemy units north of the Kupiansk-Svatove section of the H26 highway.

Throughout the first 10 days of December, the situation along the stretch of the front from the state border to Bilohorivka remained largely unchanged, apart from Russia's continuous strengthening of defensive fortifications along the Svatove–Kreminna line, the creation of a reserve defensive line in the Starobilsk area, and the redeployment of the most combat-capable VDV units to the Kupiansk and Lyman directions. By 8 December, Russian forces had completed the construction of an almost continuous 60km trench system between Svatove and the Russian border. Along the defensive line near this town, the Russian grouping was reinforced with units of the 1st Guards Tank Army.

Countering the enemy's build-up of defensive capabilities and creating conditions for the continuation of offensive actions on these axes, the Defence Forces of Ukraine on 9–10 December carried out precision strikes against enemy positions and logistics, and resumed offensive actions on selected sectors of the front. On 13 December, Ukrainian forces liberated Tabaivka in the Kharkiv Oblast and restored control over the Kupiansk-Svatove section of the H26 highway.

During the second half of December, Ukrainian forces conducted limited offensive actions aimed at identifying weak points in the enemy's defensive positions along the entire frontline. The Russians also attempted offensive actions on the Kupiansk axis in an effort to regain previously lost positions. These attempts proved unsuccessful: Ukrainian units held firm in defence and carried out assault operations. As a result, on 21–22 December, Ukrainian forces not only halted Russian attacks on the Kupiansk axis but also liberated the settlements of Dvorichna, Novomlynsk, and Tavilzhanka. On 30 December, on the Svatove axis, assault groups of the 'Kraken' special unit, supported by artillery and in cooperation with units of the 92nd Separate Mechanised Brigade, cleared Novoselivske of occupiers. Approximately 20km remained to Svatove.

Thus, during the third stage of the Slobozhanska Offensive Operation, the Defence Forces of Ukraine came almost right up to the Svatove–Kreminna line, preventing the enemy from consolidating along the barrier line of the Oskil and Zherebets rivers. In the course of assault operations, Ukrainian forces advanced by 20km and liberated seven settlements. These figures appear modest against the backdrop of the successes achieved in September. In practice, by the end of December 2022, the Defence Forces of Ukraine were no longer able to conduct large-scale offensive operations. This was due primarily to the lack of reserves that could timely replenish frontline units with personnel, weapons, and military equipment, as well as enable the rotation of troops exhausted by nearly three months of intense fighting. Adverse weather conditions also took their toll: heavy rains made the movement of wheeled vehicles outside populated areas extremely difficult.

Oleksandr Syrskyi recalled those events as follows:

> Probably the most dramatic and tense moments were when we could see Kreminna and Svatove right in front of us, but we could no longer move forward, even though the enemy presence there was minimal. We simply did not have reserves; equipment was breaking down. Unfortunately, we were taking losses among our servicemen. And then the rains began – this was the main factor that stopped us. Roads literally turned into solid mud, and all wheeled vehicles came to a halt. Everything we could do with this grouping, we did – everything and even more.[120]

Consequences of the Russian occupation

The successful conduct of the Slobozhanska Offensive Operation led to the almost complete liberation of the Kharkiv Oblast (as well as parts of the Donetsk and Luhansk oblasts). Russian occupying forces were pushed back from Kharkiv, significantly reducing the threat of shelling. The enemy lost the ability to use the most convenient railway lines for supplying its troops; Valuyki–Kupiansk and Belgorod–Vovchansk–Kupiansk. However, the consequences of the operation are not limited to purely military-strategic aspects. The humanitarian dimension was no less, perhaps even more, important: the liberation of tens of thousands of civilians from the harsh Russian occupation regime.

In nearly every liberated city or village, graves were found containing civilians and prisoners of war tortured by the Russians. In a forest near Izium, Ukrainian servicemen discovered 447 graves (425 civilians; 215 women, 194 men, five children, and 11 persons whose sex could not be determined; 22 servicemen). After exhumations began, it became clear that the majority of the dead bore signs of violent death, and 30 showed evidence of torture.[121] In that forest, the Russians hastily created a cemetery where they buried mainly civilians who had died during the capture of the city and were repressed after the occupation. Entire families, including children, were among the victims; some of the deceased had their hands tied, indicating execution. President of Ukraine Volodymyr Zelensky compared the discovery in Izium to the massacre in Bucha and the mass killing of civilians in Mariupol.[122] Over more than half a year of occupation, the Russians killed more than a thousand civilians in Izium alone and destroyed most of the city's infrastructure. Before the occupation, Izium had a population of about 46,000; after liberation, fewer than 20,000 remained.[123] According to Ukraine's Minister of Internal Affairs Denys Monastyrskyi, as of 29 October 2022, 765 people killed during the occupation had been discovered in the Kharkiv Oblast, of whom only 453 had been identified.[124]

Exhumation of bodies from mass graves in liberated Lyman. (National Police of Ukraine)

Mass graves were also discovered in the parts of the Donetsk Oblast liberated during the Slobozhanska Offensive Operation. On 9 October, it was reported that since 29 September, 87 bodies had been found in the liberated settlements of Donetsk Oblast, of which 38 civilians had already been identified.[125] The work of locating burial sites of victims of the occupiers continued. Within the territory of the Lyman united territorial community, 132 individual graves were discovered, from which 134 civilian bodies were exhumed, including one child, as well as two servicemen. In addition, two mass graves were found (one of them in Lyman itself): 146 people in total, including 111 civilians (among them four children) and 35 servicemen. Even a year after liberation, more than 50 of the deceased remained unidentified.[126] Before the full-scale invasion, the Lyman territorial community had a population of 43,000; by spring 2023, only 9,500 remained.[127] Civilians were forced to leave the de-occupied territories due to the destruction of housing and infrastructure, as well as the constant threat of shelling.

Infrastructure losses were enormous – over 30,000 destroyed facilities, including both apartment buildings and private homes. Power lines, gas pipelines, water supply and sewage systems were destroyed. In Kupiansk, for example, 60 percent of buildings were destroyed, and all major industrial enterprises ceased operations: the meat-processing plant, the milk-canning plant, the Kulynychi bakery, and the Norven fish-processing enterprise.[128]

Reconstruction of the railway bridge connecting Kupiansk and Kharkiv. (lb.ua)

Oleh Syniehubov, Head of the Kharkiv Regional Civil-Military Administration, noted:

> The first challenge was to restore electricity. For example, in the cities of Izium and Balakliia, we restored power a month after the de-occupation of these territories. However, we simply submitted the request, and in some places we began to restore and actually build power lines from scratch, because there, again, substations, power poles, wires – everything was completely destroyed. And, of course, this is related to demining, because without demining we cannot do this.[129]
>
> Over the course of a year, we managed to restore 90 percent of the power supply to settlements in the de-occupied territories. The remaining 10 percent are settlements located near the line of contact, which were under constant shelling, as well as those where demining has not been completed due to the specific landscape (swampy terrain, tall vegetation, etc).[130]

Firefighting at the Kharkiv Thermal Power Plant-5 on the evening of 11 September 2022. (State Emergency Service of Ukraine)

Shelling of civilian infrastructure continued even after the start of the Slobozhanska Offensive Operation. The choice of targets makes it difficult to speak of any military expediency. Not only bridges and other elements of road infrastructure were affected – whose destruction or damage could have delayed the Ukrainian advance – but also facilities directly linked to sustaining civilian life. On the evening of 11 September 2022, Russian forces shelled Kharkiv Thermal Power Plant No. 5, which led to a temporary loss of electricity supply in several regions at once. At the same time, according to Ukraine's Minister of Energy Herman Halushchenko, the Zmiiv Thermal Power Plant (Chuhuiv district) and three high-voltage substations were shelled; 40 substations of various voltage levels were de-energised, two 750kV overhead power lines and five 330kV overhead power lines were disconnected.[131] The consequences of these strikes were eliminated within a few hours. However, they became a harbinger of a series of Russian aerial and missile attacks on Ukraine's energy system in the autumn–winter of 2022. The Russian military-political leadership calculated that this would increase socio-political tension within Ukrainian society and force Ukraine to capitulate, but these calculations did not come true.

Mines and other explosive remnants of war (such as unexploded shells and bombs) posed a threat not only to infrastructure recovery but also to everyday economic activity, above all agricultural fieldwork. From the beginning of Russia's full-scale invasion until 16 October 2023, 236 incidents involving civilians detonating explosive devices were recorded in the Kharkiv Oblast, resulting in 45 fatalities and 227 injured.[132]

The data presented here reflect only some aspects of the losses suffered by the Kharkiv Oblast as a result of Russian aggression. To these must be added the destruction of cultural heritage sites, industrial enterprises, educational institutions, medical facilities, and more. In our view, this extremely important and painful subject merits a separate, dedicated study.

Mines and unexploded ammunition left on the battlefields continued to cause civilian casualties. In this case, which occurred on 18 October 2023, the farmer did not survive. (State Emergency Service of Ukraine)

CONCLUSIONS

In summing up our work, it is easy to succumb to the temptation to focus attention on the events of September 2022 and on the brilliantly executed Slobozhanska Offensive Operation. However, the fighting in the Kharkiv Oblast in 2022 cannot be reduced to this operation alone. The Kharkiv Defensive Operation, conducted under conditions of a rapid enemy advance – when the adversary enjoyed superiority in artillery and air power – disrupted the plans of the Russian military-political leadership to occupy the Kharkiv Oblast and advance to the Dnipro River. A key role in this outcome was played by the successful defence of the city of Kharkiv itself, organised through the mobilisation of all available forces, including military higher educational institutions, Territorial Defence units, and voluntary territorial formations (DFTG). The enemy suffered significant losses. However, unlike the northern regions of Ukraine, from which occupying forces were pushed out relatively quickly, the Russian command sought to retain control over the Kharkiv Oblast. There was a certain logic to this approach. Having been forced to abandon the idea of seizing Kyiv and all of Left-bank Ukraine, the Russian command set itself a more limited objective: the capture of Donbas and the encirclement of the Ukrainian Joint Forces grouping. Within these plans, Kharkiv Oblast – more precisely, its occupied eastern part – was transformed into a bridgehead from which a strike was to be delivered against the northern flank and rear of the Joint Forces grouping. The importance of the Kharkiv Oblast for the logistics of the Russian strike grouping was also exceptional: its territory contained the shortest routes connecting this grouping with central Russia, and these routes possessed high throughput capacity. The successful actions of the Ukrainian Defence Forces in the southern Kharkiv Oblast and in the adjacent areas of the Donetsk Oblast, which unfolded after the completion of the Kharkiv Defensive Operation, prevented the Russians from realising these plans.

Thanks to the efforts of the Ukrainian Defence Forces, by the end of August 2022 favourable conditions had emerged for a transition from strategic defence to the offensive. This was realised in the form of two successful offensive operations; the Slobozhanska and the Kherson operations. During the Slobozhanska offensive, Ukrainian mechanised and air assault brigades demonstrated their ability to conduct decisive raiding actions, which require initiative from tactical-level commanders, well-prepared equipment, and a high level of personnel training. Even Territorial Defence formations displayed a sufficient level of preparedness and the capacity to act creatively and proactively on the battlefield. According to military expert Viktor Kevlyuk, 'unlike our enemy, who over 200 days of war failed to surprise anyone even once with operational innovations, Ukrainian headquarters enriched the treasury of military art with a brilliant example of a modern interpretation of an offensive operation by an operational grouping of forces, the core of which is a deep raid by mechanised brigades'.[1] All of this enabled Ukraine's military and political leadership to begin planning and preparing the next strategic offensive operation, which was to be carried out during the spring–summer campaign of 2023 (an analysis of the course and results of that operation lies beyond the scope of this study). The successful execution of the Kharkiv Defensive Operation and the conduct of the Slobozhanska offensive constituted a significant contribution to the disruption of Russia's blitzkrieg plans.

BIBLIOGRAPHY

057.ua editors, 'Від добровольців до елітного формування. Історія харківського спецпідрозділу ГУР «Кракен»' ['From volunteers to an elite unit. The history of the Kharkiv special forces unit GUR "Kraken"'], Main Intelligence Directorate of Ukraine (25 November 2022), <https://gur.gov.ua/content/vid-dobrovoltsiv-do-elitnoho-formuvannia-istoriia-kharkivskoho-spetspidrozdilu-hur-kraken.html>

Artymyshyn, P. I. and Solyar, I. Y., 'Проєкт «Новоросія» В Контексті Сучасної Російсько-Української Війни' ['The "Novorossiya" project in the context of the modern Russian-Ukrainian war'], (Riga: Baltija Publishing, 2022) <https://doi.org/10.30525/978-9934-26-223-4-51>

Axe, David, 'Lyman, A Supply Hub In Eastern Ukraine, Is The Last Place A Russian Soldier Wants To Be Right Now', *Forbes* (25 September 2022), <https://www.forbes.com/sites/davidaxe/2022/09/25/lyman-a-supply-hub-in-eastern-ukraine-is-the-last-place-a-russian-soldier-wants-to-be-right-now/?sh=13877c191713>

Axe, David, 'Russian Troops Are Dashing Around Ukraine Trying To Block Ukrainian Counterattacks', *Forbes* (8 September 2022), <https://www.forbes.com/sites/davidaxe/2022/09/08/russian-troops-are-dashing-around-ukraine-trying-to-block-ukrainian-counterattacks/?sh=2d75ed4f1cbb>

Baibak, Angelica, 'Слобожанський контрнаступ: у ЗСУ пояснили, чому не вдалося втілити плани дійти до Сватового' ['Slobozhanshchyna counteroffensive: the Armed Forces of Ukraine explained why they failed to reach Svatove'], 24 Kanal (28 October 2023), <https://24tv.ua/slobozhanskiy-kontrnastup-zsu-poyasnili-shho-zupinilo-nastup_n2420719>

Balachuk, Iryna, 'In Izium 447 bodies exhumed, many women and children', *Ukrainska Pravda* (23 September 2022), <https://www.pravda.com.ua/news/2022/09/23/7368817/>

Balachuk, Iryna, 'Вийшли в лоб 2 танками: захисник розповів, як у лютому знищили велику колону росіян під Харковом' ['They came out with two tanks: a defender recounted how a large column of Russians was destroyed near Kharkiv in February'], *Ukrainska Pravda* (11 June 2022), <https://www.pravda.com.ua/news/2022/06/11/7351882/>

Batacchi, P. and Mottola, A., 'Ucraina, Putin in difficoltà e lo spettro nucleare', *Rivista Italiana Difesa*, 11 (2022), pp.25–33

Batacchi, P. and Mottola, A., 'Un'analisi preliminare della guerra in Ucraina' ['An initial analysis of the war in Ukraine'], *Rivista Italiana Difesa*, 4 (2022), pp.24–46

Berezhansky, Ihor, 'Пропагандисти РФ заявили, що самарський і башкирський СОБРи у Балаклії потрапили в оточення' ['Russian propagandists claimed that the Samara and Bashkir

SOBR units in Balakliia were surrounded'], *TCH* (7 September 2022), <https://tsn.ua/ato/propagandisti-rf-zayavili-scho-samarskiy-i-bashkirskiy-sobr-u-balakliyi-potrapili-v-otochennya-2152945.html>

Bezpalko, Ulyana, 'Війна, мобілізація та ескалація. Чого чекати від Путіна на 9 травня' ['War, mobilisation and escalation. What to expect from Putin on 9 May'], *RBC-Ukraine* (5 May 2022), <https://www.rbc.ua/ukr/news/voyna-mobilizatsiya-eskalatsiya-zhdat-putina-1651697728.html>

Bilchenko, Yulia, 'ЗСУ увійшли до Дробишева під Лиманом' ['The Armed Forces of Ukraine entered Drobyshev near Lyman'], Antikor (30 September 2022), <https://antikor.info/articles/578061-vsu_voshli_v_drobyshev_pod_limanom>

Boiko, Oleksandr, 'Повномасштабне вторгнення Росії в Україну: перебіг основних фаз війни' ['Russia's full-scale invasion of Ukraine: a timeline of the main phases of the war'], in A. Kiridon and A. Ivanenko (eds), *Російсько-українська війна. Енциклопедичний глосарій, Вип. 1 [Full-scale invasion of Ukraine. Encyclopaedic Glossary, Issue 1]* (Kyiv: Encyclopaedic Publishing House, 2024), pp.28–64

Boyko, Maria, 'Зруйновані будівлі, відсутність електрики та їжі: який вигляд має перше звільнене селище на Луганщині (відео)' ['Destroyed buildings, no electricity or food: what the first liberated village in Luhansk region looks like (video)', *TCH* (1 November 2022), <https://tsn.ua/ato/zruynovani-budivli-vidsutnist-elektriki-ta-yizhi-yak-viglyadaye-pershe-zvilnene-selische-na-luganschini-video-2192566.html>

Butusov, Yuriy, 'Балаклійський прорив' ['Balakliia breakthrough'], *Censor.net* (13 September 2022), <https://censor.net/ru/resonance/3366735/balaklyiskiyi_proriv>

Case No. 642/1618/22, Leninsky District Court of Kharkiv (8 December 2022), <https://reyestr.court.gov.ua/Review/107759505>

Centre for Military History Research of the Armed Forces of Ukraine (CMHRAFU), *Рік війни за свободу: воєнно-історичний нарис російсько-української війни (24.02.2022 – 24.02.2023) [A Year of War for Freedom: A Military-Historical Essay on the Russian-Ukrainian War (24 February 2022-24 February 2023)]*, Book I (Kyiv: Lira-K Publishing House, 2023)

Cielma, Mariusz, 'Bitwa o Donbas i upadek Mariupola' ['The Battle for Donbas and the Fall of Mariupol'], *Nowa Technika Wojskowa*, 5 (2022), pp.10–14

Cielma, Mariusz, 'Przed bitwą wszystkich bitew. Wojna w Ukrainie' ['Before the Battle of All Battles. War in Ukraine'], *Nowa Technika Wojskowa*, 4 (2022), pp.8–13

CMHRAFU, *Рік війни за свободу: воєнно-історичний нарис російсько-української війни (24.02.2022 – 24.02.2023) [A Year of War for Freedom: A Military-Historical Essay on the Russian-Ukrainian War (24 February 2022-24 February 2023)]*, Book II (Kyiv: Lira-K Publishing House, 2023)

CMHRAFU, *Рік війни за свободу: воєнно-історичний нарис російсько-української війни (24.02.2022 – 24.02.2023) [A Year of War for Freedom: A Military-Historical Essay on the Russian-Ukrainian War (24 February 2022-24 February 2023)]*, Book III (Kyiv: Lira-K Publishing House, 2023)

Cooper, Tom et al., *War in Ukraine, Volume 2: Russian Invasion, February 2022* (Warwick: Helion, 2023)

Department of Defense, *Department of Defense Dictionary of Military and Associated Terms. Joint Pub 1-02* (Washington, DC: US DoD, 2008)

Dim, Nestor, 'Мер Балаклії на Харківщині пішов на співпрацю з окупантами' ['The mayor of Balakliia in the Kharkiv region has agreed to cooperate with the occupiers'], *Novynarnia* (28 March 2022), < https://novynarnia.com/2022/03/28/mer-balakliyi-na-harkivshhyni-pishov-na-spivpraczyu-z-okupantamy/>

Doroshenko, Anastasia and Alekseeva, Victoria, 'У Лимані на Донеччині триває ідентифікація та встановлення причин смерті загиблих людей під час окупації — прокуратура' ['In Lyman, Donetsk Oblast, the identification and determination of the causes of death of people who died during the occupation is continuing, according to the prosecutor's office'], *Suspilne Donbas* (30 May 2024), <https://suspilne.media/donbas/757389-u-limani-na-doneccini-trivae-identifikacia-ta-vstanovlenna-pricin-smerti-zagiblih-ludej-pid-cas-okupacii-prokuratura/>

Drabok, Maksym and Sotnikov, Daniil, 'Аналітики про наказ Зеленського повернути південь України' ['Analysts on Zelensky's order to retake southern Ukraine'], *DW.com* (15 July 2022), <https://www.dw.com/uk/bytva-voli-viiskovi-analityky-pro-nakaz-zelenskoho-povernuty-pivden-ukrainy/a-62487441>

Drapatiy, Mykhailo, *«Кров Дніпром Тече»: Херсонська наступальна операція ["Blood Flows Through the Dnieper": The Kherson Offensive Operation]* (Kyiv: CMHRAFU, 2023)

Drozdov, Yegor, 'Минобороны: союзные войска РФ покинули Красный Лиман' ['Ministry of Defence: Russian allied forces have left Krasny Lyman'], *Ura.ru* (1 October 2022), <https://ura.news/news/1052591478>

F., Mick and Jenzen-Jones, N.R., 'Russian POM-3 anti-personnel landmines documented in Ukraine', *Armament Research Service* (15 April 2022), <https://armamentresearch.com/russian-pom-3-anti-personnel-landmines-documented-in-ukraine-2022/>

Fartushkov, Andriy and Kholodov, Pavlo, '«Яким треба бути ідіотом, щоб зайти однією ротою» – комбриг Павло Федосенко про битву за Харків' ['"How stupid do you have to be to go in with just one company?" – Brigade Commander Pavlo Fedosenko on the battle for Kharkiv'], *Radio Liberty* (9 July 2023), <https://www.radiosvoboda.org/a/zsu-bytva-za-kharkiv/32493407.html>

Fedorkova, Tatyana and Getsko, Valeria, '"Цю війну ми вже програли", — Максим Криштоп, полонений у Харкові російський льотчик' ['"We have already lost this war," says Maxim Kryshtop, a Russian pilot captured in Kharkiv'], <https://suspilne.media/216424-cu-vijnu-mi-vze-prograli-maksim-kristop-polonenij-u-harkovi-rosijskij-lotcik/>

Gaevska, Alina, 'Зеленський офіційно підтвердив звільнення Балаклії на Харківщині від російських окупантів' ['Zelensky officially confirmed the liberation of Balakliia in the Kharkiv region from Russian occupiers'], *Suspilne Kharkiv* (8 September 2022), <https://suspilne.media/279825-zelenskij-oficijno-pidtverdiv-zvilnenna-balaklii-na-harkivsini-vid-rosijskih-okupantiv/>

Gaevska, Alina, 'ЗСУ зайшли до Куп'янська Харківської області, над містом — українські прапори' ['Ukrainian Armed Forces enter Kupiansk in Kharkiv Region, Ukrainian flags fly over the city'], *Suspilne Kharkiv* (10 September 2022), <https://suspilne.media/280311-zsu-zajsli-do-kupanska-harkivskoi-oblasti-nad-mistom-ukrainski-prapori/>

Gawęda, Marcin, 'Wojna rosyjsko-ukraińska cz. 1' ['The Russian-Ukrainian War, Part 1'], *Wojsko i Technika*, 3 (2022), pp.16–24

Gawęda, Marcin, 'Wojna rosyjsko-ukraińska Cz. 2' [The Russian-Ukrainian War Part 2], *Wojsko i Technika*, 4 (2022), pp.12–20

Gawęda, Marcin, 'Wojna rosyjsko-ukraińska Cz. 3' ['The Russian-Ukrainian War Part 3], Wojsko i Technika, 5 (2022), pp.32–41.

Gawęda, Marcin, 'Wojna rosyjsko-ukraińska cz. 7' ['The Russian-Ukrainian War, Part 7'], *Wojsko i Technika*, 10 (2022), pp.38–47

Gema, Mykhailo, 'На Харківщині загинув гауляйтер важливого для росіян селища Великий Бурлук: його авто підірвали' ['The Gauleiter of the village of Velykyi Burluk, which is important for the Russians, was killed in the Kharkiv region: his car was blown up'], *24 Kanal* (11 July 2022), <https://24tv.ua/harkivshhini-zaginuv-gaulyayter-vazhlivogo-dlya-rosiyan-selishha_n2092329>

'General mobilisation announced in the "DPR" and "LPR"', *DW.com* (19 February 2022), <https://www.dw.com/ru/v-dnr-objavili-vseobshhuju-mobilizaciju/a-60839410>

General Staff of the Armed Forces of Ukraine, 'Оперативна інформація станом на 24.00 06.03.2022…' ['Operational information on 24.00, 06.03.2022…'] [Facebook post], 6 March 2022, <https://www.facebook.com/GeneralStaff.ua/posts/266469205666165>

Golovko, Volodymyr, *Вторгнення. 2022. Широкомасштабна агресія Росії проти України [Invasion. 2022. Russia's large-scale aggression against Ukraine]* (Kyiv: Institute of History of Ukraine, National Academy of Sciences of Ukraine, 2023)

Gorbunov, Dmitry, 'Генерал-майор Олег Мікац та полковник Сергій Гузченко – почесні громадяни Харкова' ['Major General Oleh Mikats and Colonel Serhii Huzchenko – honorary citizens of Kharkiv'], ArmyInform (24 August 2022), <https://armyinform.com.ua/2022/08/24/general-major-oleg-mikacz-ta-polkovnyk-sergij-guzchenko-staly-pochesnymy-gromadyanamy-harkova/>

Harasym, Andriy and Kelm, Nadia, 'Більше води. Як Сіверський Донець вдалося зробити неприступною перепоною' ['More water. How the Siverskyi Donets River became an impenetrable barrier'], *Texty.org.ua* (28 June 2022), <https://texty.org.ua/articles/107064/golubyj-val-yak-siverskyj-donec-vdalosya-zrobyty-neprystupnoyu-pereponoyu/>

Hird, Karolina, Barros, George, Philipson, Layne, and Kagan, Frederick W., 'Russian Offensive Campaign Assessment, September 6, 2022', Institute for the Study of War (7 September 2022), <https://www.understandingwar.org/backgrounder/russian-offensive-campaign-assessment-september-6>

Hird, Karolina, Mappes, Grace, Barros, George, Philipson, Layne, Clark, Mason, Russian Offensive Campaign Assessment, September 7, 2022', Institute for the Study of War (8 September 2022), <https://www.understandingwar.org/ backgrounder/russian-offensive-campaign-assessment-september-7>

Ivanets, Oksana, 'Як у лютому Сили оборони Харкова знищили спецназ рф у школі № 134' ['How in February the Kharkiv Defence Forces destroyed Russian special forces at school No. 134'], ArmyInform (2 September 2022), <https://armyinform.com.ua/2022/09/02/yak-u-lyutomu-syly-oborony-harkova-znyshhyly-specznaz-rf-u-shkoli-%e2%84%96-134/>

Ivanitsky, Alexander, 'На Харьковщине подсчитали трофейную технику России' ['Russia's captured equipment counted in Kharkiv region'], *Korrespondent.net* (14 September 2022), <https://korrespondent.net/ukraine/4516167-na-kharkovschyne-podschytaly-trofeinuui-tekhnyku-rossyy>

Kevlyuk, Viktor, 'Український наступ. Що сталося на Слобожанщині?' ['Ukrainian offensive. What happened in Slobozhanshchyna?'], *LB.ua* (14 September 2022), <https://lb.ua/society/2022/09/14/529296_ukrainskiy_nastup_shcho_stalosya.html>

Kharuk, A, 'Obrona Charkowa' ['Defence of Kharkiv'], *Nowa Technika Wojskowa*, 16 special issue (2023), pp.12–21.

Kharuk, A. and Zelenyi, V.I., 'Офіційні українські видання про російсько-українську війну та їх використання в історичних дослідженнях' ['Official Ukrainian publications on the Russian-Ukrainian war and their use in historical research'], Military Scientific Bulletin, 40 (2023), pp.202–216

Kharuk, A., 'Bitwy o Białohoriwkę' ['Battles for Bilohorivka'], *Nowa Technika Wojskowa*, special issue 17 (2023), pp.4–11

Kharuk, A., 'Dwie bitwy o Łyman 23 maja – 2 października 2022 r.' ['Two battles for Lyman. 23 May – 2 October 2022'], *Nowa Technika Wojskowa*, 17 special issue (2023), pp.12–19

Kharuk, A., 'Слобожанська наступальна операція: передумови і перший етап (6-12 вересня 2022 р.)' ['The Slobozhansky Offensive Operation: Preconditions and First Stage (6-12 September 2022)'], *Ukrainian Historical Journal*, 1 (2023), pp.5–19

Kharuk, A., 'Харківська оборонна операція (24 лютого — 14 травня 2022 р.)' ['The Kharkiv defensive operation (24 February – 14 May 2022)'], *Ukrainian Historical Journal*, 5 (2023), pp.23–34

Kharuk, A., 'Як Використовувати Російські Джерела Для Вивчення Російсько-Української Війни?' ['How to use Russian sources to study the Russian-Ukrainian war?'], *Problems of the Humanities: Collection of Scientific Works of the Ivan Franko State Pedagogical University of Drohobych, History Series*, 13:55 (2023), pp.345–346

Khlon, S., Pahiria, O., and Poltorakov, O., *"Східна брама держави", Оборона Харкова (24 лютого 14 травня 2022 р.) [The Eastern Gate of the State, The Defence of Kharkiv (24 February – 14 May 2022)]* (Kyiv: CMHRAFU, no date)

Khmelnytska, Vera, '"Фурами майно вивозили, нові авто крали": мобілізовані з ОРДЛО влаштували бунт на Харківщині ' ['"They took away our property in trucks and stole new cars": mobilised soldiers from the ORDLO staged a riot in the Kharkiv region'], *TCH* (8 September 2022), <https://tsn.ua/ato/furami-mayno-vivozili-novi-avto-krali-mobilizovani-z-ordlo-vlashtuvali-bunt-na-harkivschini-2153836.html>

Khmilevska, Viktoriia, 'У ЗСУ підтвердили звільнення п›яти населених пунктів біля Лиману (карта)' ['The Armed Forces of Ukraine confirmed the liberation of five settlements near Lyman'], *Mirror of the Week* (1 October 2022), <https://zn.ua/ukr/UKRAINE/u-zsu-pidtverdili-zvilnennja-pjati-naselenikh-punktiv-bilja-limanu-.html>

Khomenko, Svyatoslav, 'ХНР: Харьковская неудавшаяся республика' ['KNR: Kharkiv's failed republic'], BBC News Russian Service (8 April 2015)

Komarov, Dmytro and Kruglyak, Danilo, 'Контрнаступальна операція Збройних сил України на Харківському напрямку у 2022 році: досвід та стратегічне значення' ['Counteroffensive operation of the Armed Forces of Ukraine in the Kharkiv direction in 2022: experience and strategic significance'], *Bulletin of Taras Shevchenko National University of Kyiv. History*, 157:2 (2023), pp.38–43

Korepanov, V. O. and Shumov, V. V., 'Моделирование военных, боевых и специальных действий' ['Modelling military, combat and special operations'], Military Thought, 1 (2023), pp.39–40.

Kostyk, Antonina, 'За два дні львівські десантники пройшли понад 150 кілометрів в тилу противника' ['In two days, Lviv paratroopers covered more than 150 kilometres behind enemy lines'], *Tvoe Misto* (12 September 2022), <https://tvoemisto.tv/news/za_dva_dni_lvivski_desantnyky_proyshly_ponad_150_kilometriv_v_tylu_protyvnyka_137170.html>

Koval, M. V. (ed.), *Рік незламності: крах операції "Z" : Монографія [A Year of Resilience: The Collapse of Operation Z: Monograph]* (Kyiv: National Defence University of Ukraine, 2023)

Kozatskyi, Sanya, 'Зенітні установки «Gepard» працюють на Харківщині' ['Gepard anti-aircraft systems are operating in the Kharkiv region'], *Militarnyi* (26 September 2022), <https://mil.in.ua/ uk/news/zenitni-ustanovky-gepard-pratsyuyut-na-harkivshhyni/>

Krebs, Katharina, Liakos, Chris, and Kolirin, Lianne, 'Russia suspends "partial mobilisation" of citizens for Ukraine war', CNN (1 November 2022), <https://edition.cnn.com/2022/10/31/europe/russian-mobilization-suspended-intl/index.html>

Kryshtun, Ihor, 'Ато: Як Все Починалося' ['ATO: how it all began'], Army FM (14 April 2018), <https://www.armyfm.com.ua/-ato-jak-vse-pochinalosja-/>

Kwasek, T., 'Rosyjskie Wojska Powietrznodesantowe' ['Russian Airborne Forces'], *Nowa Technika Wojskowa*, 15 (2023), pp.22–31

Landa, Volodymyr and Gnennyi, Konstantin, 'Операція на 9000 визволених кв. км і $670 млн знищеної техніки РФ: контрнаступ на Харківщині в цифрах' ['Operation to liberate 9,000 square kilometres and destroy $670 million worth of Russian equipment: the counteroffensive in Kharkiv Region in figures'], *Forbes Ukraine* (12 September 2022), <https://forbes.ua/war-in-ukraine/operatsiya-na-9000-vizvolenikh-kv-km-i-670-mln-znishchennoi-tekhniki-rf-kontrnastup-na-kharkivshchini-u-tsifrakh-12092022-8285>

Liskovych, Myroslav, 'Успіх ЗСУ на Харківщині: подібне в історії війн бувало, але дуже нечасто' ['Success of the Armed Forces of Ukraine in Kharkiv region: similar events have occurred in the history of wars, but very rarely'], *Ukrinform* (17 September 2022), <https://www.ukrinform.ua/rubric-ato/3573458-uspih-zsu-na-harkivsini-podibne-v-istorii-vijn-buvalo-ale-duze-necasto.html>

Listopad, Artem, 'Подвійний злочин: в 50-х радянська влада створила Оскільське водосховище, знищивши все живе навколо, а в 2022–му окупанти його підірвали, вдруге зруйнувавши еко-систему. Чи понесе росія відповідальність за екоцид на Харківщині?' ['A double crime: in the 1950s, the Soviet authorities created the Oskil Reservoir, destroying all life around it, and in 2022, the occupiers blew it up, destroying the ecosystem for the second time. Will Russia be held responsible for ecocide in the Kharkiv region?'], *Ursa Media* (4 March 2024), <https://ursamedia.com.ua/history/podvijnyj-zlochyn-chy-ponese-rosiyja-vidpovidalnist-za-ecozid-na-kharkivshuni/>

Lyutyi, Kyrylo, 'Окупанти втекли з Куп›янська та оголосили про перенесення "столиці" захопленої Харківщини до Вовчанська' ['The occupiers fled Kupiansk and announced the transfer of the "capital" of the occupied Kharkiv region to Vovchansk'], *Oboz.ua* (9 September 2022), <https://war.obozrevatel.com/ukr/okupanti-vtekli-z-kupyanska-ta-ogolosili-pro-perenesennya-stolitsi-zahoplenoi-harkivschini-do-vovchanska.htm>

Masliychuk, Volodymyr, *Слобідська Україна [Sloboda Ukraine]* (Kyiv, 2008)

McDonald, Scott, 'What is Russia's 3rd Army Corps? New unit moving to front lines', *Newsweek* (28 August 2022), <https://www.newsweek.com/what-russias-3rd-army-corps-new-unit-moving-front-lines-intel-1737651>

Mikhalevska, Kateryna, 'ОКУПОВАНІ: Куп'янськ. Життя під загрозою повторної окупації' ['Occupied: Kupiansk. Life under threat of new occupation'], *LB.ua* (26 January 2024), <https://lb.ua/news/2024/01/26/595391_okupovani_kupyansk_zhittya_pid.html>

Military Scientific Directorate of the General Headquarters of the Armed Forces of Ukraine, *Dictionary of Military Terms and Abbreviations* (Kyiv: Ukrainian Ministry of Defence, 2020)

Miroshnichenko, Yevhen, '«Ми були першими з добровольчих підрозділів, які прийшли на допомогу Збройним Силам України 24 лютого». Інтерв›ю з начальником штабу Фрайкорпу Богданом Войцеховським' ['"We were the first volunteer units to come to the aid of the Armed Forces of Ukraine on 24 February." Interview with Bogdan Voitsekhovsky, Chief of Staff of the Freikorps'], *057.ua* (24 November 2022), <https://www.057.ua/news/3501898/mi-buli-persimi-z-dobrovolcih-pidrozdiliv-aki-24-lutogo-prijsli-na-dopomogu-zsu-intervu-z-nacalnikom-stabu-frajkoru-bogdanom-vojcehovskim-foto>

Murphy, Matt, '"Нам потрібні штурмовики". Як ПВК «Вагнер" вербує в›язнів на війну в Україні' ['"We need assault troops." How the Wagner Group recruits prisoners for the war in Ukraine'], BBC News Ukraine (15 September 2022), <https://www.bbc.com/ukrainian/features-62917466>

Naiev, Serhiy, *«Чия Відвага, Того й Перемога»: Битва за Білогорівський плацдарм (08 – 14 травня 2022 року) ['"Whose courage is the victory": The battle for the Bilohorivsky bridgehead (8–14 May 2022)'].* (Kyiv: CMHRAFU, no date)

National Defence University of Ukraine, *Хроніка війни, Частина II (Російсько-українська війна, 27.03- 25.04.2022) [Chronicle of the War, Part II (Russian-Ukrainian war, 27 March – 25 April 2022)]* (Kyiv: Ivan Chernyakhovsky National Defence University [now National Defence University of Ukraine], 2022)

National Defence University of Ukraine, *Хроніка війни, частина I (перші 30 діб російсько-української війни, 24.02-26.03.2022) [Chronicle of the War, Part I (the first 30 days of the Russian-Ukrainian War, 24 February – 26 March 2022)]* (Kyiv: Ivan Chernyakhovsky National Defence University [now National Defence University of Ukraine], 2022)

National Defence University of Ukraine, *Хроніка війни, Частина III (російсько-українська війна 26.04-26.05.2022) [Chronicle of the War, Part III (Russian-Ukrainian war, 26 April – 26 May 2022)]* (Kyiv: Ivan Chernyakhovsky National Defence University [now National Defence University of Ukraine], 2022)

Nazarova, Anna, 'ЗСУ звільнили ще один населений пункт на Донеччині (ВІДЕО)' ['The Armed Forces of Ukraine liberated another settlement in Donetsk Region (Video)'], *Free Radio* (5 September 2022), <https://freeradio.com.ua/zsu-zvilnyly-shche-odyn-naselenyi-punkt-na-donechchyni-video/>

Novik, Pavlo and Lisichkin, Yevhen, 'Вкрадене українське зерно: фірми, схеми та механізм санкцій' ['Stolen Ukrainian grain: companies, schemes and sanctions mechanisms'], Kharkiv Anti-Corruption Centre (18 April 2024), <https://anticor-kharkiv.org/our-work/vkradene-ukrainske-zerno-firmy-skhemy-ta-mekhanizm-sanktsiy/>

Novik, Pavlo, 'Як харківські колаборанти зафільмували свою брехню та показали нових "посіпак"' ['How Kharkiv collaborators filmed their lies and showed off their new "henchmen"'], Media Literacy in the Regions of Ukraine (19 June 2023), <https://milukraine.net/2023/06/6616/>

Office of the Commander-in-Chief of the Armed Forces of Ukraine; Ukrainian General Staff, and Centre for Military History Research of the Armed Forces of Ukraine; Shaptala, Serhiy, Khlon, Serhiy, and Pahiria, Oleksandr, et al., *Історія війни: реалії та уроки, стратегія майбутнього [History of the War: Realities and Lessons, Strategy for the Future]* (Kyiv: Lira K Publishing House/CMHRAFU, 2023)

Ogarkov, Nikolai (chair) et al., *Soviet Military Encyclopaedia, Volume 4* (Moscow: Soviet Ministry of Defence, 1979)

Oleshko, Natalia, 'Український Рух Опору На Харківщині У Повномасштабній Російсько-Українській Війні 2022 Року' ['The Ukrainian resistance movement in the Kharkiv region during the full-scale Russian-Ukrainian war of 2022'], *Current issues in modern science*, 6:12 (2023), pp.643–659

Pavlenko, Olena, 'Гауляйтери Харківської області: хто і як зрадив Україну' ['Gauleiters of the Kharkiv Region: Who Betrayed Ukraine and How'], *Kharkiv Today* (1 June 2022), <https://2day.kh.ua/ua/kharkow/haulyaytery-kharkivskoyi-oblasti-khto-i-yak-zradyv-ukrayinu>

Pavlenko, Olena, 'Нові гауляйтери Харківської області. Як змінюється влада на окупованих територіях' ['New Gauleiters of Kharkiv Region. How power is changing in the occupied territories'], *Kharkiv Today* (8 July 2022), <https://2day.kh.ua/ua/kharkow/novi-haulyaytery-kharkivskoyi-oblasti-yak-zminyuyetsya-vlada-na-okupovanykh-terytoriyakh>

Pertsev, Andrey, 'Кремль «поставил на стоп» референдумы о «присоединении» оккупированных территорий к России, утверждают источники «Медузы» Их «отложили на неопределенный срок» из-за успешного украинского контрнаступления' ['The Kremlin has "put on hold" referendums on the "annexation" of occupied territories to Russia, according to sources at Meduza'], *Meduza* (11 September 2022), <https://meduza.io/feature/2022/09/11/kreml-postavil-na-stop-referendumy-o-prisoedinenii-okkupirovannyh-territoriy-k-rossii-utverzhdayut-istochniki-meduzy>

Petrenko, Roman, 'ЗСУ звільнили Борову на Харківщині' ['The Armed Forces of Ukraine liberated Borova in the Kharkiv region'], *Ukrainska Pravda* (3 October 2022), <https://www.pravda.com.ua/news/2022/10/3/7370187/>

Poberezhnyi, Vitaliy, 'Як Піски-Радьківські чинили опір окупації' ['How Pisky-Radkivski resisted the occupation'], *Ukrainer* (8 March 2023), <https://www.ukrainer.net/pisky-radkivski/>

Pyrih, Volodymyr, 'Росіяни з комплексів ППО масовано вдарили по Чугуєву' ['Russians launched a massive strike on Chuhuiv from air defence systems'], Zaxid.net (25 July 2022), <https://zaxid.net/udar_po_chuguyevu_25_lipnya_2022_naslidki_foto_detali_n154679>

Reznikova, Kateryna, 'Путеводитель по российским оккупантам и украинским коллаборационистам' ['A guide to the Russian occupiers and Ukrainian collaborators'], Proekt Media (29 September 2022), <https://www.proekt.media/guide/kto-rukovodit-okkupirovannymi-territoriyami-ukrainy/>

Roschina, Olena, 'На Харківщині звільнили Куп'янськ-Вузловий, ще 6% області – під окупацією' ['Kupiansk-Vuzlovyi has been liberated in Kharkiv region, with 6% of the region still under occupation'], *Ukrainska Pravda* (27 September 2022), <https://www.pravda.com.ua/news/2022/09/27/7369277/>

Rovenský, D., '"Hot" Ukrainian Dawn. Counteroffensives in Kherson and Kharkiv', ATM, 10 (2022), pp.8–11

Safronov, Taras, 'На Луганщині ЗСУ зачистили від окупантів Білогорівку' ['In Luhansk region, the Armed Forces of Ukraine cleared Bilohorivka of occupiers'], *Militarnyi* (19 September 2022), <https://mil.in. ua/uk/news/na-luganshhyni-zsu-zachystyly-vid-okupantiv-bilogorivku/>

Safronov, Taras, 'На Харківщині знайшли уламки збитого Су-25 ПКС Росії' ['Debris from a downed Russian Su-25 found in Kharkiv region'], *Militarnyi* (11 September 2022), <https://mil.in.ua/uk/news/na-harkivshhyni-znajshly-ulamky-zbytogo-su-25-pks-rosiyi/>

Safronov, Taras, 'Українські військові відбили атаку росіян на село Заводи' ['Ukrainian military repelled Russian attack on the village of Zavody'], *Militarnyi* (25 April 2022), <https://mil.in.ua/uk/news/ukrayinski-vijskovi-vidbyly-ataku-rosiyan-na-selo-zavody/>

Segida, E. Yu., Redin, V. I., and Chaban, M. T., *Geography of Kharkiv Region* (Kharkiv: Kharkiv National University, 2012)

Shcheglova, Agata, '«Никакой паники нет» и СОБР в окружении. Украина перешла в наступление на важный для снабжения российской армии город Балаклею — главное' ['"No panic" and SOBR surrounded. Ukraine has launched an offensive on the city of Balakliia, which is important for supplying the Russian army – the main thing'], *Mediazona* (7 September 2022), <https://zona.media/article/2022/09/07/balakleya>

Shevchenko, Artem, *Воєнна розвідка України. У небі, на морі, на землі [Military Intelligence of Ukraine: In the Sky, at Sea, on Land]* (Kyiv: Yakaboo Publishing, 2023)

Shopynskyi, Bohdan and Nadtoka, Oleksander, *Слобожанська Наступальна Операція Сил Оборони України: перебіг та результати (6 вересня – 1 жовтня 2022 р.) ['Slobozhanshchyna offensive operation of the Armed Forces of Ukraine: progress and results (6 September – 1 October 2022)']*, CMHRAFU (19 March 2024), <https://milhistory.zsu.gov.ua/operatsiyi-syl-oborony-ukrayiny/slobozhanska-nastupalna-operaciya-perebih-ta-rezultaty>

Shulman, Alexander, 'Підполковник Роман Зуй: Коли росіяни відмовились здатися, я їх просто розстріляв з танка' ['Lieutenant Colonel Roman Zuy: When the Russians refused to surrender, I simply shot them from my tank'], ArmyInform (26 February 2024), <https://armyinform.com.ua/2024/02/26/pidpolkovnyk-roman-zuj-koly-rosiyany-vidmovylys-zdatysya-ya-yih-prosto-rozstrilyav-z-tanka/>

Silaeva, Anna, 'Харків: щонайменше 97 у лікарні після "мирного мітингу патріотів"' ['Kharkiv: at least 97 people hospitalised after a "peaceful patriotic rally"'], BBC News Ukraine (1 March 2014), <https://www.bbc.com/ukrainian/news/2014/03/140301_kharkiv_az>

Solodovnik, Maria, Kryvko, Roman, and Kryvonis, Tetiana, '"Залужний обіцяв, що все буде добре". Спогади Синєгубова про контрнаступ ЗСУ на Харківщині' ['"Zaluzhny promised that everything would be fine." Sinehubov's memories of the Ukrainian Armed Forces' counteroffensive in the Kharkiv region'], *Suspilne Kharkiv* (21 September 2023), <https://suspilne.

media/kharkiv/577361-zaluznij-obicav-so-vse-bude-dobre-spogadi-sinegubova-pro-kontrnastup-zsu-na-harkivsini/>

Stepanenko Kateryna, and Kagan, Frederick W., 'Russian Offensive Campaign Assessment, May 13, 2022', Institute for the Study of War (13 May 2022), <https://www.understandingwar.org/backgrounder/russian-offensive-campaign-assessment-may-13>

Stepanenko, Kateryna, Hird, Karolina, Barros, George, Bailey, Riley, Kagan, Frederick W. 'Russian Offensive Campaign Assessment, 29 September, 2022', Institute for the Study of War (30 September 2022), <https://www.understandingwar.org/ backgrounder/russian-offensive-campaign-assessment-september-29>

Stepanenko, Kateryna, Hird, Karolina, Howard, Angela, Clark, Mason, 'Russian Offensive Campaign Assessment, 5 September, 2022', Institute for the Study of War (6 September 2022), <https://www.understandingwar.org/backgrounder/ russian-offensive-campaign-assessment-september-5>

Stepanenko, Kateryna, Lawlor, Katherine, Mappes, Grace, Bailey, Riley, Barros, George, Kagan, Frederick W., 'Russian Offensive Campaign Assessment, September 30, 2022', Institute for the Study of War (1 October 2022), <https://www.understandingwar.org/backgrounder/russian-offensive-campaign-assessment-september-30>

Stepanenko, Kateryna, Mappes, Grace, Barros, George, Howard, Angela, Clark, Mason, 'Russian Offensive Campaign Assessment, 10 September, 2022', Institute for the Study of War (11 September 2022), <https://understandingwar.org/research/russia-ukraine/russian-offensive-campaign-assessment_11-27/>

Stepanenko, Kateryna, Mappes, Grace, Barros, George, Philipson, Layne, and Clark, Mason, 'Russian Offensive Campaign Assessment, 8 September, 2022', Institute for the Study of War (9 September 2022), <https://www.understandingwar.org/backgrounder/russian-offensive-campaign-assessment-september-8>

Stepanenko, Kateryna, Mappes, Grace, Barros, George, Philipson, Layne, and Clark, Mason, 'Russian Offensive Campaign Assessment, 9 September, 2022', Institute for the Study of War (10 September 2022), <https://www.understandingwar.org/backgrounder/russian-offensive-campaign-assessment-september-9>

Stepura, Anton and Galasyuk, Anastasia, 'У Лиманській громаді за рік після звільнення не встановили дані понад 50 людей, чиї тіла знайшли у похованнях' ['In the Lyman community, a year after liberation, more than 50 people whose bodies were found in the graves remain unidentified'], *Suspilne Donbas* (30 September 2023), <https://suspilne.media/donbas/582303-u-limanskij-gromadi-za-rik-pisla-zvilnenna-ne-vstanovili-dani-ponad-50-ludej-cii-tila-znajsli-u-pohovannah/>

Strembski, Marcin, 'Wojna powietrza nad Ukrainą 24 sierpnia – 23 września 2022' ['Air war over Ukraine, 24 August – 23 September 2022'], Lotnictwo, 10 (2022), p.31

Strembski, Marcin, 'Wojna powietrzna, 24 marca – 23 kwietnia 2022' ['Air War, 24 March – 23 April 2022, *Lotnictwo*, 4 (2022), pp.16–29

Strembski, Marcin,'Wojna powietrzna, 24 lutego – 23 marca 2022' ['Air War, 24 February – 23 March 2022'], *Lotnictwo* 3 (2022). pp.16–31

Thorkill, 'Przepis na katastrofę. Rajd w głąb śródmieścia Charkowa 2 Brygady Specnazu 27 lutego 2022 r.' ['A recipe for disaster. Raids into the centre of Kharkiv by the 2nd Spetsnaz Brigade on 27 February and 5 March 2022'], *Thorkill Blog* (12 April 2023), <https://thorkillblog.blogspot.com/2023/04/przepis-na-katastrofe-rajdy-w-gab.html>

Townsend, Mark, Tondo, Lorenzo, and Koshiw, Isobel, 'Ukrainian counter-offensive in north-east inflicts a defeat on Moscow', *The Guardian* (10 September 2022), <https://www.theguardian.com/world/2022/sep/10/ukrainian-forces-kupiansk-advances-north-east-russia-izyum>

Trystan, Andriy, *Прийшла війна… [The War Has Come…]* (Lviv: Apriori Publishing, 2023)

Tsomyik, Hanna. and Mavrichev, Vyacheslav, 'Російський артобстріл Харкова вранці 30 серпня: фото наслідків' ['Russian artillery shelling of Kharkiv on the morning of 30 August: photos of the aftermath'], *Suspilne Kharkiv* (30 August 2022), <https://suspilne.media/kharkiv/276443-artilerijski-obstrili-harkova-vranci-30-serpna-foto-naslidkiv/>

Tsomyik, Hannah, '"Козача Лопань на Харківщині — під контролем ЗСУ» — голова громади' ["Kozacha Lopan in the Kharkiv region — under the control of the Armed Forces of Ukraine" — head of the community'], *Suspilne Kharkiv* (11 September 2022), <https://suspilne.media/280628-kozaca-lopan-na-harkivsini-pid-kontrolem-zsu-golova-gromadi/>

Tukmakov, O.G., 'Основные направления совершенствования военно-политической работы при подготовке операций' ['Main directions for improving military-political work in the preparation of operations'], Military Thought, 2 (2023), pp.38–48

Tymokhin, A., 'Его нельзя бросить, его нельзя эвакуировать. Куда ставить запятую? Обзор армии и флота' ['You can't abandon it, you can't evacuate it. Where to put the comma?'], *Army and Navy Review*, 2 (2023), pp.58–59

Tyshchenko, Kateryna, 'Russian authorities urge residents of the occupied areas of Kharkiv Oblast to "evacuate"', *Ukrainska Pravda* (10 September 2022), <https://www.pravda.com.ua/eng/news/2022/09/10/7366932/>

Venkina, Ekaterina and Guba, Roman, 'Зеленський наказав відвоювати південь України – Резніков' ['Zelensky ordered to recapture southern Ukraine – Reznikov'], *DW.com* (11 July 2022), <https://www.dw.com/uk/zelenskyi-nakazav-vidvoiuvaty-pivden-ukrainy-reznikov/a-62432972>

Yakushko, Oksana, 'Найкритичніший день. Як 27 лютого відбувався бій за центр Харкова' ['The most critical day. How the battle for the centre of Kharkiv unfolded on 27 February'], *Objectiv* (13 February 2023), <https://www.objectiv.tv/uk/objectively/2023/02/13/samyj-kriticheskij-den-kak-27-fevralya-prohodil-boj-za-tsentr-harkova/>

Yevseyev, I. G., Maraev, V. R., Skryabin, O. L., and Khalimanenko, K., *Харківська наступна опера 2022 року: Військово-історичний шедевр [Kharkiv Offensive Operation 2022: A Military-Historical Essay]* (Kyiv: Research and Development Centre of the Armed Forces of Ukraine, 2025)

Zaluzhnyi, Valerii (chair) et al., *Воєнно-історичний опис російсько-української війни (лютий–березень 2022 року) [Military-historical description of the Russian-Ukrainian war (February-March 2022)]* (Kyiv: Ukrainian Ministry of Defence and Ukrainian General Staff, 2022)

Zaluzhnyi, Valerii (chair) et al., *Воєнно-Історичний Опис Російсько-Української Війни (вересень 2022 року) [Military-historical description of the Russian-Ukrainian war (September 2022)]* (Kyiv: Ukrainian Defence Ministry and Ukrainian General Staff, 2022)

Zaluzhnyi, Valerii (chair) et al., *Воєнно-Історичний Опис Російсько-Української Війни (жовтень 2022 року) [Military-historical description of the Russian-Ukrainian war (October 2022)]* (Kyiv: Ukrainian Defence Ministry and Ukrainian General Staff, 2022)

Zaluzhnyi, Valerii (chair) et al., *Воєнно-Історичний Опис Російсько-Української Війни (листопад 2022 року) [Military-historical description of the Russian-Ukrainian war (October 2022)]* (Kyiv: Ukrainian Defence Ministry and Ukrainian General Staff, 2022)

Zaluzhnyi, Valerii (chair) et al., *Воєнно-Історичний Опис Російсько-Української Війни (квітень 2022 року) [Military-historical description of the Russian-Ukrainian war (April 2022)]* (Kyiv: Ukrainian Defence Ministry and Ukrainian General Staff, 2022)

Zaluzhnyi, Valerii (chair) et al., *Воєнно-Історичний Опис Російсько-Української Війни (травень 2022 року) [Military-historical description of the Russian-Ukrainian war (May 2022)]* (Kyiv: Ukrainian Defence Ministry and Ukrainian General Staff, 2022)

Zaluzhnyi, Valerii (chair) et al., *Воєнно-Історичний Опис Російсько-Української Війни (червень 2022 року) [Military-historical description of the Russian-Ukrainian war (June 2022)]* (Kyiv: Ukrainian Defence Ministry and Ukrainian General Staff, 2022)

Zaluzhnyi, Valerii (chair) et al., *Воєнно-Історичний Опис Російсько-Української Війни (липень 2022 року) [Military-historical description of the Russian-Ukrainian war (July 2022)]* (Kyiv: Ukrainian Defence Ministry and Ukrainian General Staff, 2022)

Zaluzhnyi, Valerii (chair) et al., *Воєнно-Історичний Опис Російсько-Української Війни (серпень 2022 року) [Military-historical description of the Russian-Ukrainian war (August 2022)]* (Kyiv: Ukrainian Defence Ministry and Ukrainian General Staff, 2022)

Zgurets, Serhiy, ‘Напередодні битви за Донбас: скільки військ, зброї та на яких напрямках збирає армія рашистів (аналіз)’ [‘On the eve of the battle for Donbas: how many troops and weapons are the Russian forces gathering, and in which directions (analysis)’], *Defense Express* (14 April 2022), <https://defence-ua.com/army_and_war/naperedodni_bitvi_za_donbas_skilki_vijsk_zbroji_ta_na_jakih_naprjamkah_zbiraje_armija_rashistiv_analiz-6941.html>

Zhirokhov, Mykhailo, *Війна в повітрі. Україна, лютий-травень 2022 [War in the Air: Ukraine, February–May 2022]* (Chernihiv: Princely Val, 2022)

Zmiyevsky, G. A., Pugach, V. V., and Chepurny, V. P., ‘Застосування сучасних форм наступального маневну на прикладі досвіду харківської наступальної операції’ [‘The use of modern forms of offensive manoeuvres on the example of the Kharkiv offensive operation’] *Military Affairs and National Security*, 151 (2023), pp.761–766

‘Балаклія довго чекала. Що відбувається навколо міста?’ [‘Balakliia waited a long time. What is happening around the city?’], *Kharkiv Today* (7 September 2022), <https://2day.kh.ua/ua/kharkow/balakliya-dovho-chekala-shcho-vidbuvayetsya-navkolo-mista>

‘“Бросили ребят, как кусок мяса, на растерзание”. Родные военных из Калининградской области рассказывают, как они попали в плен под Харьковом’ [‘“They threw the boys, like pieces of meat, to be torn apart.” Relatives of soldiers from the Kaliningrad region tell how they were captured near Kharkiv’], *Current Time* (14 September 2022) <https://www.currenttime.tv/a/brosili-rebyat-kak-kusok-myasa-na-rasterzanie-rodnye-voennyh-iz-kaliningradskoy-oblasti-rasskazyvayut-kak-oni-popali-v-plen-pod-harkovom/32031548.html>

‘В Бурятии формируется именное подразделение контрактников «Байкал»’ [‘A special unit of contract soldiers called “Baikal” is being formed in Buryatia’], *Baikal Daily* (27 July 2022) <https://www.baikal-daily.ru/news/16/439794/>

‘В Украине почти полностью уничтожили батальон «боевых бурят» из РФ’ [‘In Ukraine, a battalion of “combat Buryats” from the Russian Federation has been almost completely destroyed’], *Charter 97* (27 October 2022), <https://charter97.org/ru/news/2022/10/27/521672/>

‘“Вивезли до Бєлгорода на “перевиховання”: викраденого під Куп’янськом блогера Сергія Строєва другий рік шукає родина’ [‘“Taken to Belgorod for ‘re-education’: the family of Sergei Stroev, a blogger kidnapped near Kupiansk, has been searching for him for two years’], ZMINA (3 November 2023), <https://zmina.info/news/vash-syn-borzyj-my-jogo-vyvezly-do-byelgoroda-na-perevyhovannya-take-pochula-maty-sergiya-stroyeva-blogera-vid-jogo-vykradachiv/>

‘“Війна показала справжні обличчя». Як живе тимчасово окупований Куп›янськ на Харківщині’ [‘“The war has revealed true faces.” How life is in the temporarily occupied town of Kupiansk in the Kharkiv region’], *Suspilne Kharkiv* (19 March 2022), <https://suspilne.media/kharkiv/218803-vijna-pokazala-spravzni-oblicca-ak-zive-timcasovo-okupovanij-kupansk-na-harkivsini/>

‘Воїни волинської 14-ї ОМБР показали звільнений Куп›янськ (фото)’ [‘Soldiers of the Volyn 14th OMBR showed the liberated Kupiansk’], *Konkurent* (15 September 2022), <https://konkurent.ua/publication/103747/voini-volinskoi-14-i-ombr-pokazali-zvilneniy-kupyansk-foto/>.

‘Жадана били бітами по голові і вимагали стати на коліна. Він послав їх на х…’ [‘Zhadan was beaten on the head with bats and forced to kneel. He told them to f*** off’], *iPress* (1 March 2014), <https://ipress.ua/news/zhadana_byly_bitamy_po_golovi_i_vymagaly_staty_na_kolina_vin_poslav_ih_na_h_51444.html>

‘З’явились підтвердження, що ЗСУ зайшли в Старий Караван на Донеччині’ [‘“Confirmation Emerges That the Armed Forces of Ukraine Entered Staryi Karavan in Donetsk Region.”’], *Ukrainian View* (8 September 2022), <https://ukrpohliad.org/news/z-yavylys-pidtverdzhennya-shho-zsu-zajshly v staryj karavan-na-donechchyni.html>

и специальных действий’ [‘Modelling military, combat and special operations’], *Military Thought*, 1 (2023), pp.39–40

‘Із Харкова залізницею евакуювали вже понад 600 тисяч людей, – голова ОДА’ [‘More than 600,000 people have already been evacuated from Kharkiv by rail, according to the head of the Regional State Administration’], *Rubryka* (8 March 2022), <https://rubryka.com/2022/03/08/iz-harkova-zaliznytseyu-evakuyuvaly-vzhe-ponad-600-tysyach-lyudej-golova-oda/>

‘Кількість загиблих від удару по Харківській обладміністрації збільшилась до 29’ [‘The death toll from the strike on the Kharkiv regional administration has risen to 29’], *The New Voice of Ukraine* (2 April 2022), < https://nv.ua/ukr/kharkiv/boji-za-harkiv-pid-chas-obstrilu-harkivskoji-oda-zaginuli-29-lyudey-novini-harkova-50230576.html>

‘Куп›янськ, Ізюм, Балаклія. Як наступають ЗСУ на Харківщині і чи буде великий котел’ [‘Kupiansk, Izium, Balakliia. How the Armed Forces of Ukraine are advancing in the Kharkiv region and whether there will be a large encirclement’], BBC News Ukraine (10 September 2022), <https://www.bbc.com/ukrainian/features-62860946>

‘Ми будемо звільняти рідну землю до останнього сантиметра — Валерій Залужний’ [‘We will liberate our native land to the last centimetre – Valerii Zaluzhny’], ArmyInform (1 December 2022), <https://armyinform.com.ua/2022/12/01/my-budemo-zvilnyaty-ridnu-zemlyu-do-ostannogo-santymetra-valerij-zaluzhnyj/>

‘Міноборони: військових РФ відтіснили до держкордону на Харківщині’ [‘Ministry of Defence: Russian troops pushed back to the state border in Kharkiv region’], *Radio Liberty* (16 May 2022), <https://www.radiosvoboda.org/a/news-kharkivska-oblast-viyskovi-kordon/31852249.html>

‘МО РФ: задействованным в спецоперации подразделениям предоставили возможность отдохнуть’ [‘Russian Ministry of Defence: Units involved in special operations were given the opportunity to rest’], TASS (7 July 2022), <https://tass.ru/armiya-i-opk/15150167>

‘Мобілізовані у “Л/ДНР” не мають бажання воювати: боєздатність підрозділів дуже низька’ [‘Those mobilised in the “L/DNR” have no desire to fight: the combat capability of the units is very low’], *Suspilne* (26 September 2022), <https://suspilne.media/285804-mobilizovani-u-ldnr-ne-maut-bazanna-vouvati-boezdatnist-pidrozdiliv-duze-nizka/>

‘На Харківщині виявили тіла понад 760 загиблих під час окупації’ [‘The bodies of more than 760 people killed during the occupation were found in the Kharkiv region’], *Mykolaivksa Pravda* (30 October 2022), <https://www.nikpravda.com.ua/na-harkivshhyni-vyyavyly-tila-ponad-760-zagyblyh-pid-chas-okupatsiyi/>

‘На Харківщині підірвався на міні і загинув тракторист’ [‘A tractor driver was killed when he hit a mine in the Kharkiv region’], *Ukrinform* (17 October 2023), <https://www.ukrinform.ua/rubric-regions/3775204-na-harkivsini-pidirvavsa-na-mini-i-zaginuv-traktorist.html>

‘Найцінніші трофеї ЗСУ на Харківщині: чому один “Зоопарк” та «Орлан-10» цінніші за танкову роту’ [‘The most valuable trophies of the Armed Forces of Ukraine in the Kharkiv region: why one “Zoo” and “Orlan-10” are more valuable than a tank company’], *Defense Express* (14 September 2022), <https://defence-ua.com/weapon_and_tech/najtsinnishi_trofeji_zsu_na_harkivschini_chomu_odin_zoopark_ta_orlan_10_tsinnishi_za_tankovu_rotu-8910.html>

‘“Ненастоящие» военные. Вернувшиеся из Украины добровольцы остались без обещанных привилегий и денег’ [‘“Fake” soldiers. Volunteers who returned from Ukraine were left without the promised privileges and money’], *Radio Liberty* (11 August 2022), <https://www.svoboda.org/a/31980270.html>

‘Окупанти посилили терор і заборонили людям виходити на вулиці у селах поблизу Балаклії’ [‘The occupiers have intensified their terror and banned people from going out on the streets in villages near Balakliia’], *Kharkiv Today* (7 September 2022), <https://2day.kh.ua/ua/kharkow/okupanty-posylyly-teror-i-zaboronyly-lyudyam-vykhodyty-na-vulytsi-u-selakh-poblyzu>

‘Окупанти призначили колишнього міліціонера головним в Ізюмі’ [‘The occupiers have appointed a former police officer as head of Izium’], *Kharkiv Today* (25 April 2022), <https://2day.kh.ua/ua/kharkow/okupanty-pryznachyly-kolyshnoho-militsionera-holovnym-v-izyumi>

‘Перелом: ЗСУ звільнили більше половини територій, захоплених РФ після 24.02.2022’ [‘Turning point: The Armed Forces of Ukraine have liberated more than half of the territories captured by the Russian Federation after 24 February 2022’], *Militarnyi* (14 November 2022), <https://mil.in.ua/uk/news/perelom-zsu-zvilnyly-bilshe-polovyny-terytorij-zahoplenyh-rf-pislya-24-02-2022/>

‘Поліція повідомила про ексгумацію перших 20 тіл на місці масового поховання в Лимані’ [‘Police reported the exhumation of the first 20 bodies at a mass grave in Lyman’], *Radio Liberty* (9 October 2022), < https://www.radiosvoboda.org/a/news-politsia-ekshumatsia-lyman/32072127.html>

‘Рашисти переходять до масового використання ЗРК С-300 для ударів по містах: чи є захист’[‘The Rashists are moving to the mass use of S-300 air defence systems to strike cities: is there any protection?’], *Defense Express* (9 July 2022), <https://defence-ua.com/minds_and_ideas/rashisti_perehodjat_do_masovogo_vikoristannja_zrk_s_300_dlja_udariv_po_mistah_chi_je_zahist-8096.html>

‘Рашисти почали з ЗРК С-300 обстрілювати й Харківщину: одну ракету вдалось збити (фото)’ [‘The Rashists began firing at the Kharkiv region with S-300 air defence systems: one missile was shot down’], *Defense Express* (13 July 2022), <https://defence-ua.com/news/rashisti_pochali_z_zrk_s_300_obstriljuvati_j_harkivschinu_odnu_raketu_vdalos_zbiti_foto-8144.html>

‘Рік тому Збройні Сили України звільнили Ізюм’ [‘A year ago, the Armed Forces of Ukraine liberated Izium’], *Christians for Ukraine* (10 September 2023), <URL:https://media.c4u.org.ua/calendar/2236>

‘Росіяни та OSINT-дослідники підтвердили втрату двох Су-34 ПКС РФ’ [‘Russians and OSINT researchers have confirmed the loss of two Su-34s belonging to the Russian Air Force’], *Militarnyi* (25 September 2022), <https://mil.in.ua/uk/news/rosiyany-ta-osint-doslidnyky-pidtverdyly-vtratu-dvoh-su-34-pks-rf/>

‘Сепарастист став заступником гауляйтера окупованої Харківщини’ [‘Separatist becomes deputy gauleiter of occupied Kharkiv region’], *Kharkiv Today* (29 June 2022), <https://2day.kh.ua/ua/politika/separastyst-stav-zastupnykom-haulyaytera-okupovanoyi-kharkivshchyny>

‘Справу про викрадення загарбниками депутата-ветерана з Куп’янська розгляне ЄСПЛ’ [‘The case of the abduction of a veteran deputy from Kupiansk by invaders will be considered by the ECHR’], *Ukrinform* (9 June 2023), <https://www.ukrinform.ua/rubric-society/3720587-spravu-pro-vikradenna-zagarbnikami-deputataveterana-z-kupanska-rozglane-espl.html>

‘Турчинов розповів, чому в 2014-му вдалося запобігти окупації Харкова, але не Донецька й Луганська’ [‘Turchynov explained why it was possible to prevent the occupation of Kharkiv in 2014, but not Donetsk and Luhansk’], Radio Liberty (18 April 2021), <https://www.radiosvoboda.org/a/news-turchynov-2014-kharkiv-donetsk-luhansk/31209670.html>

‘У ЗСУ підтвердили звільнення села Торське на Донеччині’ [‘The Armed Forces of Ukraine confirmed the liberation of the village of Torske in Donetsk Region’], *Radio Liberty* (2 October 2022), <https://www.radiosvoboda.org/a/news-torske-zvilnennya/32061994.html>

'У Нацгвардії підтвердили звільнення Святогірська' ['The National Guard of Ukraine confirmed the liberation of the city of Svyatogorsk in the Donetsk region'], *Ukrinform* (12 September 2022), <https://www.ukrinform.ua/rubric-ato/3570062-u-nacgvardii-pidtverdili-zvilnenna-svatogirska.html>

'У Харкові на місцевий Майдан напали члени "Оплоту"' ['In Kharkiv, members of Oplot attacked the local Maidan'], *Ukrainska Pravda* (23 February 2014), <http://www.pravda.com.ua/news/2014/02/23/7015899/>

'У Харкові ракетний удар зруйнував депо метрополітену' ['In Kharkiv, a missile strike destroyed a metro depot'], *Defense Express* (14 July 2022), <https://2day.kh. ua/ua/kharkow/u-kharkovi-raketnyy-udar-zruynuvav-depo-metropolitenu>

'Удари по Харкову: все, що відомо про атаку Росії на енергосистему' ['Strikes on Kharkiv: everything we know about Russia's attack on the power grid'], BBC News Ukraine (12 September 2022), <https://www.bbc.com/ukrainian/news-62873359>

'"Українцям важливіше за все свобода", — командир "Хартії" Всеволод Кожемяко' ['"Freedom is the most important thing for Ukrainians," Khartia commander Vsevolod Kozhemyako'], *Kharkiv Today* (20 October 2022), <https://2day.kh.ua/ua/kharkow/ukrayintsyam-vazhlyvishe-za-vse-svoboda-komandyr-khartiyi-vsevolod-kozhemyako>

'Харківські сепаратисти відмовилися проводити "референдум" 11 травня' ['Kharkiv separatists refused to hold a "referendum" on 11 May'], *Ukrainska Pravda* (9 May 2014), <https://www.pravda.com.ua/news/2014/05/9/7024854/>

'"Хартія" стане механізованою бригадою у складі Нацгвардії України' ['Khartia will become a mechanised brigade within the National Guard of Ukraine'], *Kharkiv Today* (20 March 2023), <https://2day.kh.ua/ua/kharkow/khartiya-stane-mekhanizovanoyu-bryhadoyu-u-skladi-natshvardiyi-ukrayiny>

'Харьков: драка ультрас и активистов с георгиевскими ленточками' ['Kharkiv: fight between ultras and activists wearing St. George's ribbons'], *Korrespondent.net* (27 April 2014), <https://korrespondent.net/ukraine/events/3355225-kharkov-draka-ultras-y-aktyvystov-s-heorhyevskymy-lentochkamy>

'Шойгу: будут мобилизованы 300 тысяч резервистов' ['Shoigu: 300,000 reservists will be mobilised'], *Radio Liberty* (21 September 2022), <https://www.svoboda.org/a/shoygu-obyavil-o-mobilizatsii-300-tysyach-rezervistov/32044077.html>

'"Якщо впаде Харків, впаде вся Україна». Репортаж з лінії фронту' ['"If Kharkiv falls, all of Ukraine will fall". Report from the front line'], BBC News Ukraine (12 March 2022), <https://www.bbc.com/ukrainian/features-60719093>

ENDNOTES

Introduction

1 The Defence Forces of Ukraine is a collective name for all military formations and bodies that defend Ukraine's sovereignty: the Armed Forces, the National Guard, the State Border Service, the National Police, etc. See, for example, Article 17 of the Law of Ukraine 'Про основи національного спротиву' ['On the Principles of National Resistance'], *Bulletin of the Verkhovna Rada*, 41 (2021), p.339. <https://zakon.rada.gov.ua/laws/show/1702-20#Text>.

2 Centre for Military History Research of the Armed Forces of Ukraine (CMHRAFU), *Рік війни за свободу: воєнно-історичний нарис російсько-української війни (24.02.2022 – 24.02.2023) [A Year of War for Freedom: A Military-Historical Essay on the Russian-Ukrainian War (24 February 2022-24 February 2023)]*, Book I (Kyiv: Lira-K Publishing House, 2023), pp.8–9.

3 Vladimir Putin, 'On the Historical Unity of Russians and Ukrainians', President of Russia (2021), <http://kremlin.ru/events/president/news/66181>.

4 A. Kharuk and V.I. Zelenyi, 'Офіційні українські видання про російсько-українську війну та їх використання в історичних дослідженнях' ['Official Ukrainian publications on the Russian-Ukrainian war and their use in historical research'], Military Scientific Bulletin, 40 (2023), pp.202–203.

5 Valerii Zaluzhnyi (chair) et al., *Воєнно-історичний опис російсько-української війни (лютий–березень 2022 року) [Military-historical description of the Russian-Ukrainian war (February-March 2022)]* (Kyiv: Ukrainian Ministry of Defence and Ukrainian General Staff, 2022), p.112; subsequent issues are monthly; our study uses issues up to and including November 2022.

6 Centre for Military History Research of the Armed Forces of Ukraine, *Рік війни за свободу... [A Year of War for Freedom...]*, Book I, pp.222–225.

7 CMHRAFU, *Рік війни за свободу: воєнно-історичний нарис російсько-української війни (24.02.2022 – 24.02.2023) [A Year of War for Freedom: A Military-Historical Essay on the Russian-Ukrainian War (24 February 2022-24 February 2023)]*, Book II (Kyiv: Lira-K Publishing House, 2023), pp.116–119.

8 Centre for Military History Research of the Armed Forces of Ukraine, *Рік війни за свободу... [A Year of War for Freedom...]*, Book II, pp.118–142.

9 National Defence University of Ukraine, *Хроніка війни, частина I (перші 30 діб російсько-української війни, 24.02-26.03.2022) [Chronicle of the War, Part I (the first 30 days of the Russian-Ukrainian War, 24 February – 26 March 2022)]* (Kyiv: Ivan Chernyakhovsky National Defence University [now National Defence University of Ukraine], 2022), p.2.

10 S. Khlon, O. Pahiria, and O. Poltorakov, *"Східна брама держави", Оборона Харкова (24 лютого 14 травня 2022 р.) [The Eastern Gate of the State, The Defence of Kharkiv (24 February – 14 May 2022)]* (Kyiv: CMHRAFU, no date).

11 Office of the Commander-in-Chief of the Armed Forces of Ukraine; Ukrainian General Staff, and Centre for Military History Research of the Armed Forces of Ukraine; Serhiy Shaptala, Serhiy Khlon, Oleksandr Pahiria, et al., *Історія війни: реалії та уроки, стратегія майбутнього [History of the War: Realities and Lessons, Strategy for the Future]* (Kyiv: Lira K Publishing House/CMHRAFU, 2023), p.131.

12 Andriy Trystan, *Прийшла війна... [The War Has Come...]* (Lviv: Apriori Publishing, 2023), p.144.

13 Mariusz Cielma, 'Przed bitwą wszystkich bitew. Wojna w Ukrainie' ['Before the Battle of All Battles. War in Ukraine'], *Nowa Technika Wojskowa*, 4 (2022), pp.8–13; Andriy Trystan, *Прийшла війна... [The War Has Come...]* (Lviv: Apriori Publishing, 2023), p.144, 'Bitwa o Donbas i upadek Mariupola' ['The Battle for Donbas and the Fall of Mariupol'], *Nowa Technika Wojskowa*, 5 (2022), pp.10–14.

14 P. Batacchi and A. Mottola, 'Ucraina, Putin in difficoltà e lo spettro nucleare', *Rivista Italiana Difesa*, 11 (2022), pp.25–33; Marcin Gawęda, 'Wojna rosyjsko-ukraińska cz. 7' ['The Russian-Ukrainian War, Part 7'], *Wojsko i Technika*, 10 (2022), pp.38–47.

15 Marcin Strembski,'Wojna powietrzna, 24 lutego – 23 marca 2022' ['Air War, 24 February – 23 March 2022'], *Lotnictwo* 3 (2022), pp.16–31; Strembski, 'Wojna powietrzna, 24 marca – 23 kwietnia 2022' ['Air War, 24 March – 23 April 2022'], *Lotnictwo*, 4 (2022), pp.16–29.

16 Mykhailo Zhirokhov, *Війна в повітрі. Україна, лютий-травень 2022 [War in the Air: Ukraine, February–May 2022]* (Chernihiv: Princely Val, 2022), p.96.

17 D. Rovenský, '"Hot" Ukrainian Dawn. Counteroffensives in Kherson and Kharkiv', ATM, 10 (2022), pp.8–11.

18 P. Batacchi and A. Mottola, 'Un'analisi preliminare della guerra in Ucraina' ['An initial analysis of the war in Ukraine'], *Rivista Italiana Difesa*, 4 (2022), pp.24–46.

19 A. Kharuk, 'Харківська оборонна операція (24 лютого — 14 травня 2022 р.)' ['The Kharkiv defensive operation (24 February – 14 May 2022)'], *Ukrainian Historical Journal*, 5 (2023), pp.23–34; P. Batacchi and A. Mottola, 'Un'analisi preliminare della guerra in Ucraina' ['An initial analysis of the war in Ukraine'], *Rivista Italiana Difesa*, 4 (2022), pp.24–46, 'Слобожанська наступальна операція: передумови і перший етап (6-12 вересня 2022 р.)' ['The Slobozhansky Offensive Operation: Preconditions and First Stage (6-12 September 2022)'], *Ukrainian Historical Journal*, 1 (2023), pp.5–19.

20 G. A. Zmiyevsky, V. V. Pugach, and V. P. Chepurny, 'Застосування сучасних форм наступального маневну на прикладі досвіду харківської наступальної операції' ['The use of modern forms of offensive manoeuvres on the example of the Kharkiv offensive operation'] *Military Affairs and National Security*, 151 (2023), pp.761–766.

21 Dmytro Komarov and Danilo Kruglyak, 'Контрнаступальна операція Збройних сил України на Харківському напрямку у 2022 році: досвід та стратегічне значення' ['Counteroffensive operation of the Armed Forces of Ukraine in the Kharkiv direction in 2022: experience and strategic significance'], *Bulletin of Taras Shevchenko National University of Kyiv. History*, 157:2 (2023), pp.38–43.

22 Oleksandr Boiko, 'Повномасштабне вторгнення Росії в Україну: перебіг основних фаз війни' ['Russia's full-scale invasion of Ukraine: a timeline of the main phases of the war'], in A. Kiridon and A. Ivanenko (eds), *Російсько-українська війна. Енциклопедичний глосарій, Вип. 1 [Full-scale invasion of Ukraine. Encyclopaedic Glossary, Issue 1]* (Kyiv: Encyclopaedic Publishing House, 2024), pp.28–64.

23 Artem Shevchenko, *Воєнна розвідка України. У небі, на морі, на землі [Military Intelligence of Ukraine: In the Sky, at Sea, on Land]* (Kyiv: Yakaboo Publishing, 2023), pp.105–136.

24 Volodymyr Golovko, *Вторгнення. 2022. Широкомасштабна агресія Росії проти України [Invasion. 2022. Russia's large-scale aggression against Ukraine]* (Kyiv: Institute of History of Ukraine, National Academy of Sciences of Ukraine, 2023), p.602.

25 M. V. Koval (ed.), *Рік незламності: крах операції «Z» : Монографія [A Year of Resilience: The Collapse of Operation Z: Monograph]* (Kyiv: National Defence University of Ukraine, 2023), p.320.

26 Tom Cooper et al., *War in Ukraine, Volume 2: Russian Invasion, February 2022* (Warwick: Helion, 2023), p.76.

27 A. Kharuk, 'Як Використовувати Російські Джерела Для Вивчення Російсько-Української Війни?' ['How to use Russian sources to study the Russian-Ukrainian war?'], *Problems of the Humanities: Collection of Scientific Works of the Ivan Franko State Pedagogical University of Drohobych, History Series*, 13:55 (2023), pp.345–346.

Chapter 1

1 Novorossiya (also Novorossiysk Region, Russian: Novorossiya) was the official name in the Russian Empire for the southern Ukrainian lands, which covered the territories annexed by the Russian Empire in the 18th century, namely the lands of the Zaporizhian Host, the Crimean Khanate and the possessions of the Ottoman Empire in the northern Black Sea region. The first mention dates back to 1764. See Volodymyr Kubiyovych (ed.), *Encyclopedia of Ukrainian Studies*, Volume 5 (Lviv: Molode Zhyttia-NTSh, 1996), pp.1788–1789.

2 P. I. Artymyshyn and I. Y. Solyar, 'Проєкт «Новоросія» В Контексті Сучасної Російсько-Української Війни' ['The "Novorossiya" project in the context of the modern Russian-Ukrainian war'], (Riga: Baltija Publishing, 2022), p.416, <https://doi.org/10.30525/978-9934-26-223-4-51>.

3 V. O. Korepanov and V. V. Shumov, 'Моделирование военных, боевых и специальных действий' ['Modelling military, combat and special operations'], *Military Thought*, 1 (2023), pp.39–40.

4 The St. George Ribbon (Russian: Георгиевская лента) is a two-colour ribbon of the Order of St. George (a Russian military decoration) consisting of three black and two yellow stripes. In Russian propaganda, it has become one of the main symbols of victory in the German-Soviet War. In Ukraine, the St. George's Ribbon has become a symbol of Russian aggression and the so-called "Russian world." See, for example, Ihor Fedyk, 'Георгіївська стрічка: поваги – нуль, максимум пропаганди' ['St. George's Ribbon: zero respect, maximum propaganda'], *Historical Truth*, <https://www.istpravda.com.ua/columns/2011/06/2/41536/>.

5 O. Turchynov, 'Постанова Верховної Ради України: 'Про самоусунення Президента України…' ['Resolution of the Verkhovna Rada of Ukraine: On the self-removal of the President of Ukraine…'], *Bulletin of the Verkhovna Rada*, No.11 (2014), p.158, <https://zakon.rada.gov.ua/laws/show/757-18#Text>.

6 Euromaidan (from *maidan*, meaning square, such as Independence Square in Kyiv) is a social movement associated with a wave of demonstrations and protests in Ukraine, the largest since independence in 1991. The protests began on 21 November 2013 due to Yanukovych's failure to sign an association agreement with the European Union. As events unfolded, the protesters' positions became more radical, with demands for the removal of the president and radical change in the country gaining popularity. The movement itself turned into nationwide protests.

7 'У Харкові на місцевий Майдан напали члени "Оплоту"' ['In Kharkiv, members of Oplot attacked the local Maidan'], *Ukrainska Pravda* (23 February 2014), <http://www.pravda.com.ua/news/2014/02/23/7015899/>.

8 Anna Silaeva, 'Харків: щонайменше 97 у лікарні після "мирного мітингу патріотів"' ['Kharkiv: at least 97 people hospitalised after a "peaceful patriotic rally"'], BBC News Ukraine (1 March 2014), <https://www.bbc.com/ukrainian/news/2014/03/140301_kharkiv_az>.

9 'Жадана били бітами по голові і вимагали стати на коліна. Він послав їх на х…' ['Zhadan was beaten on the head with bats and forced to kneel. He told them to f*** off'], *iPress* (1 March 2014), <https://ipress.ua/news/zhadana_byly_bitamy_po_golovi_i_vymagaly_staty_nakolina_vin_poslav_ih_na_h_51444.html>.

10 O. Turchynov, 'УКАЗ ПРЕЗИДЕНТА УКРАЇНИ № 223/2014' ['Decree of the President of Ukraine No.223/2014'], President of Ukraine Petro Poroshenko (2 March 2014), <https://web.archive.org/web/20140708074745/http://president.gov.ua/documents/16613.html>.

11 O. Turchynov, 'УКАЗ ПРЕЗИДЕНТА УКРАЇНИ № 224/2014' ['Decree of the President of Ukraine No.224/2014'], President of Ukraine Petro Poroshenko (2 March 2014), <https://web.archive.org/web/20140610092459/http://www.president.gov.ua/documents/16614.htmll>.

12 Interview with Nataliya Annenkova, recorded on 15 April 2014.

13 Svyatoslav Khomenko, 'ХНР: Харьковская неудавшаяся республика' ['KNR: Kharkiv's failed republic'], BBC News Russian Service (8 April 2015), <https://www.bbc.com/russian/international/2015/04/150407_kharkiv_peoples_republic>.

14 'Турчинов розповів, чому в 2014-му вдалося запобігти окупації Харкова, але не Донецька й Луганська' ['Turchynov explained why it was possible to prevent the occupation of Kharkiv in 2014, but not Donetsk and Luhansk'], Radio Liberty (18 April 2021), <https://www.radiosvoboda.org/a/news-turchynov-2014-kharkiv-donetsk-luhansk/31209670.html>.

15 A. Yatsenuk, 'Про затвердження переліку населених пунктів, на території яких здійснювалася антитерористична операція' ['On approval of the list of settlements on the territory of which the anti-terrorist operation was carried out'], Appendix to the Order of the Cabinet of Ministers of Ukraine dated October 30, 2014 No. 1053-r (2014), <https://zakon.rada.gov.ua/laws/show/1053-2014-%D1%80#Text>.

16 Ihor Kryshtun, 'Ато: Як Все Починалося' ['ATO: how it all began'], Army FM (14 April 2018), <https://www.armyfm.com.ua/-ato-jak-vse-pochinalosja-/>.

17 'Харьков: драка ультрас и активистов с георгиевскими ленточками' ['Kharkiv: fight between ultras and activists wearing St. George's ribbons'], *Korrespondent.net* (27 April 2014), <https://korrespondent.net/ukraine/events/3355225-kharkov-draka-ultras-y-aktyvystov-s-heorhyevskymy-lentochkamy>.

18 'Харківські сепаратисти відмовилися проводити "референдум" 11 травня' ['Kharkiv separatists refused to hold a "referendum" on 11 May'], *Ukrainska Pravda* (9 May 2014), <https://www.pravda.com.ua/news/2014/05/9/7024854/>.

Chapter 2

1 "Russian world" (Russian: русский мир) is a concept and a political doctrine usually defined as the sphere of military, political and cultural influence of Russia. It is a vague term, mostly used to refer to communities with a historical, cultural, or spiritual tie to Russia. This can include all ethnic Russians and Russian speakers in neighbouring states, as well as those who belong to the Russian Orthodox Church. The concept of the "Russian world" is linked to Russian neo-imperialism.

2 Khlon, Pahiria and Poltorakov, *"Східна брама держави"...* ["The Eastern Gate of the State"...], pp.2–6.

3 Zaluzhnyi (chair) et al., *Воєнно-історичний опис російсько-української війни (лютий–березень 2022 року) [Military-historical description of the Russian-Ukrainian war (February-March 2022)]*, p.72.

4 Marcin Gawęda, 'Wojna rosyjsko-ukraińska cz. 1' ['The Russian-Ukrainian War, Part 1'], *Wojsko i Technika*, 3 (2022), p.23.

5 The Federal Service of National Guard Troops of the Russian Federation (abbreviated as Rosgvardia) is a Russian federal service created in April 2016 by transforming the Internal Troops of the Ministry of Internal Affairs of the Russian Federation. It has become the largest internal security structure in Russia. See Jolanta Darczewska, 'Rosgvardiya: A Special-Purpose Force', *OSW Point of View*, 78 (2020), <https://www.osw.waw.pl/sites/default/files/PV_ENG_Rosgvardiya_net.pdf>.

6 Thorkill, 'Przepis na katastrofę. Rajd w głąb śródmieścia Charkowa 2 Brygady Specnazu 27 lutego 2022 r.' ['A recipe for disaster. Raids into the centre of Kharkiv by the 2nd Spetsnaz Brigade on 27 February and 5 March 2022'], *Thorkill Blog* (12 April 2023), <https://thorkillblog.blogspot.com/2023/04/przepis-na-katastrofe-rajdy-w-gab.html>.

7 On 30 April 2018, the anti-terrorist operation that had been ongoing in Donbas was transformed into the Joint Forces Operation (JFO). On 24 February 2022, the military units participating in the Joint Forces Operation formed the Joint Forces (JF) group. It included the operational-tactical groups "East" and "North." In June 2022, this group was transformed into several operational-tactical groups with direct subordination.

8 CMHRAFU, *Рік війни за свободу... [A Year of War for Freedom...]*, Book I, p.190.

9 CMHRAFU, *Рік війни за свободу... [A Year of War for Freedom...]*, Book I, p.193.

10 Khlon, Pahiria and Poltorakov, *"Східна брама держави"...* ["The Eastern Gate of the State"...], p.3.

11 The 92nd Mechanised Brigade was the only mechanised brigade of the Ukrainian Ground Forces that was almost entirely equipped with wheeled armoured vehicles.

12 Koval (ed.), *Рік незламності: крах операції «Z»... [A Year of Resilience: The Collapse of Operation Z...]*, p.165.

13 Case No. 642/1618/22, Leninsky District Court of Kharkiv (8 December 2022), <https://reyestr.court.gov.ua/Review/107759505>

14 Koval (ed.), *Рік незламності: крах операції «Z»... [A Year of Resilience: The Collapse of Operation Z...]*, p.166.

15 Gawęda, 'Wojna rosyjsko-ukraińska cz. 1' ['The Russian-Ukrainian War, Part 1'], p.23.

16 Dmitry Gorbunov, 'Генерал-майор Олег Мікац та полковник Сергій Гузченко – почесні громадяни Харкова' ['Major General Oleh Mikats and Colonel Serhii Huzchenko – honorary citizens of Kharkiv'], ArmyInform (24 August 2022), <https://armyinform.com.ua/2022/08/24/general-major-oleg-mikacz-ta-polkovnyk-sergij-guzchenko-staly-pochesnymy-gromadyanamy-harkova/>.

17 Trystan, *Прийшла війна... [The War Has Come...]*, p.9.

18 Unlike the brigade's linear mechanised battalions, this battalion did not have armoured vehicles. It was formed on 25 April 2014 as the 22nd Territorial Defence Battalion "Kharkiv". The battalion was formed and trained at the military training faculty of the National Technical University "Kharkiv Polytechnic Institute". On 17 November 2014, it was reorganised into the 22nd OMPB and subordinated to the 92nd OMB.

19 At present, the destruction of this helicopter has not been confirmed; it may have only been damaged.

20 Interview with Colonel Ihor Budur, recorded by the author on 14 March 2022.

21 '"Якщо впаде Харків, впаде вся Україна". Репортаж з лінії фронту' ['"If Kharkiv falls, all of Ukraine will fall". Report from the front line'], BBC News Ukraine (12 March 2022), <https://www.bbc.com/ukrainian/features-60719093>.

22 'УКАЗ ПРЕЗИДЕНТА УКРАЇНИ №167/2022' ['Decree of the President of Ukraine No. 167/2022'], President of Ukraine Volodymyr Zelensky (25 March 2022), <https://www.president.gov.ua/documents/1672022-41809>.

23 Interview with Andriy Platonov, recorded by the author on 30 August 2024.

24 Koval (ed.), *Рік незламності: крах операції «Z»... [A Year of Resilience: The Collapse of Operation Z...]*, p.166.

25 '40 окрема артилерійська бригада відзначає першу річницю з дня створення' ['The 40th Separate Artillery Brigade celebrates the first anniversary of its establishment'], Ministry of Defence Ukraine (25 May 2016), <https://web.archive.org/web/20160526115716/http://www.mil.gov.ua/news/2016/05/25/40-okrema-artilerijska-brigada-vidznachae-pershu-richniczyu-z-dnya-stvorennya--/>.

26 Iryna Balachuk, 'Вийшли в лоб 2 танками: захисник розповів, як у лютому знищили велику колону росіян під Харковом' ['They came out with two tanks: a defender recounted how a large column of Russians was destroyed near Kharkiv in February'], *Ukrainska Pravda* (11 June 2022), <https://www.pravda.com.ua/news/2022/06/11/7351882/>.

27 Khlon, Pahiria and Poltorakov, *"Східна брама держави"...* ["The Eastern Gate of the State"...], p.2.

28 A. Kharuk, 'Obrona Charkowa' ['Defence of Kharkiv'], *Nowa Technika Wojskowa*, 16 special issue (2023), p.12.

29 In the special forces of the Russian army (as, incidentally, in the Ukrainian army), a detachment is equivalent to a battalion.

30 Alexander Shulman, 'Підполковник Роман Зуй: Коли росіяни відмовились здатися, я їх просто розстріляв з танка' ['Lieutenant Colonel Roman Zuy: When the Russians refused to surrender, I simply shot them from my tank'], ArmyInform (26 February 2024), <https://armyinform.com.ua/2024/02/26/pidpolkovnyk-roman-zuj-koly-rosiyany-vidmovylys-zdatysya-ya-yih-prosto-rozstrilyav-z-tanka/>.

31 Interview with Andriy Platonov, recorded by the author on 30 August 2024.

32 Oksana Yakushko, 'Найкритичніший день. Як 27 лютого відбувався бій за центр Харкова' ['The most critical day. How the battle for the centre of Kharkiv unfolded on 27 February'], *Objectiv* (13 February 2023), <https://www.objectiv.tv/uk/objectively/2023/02/13/samyj-kriticheskij-den-kak-27-fevralya-prohodil-boj-za-tsentr-harkova/>.

33 KORD (Ukrainian: Корпус оперативно-раптової дії, Rapid Response Corps) – special police units of the main departments of the National Police in the regions, designed to directly conduct special police operations and other measures in the field of combating crime associated with an increased threat to the life and health of police officers and the likelihood of armed resistance. See 'Про затвердження Положення про підрозділи поліції особливого призначення «Корпус оперативно-раптової дії»' ['On Approval of the Regulations on Special Purpose Police Units "Corps of Operational-Sudden Action"'], Ministry of Internal Affairs of Ukraine, Order No. 958 (2018), <https://zakon.rada.gov.ua/laws/show/z1436-18#Text>.

34 DFTG (Volunteer Territorial Community Formations) – armed units created on a voluntary basis from among Ukrainian citizens residing in the territory of the relevant territorial community, designed to participate in the preparation and execution of territorial defence tasks. See D. Shmyhal, 'Про затвердження Положення про добровольчі формування територіальних громад' ['On Approval of the Regulations on Voluntary Formations of Territorial Communities'], Cabinet of Ministers of Ukraine Resolution, No. 1149 (2021), <https://zakon.rada.gov.ua/laws/show/1449-2021-%D0%BF#n11>.

35 Oksana Ivanets, 'Як у лютому Сили оборони Харкова знищили спецназ рф у школі № 134' ['How in February the Kharkiv Defence Forces destroyed Russian special forces at school No. 134'], ArmyInform (2 September 2022), <https://armyinform.com.

ua/2022/09/02/yak-u-lyutomu-syly-oborony-harkova-znyshhyly-specznaz-rf-u-shkoli-%e2%84%96-134/>.

36 Yevhen Miroshnichenko, '«Ми були першими з добровольчих підрозділів, які прийшли на допомогу Збройним Силам України 24 лютого». Інтерв›ю з начальником штабу Фрайкорпу Богданом Войцеховським' ['"We were the first volunteer units to come to the aid of the Armed Forces of Ukraine on 24 February." Interview with Bogdan Voitsekhovsky, Chief of Staff of the Freikorps'], *057.ua* (24 November 2022), <https://www.057.ua/news/3501898/mi-buli-persimi-z-dobrovolcih-pidrozdiliv-aki-24-lutogo-prijsli-na-dopomogu-zsu-intervu-z-nacalnikom-stabu-frajkoru-bogdanom-vojcehovskim-foto>.

37 057.ua editors, 'Від добровольців до елітного формування. Історія харківського спецпідрозділу ГУР "Кракен"' ['From volunteers to an elite unit. The history of the Kharkiv special forces unit GUR "Kraken"'], Main Intelligence Directorate of Ukraine (25 November 2022), <https://gur.gov.ua/content/vid-dobrovoltsiv-do-elitnoho-formuvannia-istoriia-kharkivskoho-spetspidrozdilu-hur-kraken.html>.

38 Shevchenko, *Воєнна розвідка України. У небі, на морі, на землі [Military Intelligence of Ukraine: In the Sky, at Sea, on Land]*, p.110.

39 '"Українцям важливіше за все свобода", — командир "Хартії" Всеволод Кожемяко' ['"Freedom is the most important thing for Ukrainians," Khartia commander Vsevolod Kozhemyako'], *Kharkiv Today* (20 October 2022), <https://2day.kh.ua/ua/kharkow/ukrayintsyam-vazhlyvishe-za-vse-svoboda-komandyr-khartiyi-vsevolod-kozhemyako>.

40 '"Хартія" стане механізованою бригадою у складі Нацгвардії України' ['Khartia will become a mechanised brigade within the National Guard of Ukraine'], *Kharkiv Today* (20 March 2023), <https://2day.kh.ua/ua/kharkow/khartiya-stane-mekhanizovanoyu-bryhadoyu-u-skladi-natshvardiyi-ukrayiny>.

41 National Defence University of Ukraine, *Хроніка війни, частина І...[Chronicle of the War, Part I...]*, p.16.

42 '"Війна показала справжні обличчя". Як живе тимчасово окупований Куп'янськ на Харківщині' ['"The war has revealed true faces." How life is in the temporarily occupied town of Kupiansk in the Kharkiv region'], *Suspilne Kharkiv* (19 March 2022), <https://suspilne.media/kharkiv/218803-vijna-pokazala-spravzni-oblicca-ak-zive-timcasovo-okupovanij-kupansk-na-harkivsini/>.

43 Nestor Dim, 'Мер Балаклії на Харківщині пішов на співпрацю з окупантами' ['The mayor of Balakliia in the Kharkiv region has agreed to cooperate with the occupiers'], *Novynarnia* (28 March 2022), <https://novynarnia.com/2022/03/28/mer-balakliyi-na-harkivshhyni-pishov-na-spivpraczyu-z-okupantamy/>.

44 Khlon, Pahiria and Poltorakov, *"Східна брама держави"*... ["The Eastern Gate of the State"...], p. 3.

45 'Кількість загиблих від удару по Харківській обладміністрації збільшилась до 29' ['The death toll from the strike on the Kharkiv regional administration has risen to 29'], *The New Voice of Ukraine* (2 April 2022), <https://nv.ua/ukr/kharkiv/boji-za-harkiv-pid-chas-obstrilu-harkivskoji-oda-zaginuli-29-lyudey-novini-harkova-50230576.html>.

46 Interview with Kateryna Novak, recorded on 29 June 2024; her husband, Valerii Novak, has been serving in the Kharkiv territorial defence brigade since the first days of the war.

47 'Із Харкова залізницею евакуювали вже понад 600 тисяч людей, – голова ОДА' ['More than 600,000 people have already been evacuated from Kharkiv by rail, according to the head of the Regional State Administration'], *Rubryka* (8 March 2022), <https://rubryka.com/2022/03/08/iz-harkova-zaliznytseyu-evakuyuvaly-vzhe-ponad-600-tysyach-lyudej-golova-oda/>.

48 Khlon, Pahiria and Poltorakov, *"Східна брама держави"*... ["The Eastern Gate of the State"...], p.3.

49 Andriy Fartushkov and Pavlo Kholodov, '«Яким треба бути ідіотом, щоб зайти однією ротою» – комбриг Павло Федосенко про битву за Харків' ['"How stupid do you have to be to go in with just one company?" – Brigade Commander Pavlo Fedosenko on the battle for Kharkiv'], *Radio Liberty* (9 July 2023), <https://www.radiosvoboda.org/a/zsu-bytva-za-kharkiv/32493407.html>.

50 Gawęda, 'Wojna rosyjsko-ukraińska cz. 1' ['The Russian-Ukrainian War, Part 1'], p.23.

51 General Staff of the Armed Forces of Ukraine, 'Оперативна інформація станом на 24.00 06.03.2022...' ['Operational information on 24.00, 06.03.2022...'] [Facebook post], 6 March 2022, <https://www.facebook.com/GeneralStaff.ua/posts/266469205666165>.

52 Marcin Gawęda, 'Wojna rosyjsko-ukraińska Cz. 2' [The Russian-Ukrainian War Part 2], *Wojsko i Technika*, 4 (2022), p.18.

53 Cielma, 'Przed bitwą wszystkich bitew. Wojna w Ukrainie' ['Before the Battle of All Battles. War in Ukraine'], p.10.

54 News.LIVE, 'В Ізюмі активізувались зрадники та колаборанти, — Валерій Марченко' ['Traitors and collaborators have become more active in Izium, says Valerii Marchenko'], YouTube video (25 March 2022), <https://www.youtube.com/watch?v=HGa1gtL9VbQ>.

55 Valerii Zaluzhnyi (chair) et al., *Воєнно-Історичний Опис Російсько-Української Війни (Квітень 2022) [Military-historical description of the Russian-Ukrainian war (April 2022)]* (Kyiv: Ukrainian Defence Ministry and Ukrainian General Staff, 2022), p.56.

56 The Donetsk People's Republic (DPR) is a quasi-state entity proclaimed in the Russian-occupied part of Ukraine's Donetsk Oblast on 7 April 2014 and annexed by the Russian Federation on 30 September 2022. A similar entity in the occupied part of Luhansk Oblast, the Luhansk People's Republic (LPR), was proclaimed on 27 April 2014 and annexed on 30 September 2022.

57 Andriy Harasym and Nadia Kelm, 'Більше води. Як Сіверський Донець вдалося зробити неприступною перепоною' ['More water. How the Siverskyi Donets River became an impenetrable barrier'], *Texty.org.ua* (28 June 2022), <https://texty.org.ua/articles/107064/golubyj-val-yak-siverskyj-donec-vdalosya-zrobyty-neprystupnoyu-pereponoyu/>.

58 Artem Listopad, 'Подвійний злочин: в 50-х радянська влада створила Оскільське водосховище, знищивши все живе навколо, а в 2022–му окупанти його підірвали, вдруге зруйнувавши еко-систему. Чи понесе росія відповідальність за екоцид на Харківщині?' ['A double crime: in the 1950s, the Soviet authorities created the Oskil Reservoir, destroying all life around it, and in 2022, the occupiers blew it up, destroying the ecosystem for the second time. Will Russia be held responsible for ecocide in the Kharkiv region?'], *Ursa Media* (4 March 2024), <https://ursamedia.com.ua/history/podvijnyj-zlochyn-chy-ponese-rosiyja-vidpovidalnist-za-ecozid-na-kharkivshuni/>.

59 CMHRAFU, *Рік війни за свободу... [A Year of War for Freedom...]*, Book I, p.224.

60 Koval (ed.), *Рік незламності: крах операції «Z»... [A Year of Resilience: The Collapse of Operation Z...]*, p.175.

61 National Defence University of Ukraine, *Хроніка війни, Частина ІІ (Російсько-українська війна, 27.03- 25.04.2022) [Chronicle of the War, Part II (Russian-Ukrainian war, 27 March – 25 April 2022)]*. (Kyiv: Ivan Chernyakhovsky National Defence University [now National Defence University of Ukraine], 2022), p.132.

62 Serhiy Zgurets, 'Напередодні битви за Донбас: скільки військ, зброї та на яких напрямках збирає армія рашистів (аналіз)' ['On the eve of the battle for Donbas: how many troops and weapons are the Russian forces gathering, and in which directions (analysis)'], *Defense Express* (14 April 2022), <https://defence-ua.com/army_and_war/naperedodni_bitvi_za_donbas_skilki_vijsk_zbroji_ta_na_jakih_naprjamkah_zbiraje_armija_rashistiv_analiz-6941.html>.

63 Tatyana Fedorkova and Valeria Getsko, '"Цю війну ми вже програли", — Максим Криштоп, полонений у Харкові російський льотчик' ['"We have already lost this war," says Maxim Kryshtop, a Russian pilot captured in Kharkiv'], <https://suspilne.media/216424-cu-vijnu-mi-vze-prograli-maksim-kristop-polonenij-u-harkovi-rosijskij-lotcik/>.

64 Strembski, 'Wojna powietrzna, 24 lutego...' [Air War, 24 February...'], p.27.

65 Strembski, 'Wojna powietrzna, 24 marca...' [Air War, 24 March...'], p.22.

66 Kharuk, 'Obrona Charkowa' ['Defence of Kharkiv'], p.18.

67 Mick F. and N.R. Jenzen-Jones, 'Russian POM-3 anti-personnel landmines documented in Ukraine', *Armament Research Service* (15 April 2022), <https://armamentresearch.com/russian-pom-3-anti-personnel-landmines-documented-in-ukraine-2022/>.

68 Koval (ed.), *Рік незламності: крах операції «Z»... [A Year of Resilience: The Collapse of Operation Z...]*, p.176.

69 Koval (ed.), *Рік незламності: крах операції «Z»... [A Year of Resilience: The Collapse of Operation Z...]*, p.199.

70 Ukrainian Military YouTube, 'Українські військові відбили атаку росіян у селі Заводи' ['Ukrainian military repelled Russian attack in Zavody village'], YouTube video (25 April 2022), <https://www.youtube.com/watch?v=Q1v6bpmAFtg>.

71 Taras Safronov, 'Українські військові відбили атаку росіян на село Заводи' ['Ukrainian military repelled Russian attack on the village of Zavody'], *Militarnyi* (25 April 2022), <https://mil.in.ua/uk/news/ukrayinski-vijskovi-vidbyly-ataku-rosiyan-na-selo-zavody/>.

72 Koval (ed.), *Рік незламності: крах операції «Z»... [A Year of Resilience: The Collapse of Operation Z…]*, p.200.

73 Khlon, Pahiria and Poltorakov, *"Східна брама держави"...* ["The Eastern Gate of the State"…], p.7.

74 Zaluzhnyi (chair) et al., *Воєнно-Історичний Опис Російсько-Української Війни (Квітень 2022) [Military-historical description of the Russian-Ukrainian war (April 2022)]*, p.56.

75 Marcin Gawęda, 'Wojna rosyjsko-ukraińska Cz. 3' [The Russian-Ukrainian War Part 3], Wojsko i Technika, 5 (2022), p.33.

76 Marcin Gawęda, 'Wojna rosyjsko-ukraińska Cz. 3' [The Russian-Ukrainian War Part 3], Wojsko i Technika, 5 (2022), pp.35–36.

77 Khlon, Pahiria and Poltorakov, *"Східна брама держави"...* ["The Eastern Gate of the State"…], p.7.

78 CMHRAFU, *Рік війни за свободу... [A Year of War for Freedom…]*, Book II, p.117.

79 General Staff of the Armed Forces of Ukraine, 'Оперативна інформація станом на 18.00 10.05.2022 щодо російського вторгнення…' ['Operational information as of 18.00 on 10.05.2022…'] [Facebook post], 10 May 2022, <https://www.facebook.com/GeneralStaff.ua/posts/314011584245260>.

80 The author is fully aware of the legal nullity of any acts of the "DPR" and "LPR" as well as acts of the Russian Federation concerning the temporarily occupied territories of Ukraine. However, we will sometimes have to refer to them in order to explain the logic of the actions of the occupying authorities.

81 Khlon, Pahiria and Poltorakov, *"Східна брама держави"...* ["The Eastern Gate of the State"…], p.8.

82 Kharuk, 'Obrona Charkowa' ['Defence of Kharkiv'], p.19.

83 Kateryna Stepanenko and Frederick W. Kagan, 'Russian Offensive Campaign Assessment, May 13, 2022', Institute for the Study of War (13 May 2022), <https://www.understandingwar.org/backgrounder/russian-offensive-campaign-assessment-may-13>.

84 Khlon, Pahiria and Poltorakov, *"Східна брама держави"...* ["The Eastern Gate of the State"…], pp.8–9.

85 'Міноборони: військових РФ відтіснили до держкордону на Харківщині' ['Ministry of Defence: Russian troops pushed back to the state border in Kharkiv region'], *Radio Liberty* (16 May 2022), <https://www.radiosvoboda.org/a/news-kharkivska-oblast-viyskovi-kordon/31852249.html>.

86 O. G. Tukmakov, 'Основные направления совершенствования военно-политической работы при подготовке операций' ['Main directions for improving military-political work in the preparation of operations'], Military Thought, 2 (2023), pp.47–48.

87 Shevchenko, *Воєнна розвідка України. У небі, на морі, на землі [Military Intelligence of Ukraine: In the Sky, at Sea, on Land]*, p.111.

88 Kharuk, 'Харківська оборонна операція (24 лютого — 14 травня 2022 р.)', p.32.

Chapter 3

1 Pavlenko, Olena, 'Гауляйтери Харківської області: хто і як зрадив Україну' ['Gauleiters of the Kharkiv Region: Who Betrayed Ukraine and How'], *Kharkiv Today* (1 June 2022), <https://2day.kh.ua/ua/kharkow/haulyaytery-kharkivskoyi-oblasti-khto-i-yak-zradyv-ukrayinu>.

2 'Сепарастист став заступником гауляйтера окупованої Харківщини' ['Separatist becomes deputy gauleiter of occupied Kharkiv region'], *Kharkiv Today* (29 June 2022), <https://2day.kh.ua/ua/politika/separastyst-stav-zastupnykom-haulyaytera-okupovanoyi-kharkivshchyny>.

3 'Окупанти призначили колишнього міліціонера головним в Ізюмі' ['The occupiers have appointed a former police officer as head of Izium'], *Kharkiv Today* (25 April 2022), <https://2day.kh.ua/ua/kharkow/okupanty-pryznachyly-kolyshnoho-militsionera-holovnym-v-izyumi>.

4 Pavlenko, Olena, 'Нові гауляйтери Харківської області. Як змінюється влада на окупованих територіях' ['New Gauleiters of Kharkiv Region. How power is changing in the occupied territories'], *Kharkiv Today* (8 July 2022), <https://2day.kh.ua/ua/kharkow/novi-haulyaytery-kharkivskoyi-oblasti-yak-zminyuyetsya-vlada-na-okupovanykh-terytoriyakh>.

5 Kateryna Reznikova, 'Путеводитель по российским оккупантам и украинским коллаборационистам' ['A guide to the Russian occupiers and Ukrainian collaborators'], Proekt Media (29 September 2022), <https://www.proekt.media/guide/kto-rukovodit-okkupirovannymi-territoriyami-ukrainy/>.

6 Pavlo Novik, 'Як харківські колаборанти зафільмували свою брехню та показали нових "посіпак"' ['How Kharkiv collaborators filmed their lies and showed off their new "henchmen"'], Media Literacy in the Regions of Ukraine (19 June 2023), <https://milukraine.net/2023/06/6616/>.

7 Pavlo Novik and Yevhen Lisichkin, 'Вкрадене українське зерно: фірми, схеми та механізм санкцій' ['Stolen Ukrainian grain: companies, schemes and sanctions mechanisms'], Kharkiv Anti-Corruption Centre (18 April 2024), <https://anticor-kharkiv.org/our-work/vkradene-ukrainske-zerno-firmy-skhemy-ta-mekhanizm-sanktsiy/>.

8 Kateryna Mikhalevska, 'ОКУПОВАНІ: Куп'янськ. Життя під загрозою повторної окупації' ['Occupied: Kupiansk. Life under threat of new occupation'], *LB.ua* (26 January 2024), <https://lb.ua/news/2024/01/26/595391_okupovani_kupyansk_zhittya_pid.html>.

9 'Справу про викрадення загарбниками депутата-ветерана з Куп'янська розгляне ЄСПЛ' ['The case of the abduction of a veteran deputy from Kupiansk by invaders will be considered by the ECHR'], *Ukrinform* (9 June 2023), <https://www.ukrinform.ua/rubric-society/3720587-spravu-pro-vikradenna-zagarbnikami-deputataveterana-z-kupanska-rozglane-espl.html>.

10 '"Вивезли до Бєлгорода на "перевиховання": викраденого під Куп'янськом блогера Сергія Строєва другий рік шукає родина' ['"Taken to Belgorod for 're-education': the family of Sergei Stroev, a blogger kidnapped near Kupiansk, has been searching for him for two years'], ZMINA (3 November 2023), <https://zmina.info/news/vash-syn-borzyj-my-jogo-vyvezly-do-byelgoroda-na-perevyhovannya-take-pochula-maty-sergiya-stroyeva-blogera-vid-jogo-vykradachiv/>.

11 Vitaliy Poberezhnyi, 'Як Піски-Радьківські чинили опір окупації' ['How Pisky-Radkivski resisted the occupation'], *Ukrainer* (8 March 2023), <https://www.ukrainer.net/pisky-radkivski/>.

12 Natalia Oleshko, 'Український Рух Опору На Харківщині У Повномасштабній Російсько-Українській Війні 2022 Року' ['The Ukrainian resistance movement in the Kharkiv region during the full-scale Russian-Ukrainian war of 2022'], *Current issues in modern science*, 6:12 (2023), p.653.

13 Mykhailo Gema, 'На Харківщині загинув гауляйтер важливого для росіян селища Великий Бурлук: його авто підірвали' ['The Gauleiter of the village of Velykyi Burluk, which is important for the Russians, was killed in the Kharkiv region: his car was blown up'], *24 Kanal* (11 July 2022), <https://24tv.ua/harkivshhini-zaginuv-gaulyayter-vazhlivogo-dlya-rosiyan-selishha_n2092329>.

14 General Staff of the Armed Forces of Ukraine, 'Оперативна інформація станом на 06.00 11.07.2022 щодо російського вторгнення' ['Operational information as of 06.00 on 11.07.2022 regarding the Russian invasion'], YouTube video (11 July 2022), <https://www.youtube.com/watch?v=NQLJuGGPUaY>.

15 Koval (ed.), *Рік незламності: крах операції «Z»... [A Year of Resilience: The Collapse of Operation Z…]*, p.202.

16 Ministry of Defence (UK), 'Latest Defence Intelligence update on the situation in Ukraine – 6 July 2022…' [Twitter post], 5:57 a.m., 6 July 2022, <https://x.com/DefenceHQ/status/1544546167115202560>.

17 Koval (ed.), *Рік незламності: крах операції «Z»... [A Year of Resilience: The Collapse of Operation Z…]*, p.202.

18 'МО РФ: задействованным в спецоперации подразделениям предоставили возможность отдохнуть' ['Russian Ministry of Defence: Units involved in special operations were given the opportunity to rest'], TASS (7 July 2022), <https://tass.ru/armiya-i-opk/15150167>.

19 T. Kwasek, 'Rosyjskie Wojska Powietrznodesantowe' ['Russian Airborne Forces'], *Nowa Technika Wojskowa*, 15 (2023), pp.23–24.

20 Ulyana Bezpalko, 'Війна, мобілізація та ескалація. Чого чекати від Путіна на 9 травня' ['War, mobilisation and escalation. What to expect from Putin on 9 May'], *RBC-Ukraine* (5 May 2022), <https://www.rbc.ua/ukr/news/voyna-mobilizatsiya-eskalatsiya-zhdat-putina-1651697728.html>.

21 'General mobilisation announced in the "DPR" and "LPR"', *DW.com* (19 February 2022), <https://www.dw.com/ru/v-dnr-objavili-vseobshhuju-mobilizaciju/a-60839410>.

22 Matt Murphy, '"Нам потрібні штурмовики". Як ПВК "Вагнер" вербує в'язнів на війну в Україні' ['"We need assault troops." How the Wagner Group recruits prisoners for the war in Ukraine'], BBC News Ukraine (15 September 2022), <https://www.bbc.com/ukrainian/features-62917466>.

23 Scott McDonald, 'What is Russia's 3rd Army Corps? New unit moving to front lines', *Newsweek* (28 August 2022), <https://www.newsweek.com/what-russias-3rd-army-corps-new-unit-moving-front-lines-intel-1737651>.

24 General Staff of the Armed Forces of Ukraine, 'Оперативна інформація станом на 18.00 07.07.2022 щодо російського вторгнення' ['Operational information as of 18.00 on 07.07.2022 regarding the Russian invasion'], YouTube video (7 July 2022), <https://www.youtube.com/watch?v=BQqwmMakyIw>.

25 General Staff of the Armed Forces of Ukraine, 'Оперативна інформація станом 06.00 15.08.2022 щодо російського вторгнення' ['Operational information as of 6.00 on 15.08.2022 regarding the Russian invasion'], YouTube video (15 August 2022), <https://www.youtube.com/watch?v=P7Aniwn9en8>.

26 Koval (ed.), *Рік незламності: крах операції «Z»... [A Year of Resilience: The Collapse of Operation Z...]*, pp.203–204.

27 Ministry of Defence of Ukraine, 'Оперативна інформація Генерального Штабу Збройних Сил України станом на 18:00 15.08.2022 щодо російського вторгнення' ['Operational information of the General Staff of the Armed Forces of Ukraine as of 18:00 on 15.08.2022 regarding the Russian invasion'], Government Portal (15 August 2022), <https://www.kmu.gov.ua/news/operatyvna-informatsiia-heneralnoho-shtabu-zbroinykh-syl-ukrainy-stanom-1800-15082022-shchodo-rosiiskoho-vtorhnennia>.

28 General Staff of the Armed Forces of Ukraine, 'Оперативна інформація станом 18.00 16.08.2022 щодо російського вторгнення' ['Operational information as of 6.00 on 15.08.2022 regarding the Russian invasion'], YouTube video (15 August 2022), <https://www.youtube.com/watch?v=-9kpPTr7SCE>.

29 Interview with Nadiya Zamryga, press officer of the 14th Mechanised Brigade, recorded on 31 July 2024.

30 'Рашисти переходять до масового використання ЗРК С-300 для ударів по містах: чи є захист'['The Rashists are moving to the mass use of S-300 air defence systems to strike cities: is there any protection?'], *Defense Express* (9 July 2022), <https://defence-ua.com/minds_and_ideas/rashisti_perehodjat_do_masovogo_vikoristannja_zrk_s_300_dlja_udariv_po_mistah_chi_je_zahist-8096.html>.

31 'Рашисти почали з ЗРК С-300 обстрілювати й Харківщину: одну ракету вдалось збити (фото)' ['The Rashists began firing at the Kharkiv region with S-300 air defence systems: one missile was shot down'], *Defense Express* (13 July 2022), <https://defence-ua.com/news/rashisti_pochali_z_zrk_s_300_ obstriljuvati_j_harkivschinu_odnu_raketu_vdalos_zbiti_foto-8144.html>.

32 'У Харкові ракетний удар зруйнував депо метрополітену' ['In Kharkiv, a missile strike destroyed a metro depot'], *Defense Express* (14 July 2022), <https://2day.kh. ua/ua/kharkow/u-kharkovi-raketnyy-udar-zruynuvav-depo-metropolitenu>.

33 Volodymyr Pyrih, 'Росіяни з комплексів ППО масовано вдарили по Чугуєву' ['Russians launched a massive strike on Chuhuiv from air defence systems'], Zaxid.net (25 July 2022), <https://zaxid.net/udar_po_chuguyevu_25_lipnya_2022_naslidki_foto_detali_n154679>.

34 Oleh Syniehubov, Head of the Kharkiv Regional State Administration, 'Харківщина. 25 липня...' ['Kharkiv region. July 25...'], Telegram post (25 July 2022), <https://t.me/synegubov/3753>.

35 Hanna Tsomyik and Vyacheslav Mavrichev, 'Російський артобстріл Харкова вранці 30 серпня: фото наслідків' ['Russian artillery shelling of Kharkiv on the morning of 30 August: photos of the aftermath'], *Suspilne Kharkiv* (30 August 2022), <https://suspilne.media/kharkiv/276443-artilerijski-obstrili-harkova-vranci-30-serpna-foto-naslidkiv/>.

Chapter 4

1 CMHRAFU, *Рік війни за свободу... [A Year of War for Freedom...]*, Book I, p.9.

2 See, for example, Tatyana Fedorkova, 'Контрнаступ ЗСУ на Харківщині. Текстовий онлайн' ['Counteroffensive of the Armed Forces of Ukraine in the Kharkiv region. Online Text'], *Suspilne* (6 October 2022), <https://suspilne.media/279968-kontrnastup-zsu-na-harkivsini-tekstovij-onlajn/>.

3 Komarov and Kruglyak, 'Контрнаступальна операція Збройних сил України на Харківському напрямку...' ['Counteroffensive operation of the Armed Forces of Ukraine in the Kharkiv direction in 2022...'], pp.38–43.

4 Military Scientific Directorate of the General Headquarters of the Armed Forces of Ukraine, *Dictionary of Military Terms and Abbreviations* (Kyiv: Ukrainian Ministry of Defence, 2020), p.17.

5 Department of Defense, *Department of Defense Dictionary of Military and Associated Terms. Joint Pub 1-02* (Washington, DC: US DoD, 2008), p.132.

6 Nikolai Ogarkov (chair) et al., *Soviet Military Encyclopaedia, Volume 4* (Moscow: Soviet Ministry of Defence, 1979), p.318.

7 Volodymyr Masliychuk, *Слобідська Україна [Sloboda Ukraine]* (Kyiv, 2008), pp.8–9.

8 Kateryna Stepanenko, Karolina Hird, Angela Howard, Mason Clark, 'Russian Offensive Campaign Assessment, 5 September, 2022', Institute for the Study of War (6 September 2022), <https://www.understandingwar.org/backgrounder/russian-offensive-campaign-assessment-september-5>.

9 E. Yu. Segida, V. I. Redin, and M. T. Chaban, *Geography of Kharkiv Region* (Kharkiv: Kharkiv National University, 2012), p.10.

10 Alexey Krasnov, 'Участок Купянск — Валуйки' ['Kupiansk — Valuyki section'], The Steel Ring of the Southern Railway (no date), <http://uzdlines.narod.ru/lines/line_kup1.htm>.

11 Alexey Krasnov, 'Участок Купянск — Волчанск' ['Kupiansk — Volchansk section'], The Steel Ring of the Southern Railway (no date), <http://uzdlines.narod.ru/lines/line_kup4.htm>.

12 Ekaterina Venkina and Roman Guba, 'Зеленський наказав відвоювати південь України – Резніков' ['Zelensky ordered to recapture southern Ukraine – Reznikov'], *DW.com* (11 July 2022), <https://www.dw.com/uk/zelenskyi-nakazav-vidvoiuvaty-pivden-ukrainy-reznikov/a-62432972>.

13 Maksym Drabok and Daniil Sotnikov, 'Аналітики про наказ Зеленського повернути південь України' ['Analysts on Zelensky's order to retake southern Ukraine'], *DW.com* (15 July 2022), <https://www.dw.com/uk/bytva-voli-viiskovi-analityky-pro-nakaz-zelenskoho-povernuty-pivden-ukrainy/a-62487441>.

14 Maria Solodovnik, Roman Kryvko, and Tetiana Kryvonis, '"Залужний обіцяв, що все буде добре". Спогади Синєгубова про контрнаступ ЗСУ на Харківщині' ['"Zaluzhny promised that everything would be fine." Sinehubov's memories of the Ukrainian Armed Forces' counteroffensive in the Kharkiv region'], *Suspilne Kharkiv* (21 September 2023), <https://suspilne.media/kharkiv/577361-zaluznij-obicav-so-vse-bude-dobre-spogadi-sinegubova-pro-kontrnastup-zsu-na-harkivsini/>.

15 Mykhailo Drapatiy, *"Кров Дніпром Тече": Херсонська наступальна операція ["Blood Flows Through the Dnieper": The Kherson Offensive Operation]* (Kyiv: CMHRAFU, 2023), p.8.

16 David Axe, 'Russian Troops Are Dashing Around Ukraine Trying To Block Ukrainian Counterattacks', *Forbes* (8 September 2022), <https://www.forbes.com/sites/davidaxe/2022/09/08/russian-troops-are-dashing-around-ukraine-trying-to-block-ukrainian-counterattacks/?sh= 2d75ed4f1cbb>.

17 Gawęda, 'Wojna rosyjsko-ukraińska cz. 7' ['The Russian-Ukrainian War, Part 7'], p.42.

18 '"Бросили ребят, как кусок мяса, на растерзание". Родные военных из Калининградской области рассказывают, как они попали в плен под Харьковом' ['"They threw the boys, like pieces of meat, to be torn apart." Relatives of soldiers from the Kaliningrad region tell how they were captured near Kharkiv'], *Current Time* (14 September 2022) <https://www.currenttime.tv/a/brosili-rebyat-kak-kusok-myasa-na-rasterzanie-rodnye-voennyh-

iz-kaliningradskoy-oblasti-rasskazyvayut-kak-oni-popali-v-plen-pod-harkovom/32031548.html>.

19 'Мобілізовані у "Л/ДНР" не мають бажання воювати: боєздатність підрозділів дуже низька' ['Those mobilised in the "L/DNR" have no desire to fight: the combat capability of the units is very low'], *Suspilne* (26 September 2022), <https://suspilne.media/285804-mobilizovani-u-ldnr-ne-maut-bazanna-vouvati-boezdatnist-pidrozdiliv-duze-nizka/>.

20 Vera Khmelnytska, '"Фурами майно вивозили, нові авто крали": мобілізовані з ОРДЛО влаштували бунт на Харківщині ' ['"They took away our property in trucks and stole new cars": mobilised soldiers from the ORDLO staged a riot in the Kharkiv region'], *TCH* (8 September 2022), <https://tsn.ua/ato/furami-mayno-vivozili-novi-avto-krali-mobilizovani-z-ordlo-vlashtuvali-bunt-na-harkivschini-2153836.html>.

21 Marcin Strembski, 'Wojna powietrza nad Ukrainą 24 sierpnia – 23 września 2022' ['Air war over Ukraine, 24 August – 23 September 2022'], Lotnictwo, 10 (2022), p.31.

22 Batacchi and Mottola, 'Ucraina, Putin in difficoltà e lo spettro nucleare', p.26.

23 Valerii Zaluzhnyi (chair) et al., *Воєнно-Історичний Опис Російсько-Української Війни (вересень 2022 року) [Military-historical description of the Russian-Ukrainian war (September 2022)]* (Kyiv: Ukrainian Defence Ministry and Ukrainian General Staff, 2022), p.95.

24 Batacchi and Mottola, 'Ucraina, Putin in difficoltà e lo spettro nucleare', p.27.

25 Interview with Andriy Platonov, recorded by the author on 30 August 2024.

26 Gawęda, 'Wojna rosyjsko-ukraińska cz. 7' ['The Russian-Ukrainian War, Part 7'], p.44.

27 Kharuk, 'Слобожанська наступальна операція: передумови і перший етап…' ['The Slobozhansky Offensive Operation: Preconditions and First Stage…', p.11.

28 Sanya Kozatskyi, 'Зенітні установки «Gepard» працюють на Харківщині' ['Gepard anti-aircraft systems are operating in the Kharkiv region'], *Militarnyi* (26 September 2022), <https://mil.in.ua/uk/news/zenitni-ustanovky-gepard-pratsyuyut-na-harkivshhyni/>.

29 Gawęda, 'Wojna rosyjsko-ukraińska cz. 7' ['The Russian-Ukrainian War, Part 7'], pp.42–43.

30 Yuriy Butusov, 'Балаклійський прорив' ['Balakliia breakthrough'], *Censor.net* (13 September 2022), <https://censor.net/ru/resonance/3366735/balaklyiskiyi_proriv>.

31 'Перелом: ЗСУ звільнили більше половини територій, захоплених РФ після 24.02.2022' ['Turning point: The Armed Forces of Ukraine have liberated more than half of the territories captured by the Russian Federation after 24 February 2022'], *Militarnyi* (14 November 2022), <https://mil.in.ua/uk/news/perelom-zsu-zvilnyly-bilshe-polovyny-terytorij-zahoplenyh-rf-pislya-24-02-2022/>.

32 'Балаклія довго чекала. Що відбувається навколо міста?' ['Balakliia waited a long time. What is happening around the city?'], *Kharkiv Today* (7 September 2022), <https://2day.kh.ua/ua/kharkow/balakliya-dovho-chekala-shcho-vidbuvayetsya-navkolo-mista>.

33 'Окупанти посилили терор і заборонили людям виходити на вулиці у селах поблизу Балаклії' ['The occupiers have intensified their terror and banned people from going out on the streets in villages near Balakliia'], *Kharkiv Today* (7 September 2022), <https://2day.kh.ua/ua/kharkow/okupanty-posylyly-teror-i-zaboronyly-lyudyam-vykhodyty-na-vulytsi-u-selakh-poblyzu>.

34 Shevchenko, *Воєнна розвідка України. У небі, на морі, на землі [Military Intelligence of Ukraine: In the Sky, at Sea, on Land]*, p.119.

35 Karolina Hird, George Barros, Layne Philipson, Frederick W. Kagan, 'Russian Offensive Campaign Assessment, September 6, 2022', Institute for the Study of War (7 September 2022), <https://www.understandingwar.org/backgrounder/russian-offensive-campaign-assessment-september-6>.

36 Karolina Hird, Grace Mappes, George Barros, Layne Philipson, Mason Clark, Russian Offensive Campaign Assessment, September 7, 2022', Institute for the Study of War (8 September 2022), <https://www.understandingwar.org/backgrounder/russian-offensive-campaign-assessment-september-7>.

37 Agata Shcheglova, '«Никакой паники нет» и СОБР в окружении. Украина перешла в наступление на важный для снабжения российской армии город Балаклею — главное' ['"No panic" and SOBR surrounded. Ukraine has launched an offensive on the city of Balakliia, which is important for supplying the Russian army – the main thing'], *Mediazona* (7 September 2022), <https://zona.media/article/2022/09/07/balakleya>.

38 SOBR is a "special rapid response unit," one of the territorial structures of the Russian Guard, focused on combating organised crime and anti-terrorist operations. The average size of a SOBR unit is 60 people.

39 Ihor Berezhansky, 'Пропагандисти РФ заявили, що самарський і башкирський СОБРи у Балаклії потрапили в оточення' ['Russian propagandists claimed that the Samara and Bashkir SOBR units in Balakliia were surrounded'], *TCH* (7 September 2022), <https://tsn.ua/ato/propagandisti-rf-zayavili-scho-samarskiy-i-bashkirskiy-sobr-u-balakliyi-potrapili-v-otochennya-2152945.html>.

40 Antonina Kostyk, 'За два дні львівські десантники пройшли понад 150 кілометрів в тилу противника' ['In two days, Lviv paratroopers covered more than 150 kilometres behind enemy lines'], *Tvoe Misto* (12 September 2022), <https://tvoemisto.tv/news/za_dva_dni_lvivski_desantnyky_proyshly_ponad_150_kilometriv_v_tylu_protyvnyka_137170.html>.

41 'Ми будемо звільняти рідну землю до останнього сантиметра — Валерій Залужний' ['We will liberate our native land to the last centimetre – Valerii Zaluzhny'], ArmyInform (1 December 2022), <https://armyinform.com.ua/2022/12/01/my-budemo-zvilnyaty-ridnu-zemlyu-do-ostannogo-santymetra-valerij-zaluzhnyj/>.

42 Zmiyevsky, Pugach, and Chepurny, 'Застосування сучасних форм наступального маневну…' ['The use of modern forms of offensive manoeuvres…'], p.763.

43 Army TV – Ukrainian military channel, 'БРИФІНГ ПРЕДСТАВНИКІВ СИЛ БЕЗПЕКИ ТА ОБОРОНИ УКРАЇНИ' ['Briefing of Representatives of the Security and Defence Forces of Ukraine'], YouTube video (8 September 2022), <https://www.youtube.com/watch?v=fOwJC_gXHVI&t=1054s>.

44 Ministry of Defence of Ukraine, 'Оперативна інформація Генерального Штабу Збройних Сил України станом на 06:00 09.09.2022 щодо російського вторгнення' ['Operational information of the General Staff of the Armed Forces of Ukraine as of 06:00 on 09.09.2022 regarding the Russian invasion'], Government Portal (9 September 2022), <https://www.zsu.gov.ua/new_page/631c34dad81eb05089d43bf3>.

45 'Operational Security (OPSEC)', Fortinet (2026), <https://www.fortinet.com/resources/cyberglossary/operational-security>.

46 Alina Gaevska, 'Зеленський офіційно підтвердив звільнення Балаклії на Харківщині від російських окупантів' ['Zelensky officially confirmed the liberation of Balakliia in the Kharkiv region from Russian occupiers'], *Suspilne Kharkiv* (8 September 2022), <https://suspilne.media/279825-zelenskij-oficijno-pidtverdiv-zvilnenna-balaklii-na-harkivsini-vid-rosijskih-okupantiv/>.

47 Kateryna Stepanenko, Grace Mappes, George Barros, Layne Philipson, and Mason Clark, 'Russian Offensive Campaign Assessment, 8 September, 2022', Institute for the Study of War (9 September 2022), <https://www.understandingwar.org/backgrounder/russian-offensive-campaign-assessment-september-8>.

48 Kateryna Tyshchenko, 'Russian authorities urge residents of the occupied areas of Kharkiv Oblast to "evacuate"', *Ukrainska Pravda* (10 September 2022), <https://www.pravda.com.ua/eng/news/2022/09/10/7366932/>.

49 Kyrylo Lyutyi, 'Окупанти втекли з Куп'янська та оголосили про перенесення "столиці" захопленої Харківщини до Вовчанська' ['The occupiers fled Kupiansk and announced the transfer of the "capital" of the occupied Kharkiv region to Vovchansk'], *Oboz.ua* (9 September 2022), <https://war.obozrevatel.com/ukr/okupanti-vtekli-z-kupyanska-ta-ogolosili-pro-perenesennya-stolitsi-zahoplenoi-harkivschini-do-vovchanska.htm>.

50 'Куп'янськ, Ізюм, Балаклія. Як наступають ЗСУ на Харківщині і чи буде великий котел' ['Kupiansk, Izium, Balakliia. How the Armed Forces of Ukraine are advancing in the Kharkiv region and whether there will be a large encirclement'], BBC News Ukraine (10 September 2022), <https://www.bbc.com/ukrainian/features-62860946>.

51 Kateryna Stepanenko, Grace Mappes, George Barros, Layne Philipson, and Mason Clark, 'Russian Offensive Campaign Assessment, 9 September, 2022', Institute for the Study of War (10 September 2022), <https://www.understandingwar.org/backgrounder/russian-offensive-campaign-assessment-september-9>.

52 Gawęda, 'Wojna rosyjsko-ukraińska cz. 7' ['The Russian-Ukrainian War, Part 7'], p.43.

53 Ministry of Defence of Ukraine, 'Оперативна інформація Генерального Штабу Збройних Сил України станом на 06:00 10.09.2022 щодо російського вторгнення' ['Operational information of the General Staff of the Armed Forces of Ukraine as of 06:00 on 10.09.2022 regarding the Russian invasion'], Government Portal (10 September 2022), <https://www.zsu.gov.ua/new_page/631c359ed81eb05089d43c5e>.

54 Alina Gaevska, 'ЗСУ зайшли до Куп'янська Харківської області, над містом — українські прапори' ['Ukrainian Armed Forces enter Kupiansk in Kharkiv Region, Ukrainian flags fly over the city'], *Suspilne Kharkiv* (10 September 2022), <https://suspilne.media/280311-zsu-zajsli-do-kupanska-harkivskoi-oblasti-nad-mistom-ukrainski-prapori/>.

55 Shevchenko, *Воєнна розвідка України. У небі, на морі, на землі [Military Intelligence of Ukraine: In the Sky, at Sea, on Land]*, pp.123–125.

56 Russian Ministry of Defence, 'Для достижения заявленных целей специальной военной операции по освобождению Донбасса…' ['To achieve the stated goals of the special military operation to liberate Donbas…'] [Telegram post], 15:10 p.m., 10 September 2022, <https://t.me/mod_russia/19719>, <https://, t.me/mod_russia/19720>, <https://t.me/miroshnik_r/8650>.

57 General Staff of the Armed Forces of Ukraine, 'Оперативна інформація станом 06.00 11.09.2022 щодо російського вторгнення'] ['Operational information as of 06.00 on 11.09.2022' regarding the Russian invasion'], YouTube video (11 September 2022), <https://www.youtube.com/watch?v=YuJQKBNkZJw&t=2s>.

58 General Staff of the Armed Forces of Ukraine, 'Operational information as of 18:00 11.09.2022 regarding the Russian invasion', YouTube video (11 September 2022), <https://www.youtube.com/watch?v=SelESbZWbhc>.

59 General Staff of the Armed Forces of Ukraine, 'Оперативна інформація станом 06.00 12.09.2022 щодо російського вторгнення ' ['Operational information as of 0.600 12.09.2022 regarding the Russian invasion'], YouTube video (12 September 2022), <https://www.youtube.com/watch?v=3CsZOrX1zKk>.

60 Listopad, 'Подвійний злочин…'.

61 'Найцінніші трофеї ЗСУ на Харківщині: чому один "Зоопарк" та "Орлан-10" цінніші за танкову роту' ['The most valuable trophies of the Armed Forces of Ukraine in the Kharkiv region: why one "Zoo" and "Orlan-10" are more valuable than a tank company'], *Defense Express* (14 September 2022), <https://defence-ua.com/weapon_and_tech/najtsinnishi_trofeji_zsu_na_harkivschini_chomu_odin_zoopark_ta_orlan_10_tsinnishi_za_tankovu_rotu-8910.html>.

62 Alexander Ivanitsky, 'На Харьковщине подсчитали трофейную технику России' ['Russia's captured equipment counted in Kharkiv region'], *Korrespondent.net* (14 September 2022), <https://korrespondent.net/ukraine/4516167-na-kharkovschyne-podschytaly-trofeinuui-tekhnyku-rossyy>.

63 A. Tymokhin, 'Его нельзя бросить, его нельзя эвакуировать. Куда ставить запятую? Обзор армии и флота' ['You can't abandon it, you can't evacuate it. Where to put the comma?'], *Army and Navy Review*, 2 (2023), pp.58–59.

64 Kateryna Stepanenko, Grace Mappes, George Barros, Angela Howard, and Mason Clark, 'Russian Offensive Campaign Assessment, 10 September, 2022', Institute for the Study of War (11 September 2022), <https://understandingwar.org/research/russia-ukraine/russian-offensive-campaign-assessment_11-27/>.

65 Hannah Tsomyik, '"Козача Лопань на Харківщині — під контролем ЗСУ" — голова громади' ["Kozacha Lopan in the Kharkiv region — under the control of the Armed Forces of Ukraine" — head of the community'], *Suspilne Kharkiv* (11 September 2022), <https://suspilne.media/280628-kozaca-lopan-na-harkivsini-pid-kontrolem-zsu-golova-gromadi/>.

66 Bohdan Shopynskyi and Oleksander Nadtoka, *Слобожанська Наступальна Операція Сил Оборони України: перебіг та результати (6 вересня – 1 жовтня 2022 р.) ['Slobozhanshchyna offensive operation of the Armed Forces of Ukraine: progress and results (6 September – 1 October 2022)']*, CMHRAFU (19 March 2024), <https://milhistory.zsu.gov.ua/operatsiyi-syl-oborony-ukrayiny/slobozhanska-nastupalna-operaciya-perebih-ta-rezultaty>.

67 Command of the Airborne Assault Forces of the Armed Forces of Ukraine, 'В результаті успішного контрнаступу…' ['As a result of the successful counteroffensive…'] [Facebook post], 12 September 2022, <https://www.facebook.com/watch/?v=492530292327279&ref=sharing>.

68 'У Нацгвардії підтвердили звільнення Святогірська' ['The National Guard of Ukraine confirmed the liberation of the city of Svyatogorsk in the Donetsk region'], *Ukrinform* (12 September 2022), <https://www.ukrinform.ua/rubric-ato/3570062-u-nacgvardii-pidtverdili-zvilnenna-svatogirska.html>.

69 Batacchi and Mottola, 'Ucraina, Putin in difficoltà e lo spettro nucleare', p.27.

70 Strembski, 'Wojna powietrza nad Ukrainą 24 sierpnia – 23 września 2022' ['Air war over Ukraine, 24 August – 23 September 2022'], pp.32–33.

71 'Вадим Благовісний: 299-та бригада тактичної авіації' ['Vadim Blagovisniy: 299th Tactical Aviation Brigade'], Memorial (no date), <https://www.victims.memorial/people/vadim-blagovisniy>.

72 Taras Safronov, 'На Харківщині знайшли уламки збитого Су-25 ПКС Росії' ['Debris from a downed Russian Su-25 found in Kharkiv region'], *Militarnyi* (11 September 2022), <https://mil.in.ua/uk/news/na-harkivshhyni-znajshly-ulamky-zbytogo-su-25-pks-rosiyi/>.

73 Strembski, 'Wojna powietrza nad Ukrainą 24 sierpnia – 23 września 2022' ['Air war over Ukraine, 24 August – 23 September 2022'], p.33.

74 Myroslav Liskovych, 'Успіх ЗСУ на Харківщині: подібне в історії війн бувало, але дуже нечасто' ['Success of the Armed Forces of Ukraine in Kharkiv region: similar events have occurred in the history of wars, but very rarely'], *Ukrinform* (17 September 2022), <https://www.ukrinform.ua/rubric-ato/3573458-uspih-zsu-na-harkivsini-podibne-v-istorii-vijn-buvalo-ale-duze-necasto.html>

75 Shopynskyi and Nadtoka, *Слобожанська Наступальна Операція… ['Slobozhanshchyna offensive operation…']*.

76 'We will respond to the terrorists for each of their vile acts, for each missile – we are capable of that – address by the President of Ukraine', President of Ukraine Volodymyr Zelensky (15 September 2022), <https://www.president.gov.ua/news/vidpovimo-teroristam-na-kozhnu-yihnyu-pidlist-na-kozhnu-rake-77801>.

77 Volodymyr Landa and Konstantin Gnennyi, 'Операція на 9000 визволених кв. км і $670 млн знищеної техніки РФ: контрнаступ на Харківщині в цифрах' ['Operation to liberate 9,000 square kilometres and destroy $670 million worth of Russian equipment: the counteroffensive in Kharkiv Region in figures'], *Forbes Ukraine* (12 September 2022), <https://forbes.ua/war-in-ukraine/operatsiya-na-9000-vizvolenikh-kv-km-i-670-mln-znishchennoi-tekhniki-rf-kontrnastup-na-kharkivshchini-u-tsifrakh-12092022-8285>.

78 'Воїни волинської 14-ї ОМБР показали звільнений Куп'янськ (фото)' ['Soldiers of the Volyn 14th OMBR showed the liberated Kupiansk'], *Konkurent* (15 September 2022), <https://konkurent.ua/publication/103747/voini-volinskoi-14-i-ombr-pokazali-zvilneniy-kupyansk-foto/>.

79 Serhiy Naiev, *"Чия Відвага, Того й Перемога": Битва за Білогорівський плацдарм (08 – 14 травня 2022 року) ['"Whose courage is the victory": The battle for the Bilohorivsky bridgehead (8–14 May 2022)']*. (Kyiv: CMHRAFU, no date), p.9,

80 A. Kharuk, 'Dwie bitwy o Łyman 23 maja – 2 października 2022 r.' ['Two battles for Lyman. 23 May – 2 October 2022'], *Nowa Technika Wojskowa*, 17 special issue (2023), p.13.

81 Anna Nazarova, 'ЗСУ звільнили ще один населений пункт на Донеччині (ВІДЕО)' ['The Armed Forces of Ukraine liberated another settlement in Donetsk Region (Video)'], *Free Radio* (5 September 2022), <https://freeradio.com.ua/zsu-zvilnyly-shche-odyn-naselenyi-punkt-na-donechchyni-video/>.

82 'З'явились підтвердження, що ЗСУ зайшли в Старий Караван на Донеччині' ['"Confirmation Emerges That the Armed Forces of Ukraine Entered Staryi Karavan in Donetsk Region."'], *Ukrainian View* (8 September 2022), <https://ukrpohliad.org/news/z-

yavylys-pidtverdzhennya-shho-zsu-zajshly-v-staryj-karavan-na-donechchyni.html>.

83 It should be emphasised that in the Ukrainian context, the division between the first and second lines is largely arbitrary. The Territorial Defence Forces, the National Guard of Ukraine, the State Border Guard Service and the National Police often fight on the front line. However, in terms of heavy weaponry, they are usually inferior to units of the Land Forces or Airborne Assault Forces.

84 WarGonzo, 'Срочно ВСУ переправляют технику под Красный Лиман…' ['Urgently the Ukrainian Armed Forces are transporting equipment to Krasny Lyman…'] [Telegram post], 4:05 a.m., 8 September 2022, <https://t.me/wargonzo/8198>.

85 Stepanenko, Mappes, Barros, Howard, and Clark, 'Russian Offensive Campaign Assessment, 10 September, 2022'.

86 FREEДОМ, 'Деоккупация Донецкой области. Бои за Лиман' ['De-occupation of the Donetsk region. Battles for Lyman'], YouTube video, 28 September 2022, <https://www.youtube.com/watch?v=jQNSy5YpRis>.

87 Taras Safronov, 'На Луганщині ЗСУ зачистили від окупантів Білогорівку' ['In Luhansk region, the Armed Forces of Ukraine cleared Bilohorivka of occupiers'], *Militarnyi* (19 September 2022), <https://mil.in. ua/uk/news/na-luganshhyni-zsu-zachystyly-vid-okupantiv-bilogorivku/>.

88 Maria Boyko, 'Зруйновані будівлі, відсутність електрики та їжі: який вигляд має перше звільнене селище на Луганщині (відео)' ['Destroyed buildings, no electricity or food: what the first liberated village in Luhansk region looks like (video)', *TCH* (1 November 2022), <https://tsn.ua/ato/zruynovani-budivli-vidsutnist-elektrikita-yizhi-yak-viglyadaye-pershe-zvilnene-selische-na-luganschini-video-2192566.html>.

89 A. Kharuk 'Bitwy o Białohoriwkę' ['Battles for Bilohorivka'], *Nowa Technika Wojskowa*, special issue 17 (2023), pp.10–11.

90 A. Kharuk, 'Dwie bitwy o Łyman 23 maja – 2 października 2022 r.' ['Two battles for Lyman. 23 May – 2 October 2022'], p.15.

91 Yulia Bilchenko, 'ЗСУ увійшли до Дробишева під Лиманом' ['The Armed Forces of Ukraine entered Drobyshev near Lyman'], Antikor (30 September 2022), <https://antikor.info/articles/578061-vsu_voshli_v_drobyshev_pod_limanom>.

92 Viktoriia Khmilevska, 'У ЗСУ підтвердили звільнення п'яти населених пунктів біля Лиману (карта)' ['The Armed Forces of Ukraine confirmed the liberation of five settlements near Lyman'], *Mirror of the Week* (1 October 2022), <https://zn.ua/ukr/UKRAINE/u-zsu-pidtverdili-zvilnennja-pjati-naselenikh-punktiv-bilja-limanu-.html>.

93 Kateryna Stepanenko, Karolina Hird, George Barros, Riley Bailey, Frederick W. Kagan, 'Russian Offensive Campaign Assessment, 29 September, 2022', Institute for the Study of War (30 September 2022), <https://www.understandingwar.org/backgrounder/russian-offensive-campaign-assessment-september-29>.

94 '"Ненастоящие" военные. Вернувшиеся из Украины добровольцы остались без обещанных привилегий и денег' ['"Fake" soldiers. Volunteers who returned from Ukraine were left without the promised privileges and money'], *Radio Liberty* (11 August 2022), <https://www.svoboda.org/a/31980270.html>.

95 A. Kharuk, 'Dwie bitwy o Łyman 23 maja – 2 października 2022 r.' ['Two battles for Lyman. 23 May – 2 October 2022'], p.16.

96 A. Kharuk, 'Dwie bitwy o Łyman 23 maja – 2 października 2022 r.' ['Two battles for Lyman. 23 May – 2 October 2022'], p.13.

97 'Росіяни та OSINT-дослідники підтвердили втрату двох Су-34 ПКС РФ' ['Russians and OSINT researchers have confirmed the loss of two Su-34s belonging to the Russian Air Force'], *Militarnyi* (25 September 2022), <https://mil.in.ua/uk/news/rosiyany-ta-osint-doslidnyky-pidtverdyly-vtratu-dvoh-su-34-pks-rf/>.

98 'Sunday 2 October 2022, Sukhoi Su-34…', Aviation Safety Network (no date), <https://asn.flightsafety.org/wikibase/285879>.

99 David Axe, 'Lyman, A Supply Hub In Eastern Ukraine, Is The Last Place A Russian Soldier Wants To Be Right Now', *Forbes* (25 September 2022), <https://www.forbes.com/sites/davidaxe/2022/09/25/lyman-a-supply-hub-in-eastern-ukraine-is-the-last-place-a-russian-soldier-wants-to-be-right-now/?sh=13877c191713>.

100 Kateryna Stepanenko, Katherine Lawlor, Grace Mappes, Riley Bailey, George Barros, and Frederick W. Kagan, 'Russian Offensive Campaign Assessment, September 30, 2022', Institute for the Study of War (1 October 2022), <https://www.understandingwar.org/backgrounder/russian-offensive-campaign-assessment-september-30>.

101 Yegor Drozdov, 'Минобороны: союзные войска РФ покинули Красный Лиман' ['Ministry of Defence: Russian allied forces have left Krasny Lyman'], *Ura.ru* (1 October 2022), <https://ura.news/news/1052591478>.

102 Radio Liberty, 'Украинская армия выдавливает российские войска | Донбасс Реалии' ['The Ukrainian army is squeezing out Russian troops | Donbas Realities'], YouTube video, 9 October 2022, <https://www.youtube.com/watch?v=zf_0Bbln3m4>.

103 Zelesnkiy /Official, 'Лиман' ['Lyman'] [Telegram post], 11:00 a.m., 2 October 2022, <https://t.me/V_Zelenskiy_official/3490>.

104 'У ЗСУ підтвердили звільнення села Торське на Донеччині' ['The Armed Forces of Ukraine confirmed the liberation of the village of Torske in Donetsk Region'], *Radio Liberty* (2 October 2022), <https://www.radiosvoboda.org/a/news-torske-zvilnennya/32061994.html>.

105 General Staff of the Armed Forces of Ukraine, 'Оперативна інформація станом на 18.00 26.09.2022 щодо російського вторгнення' ['Operational information as of 18.00 on 26.09.2022 regarding the Russian invasion'], YouTube video, 26 September 2022, <https://www.youtube.com/watch?v=Omhtio1Miw0>.

106 Olena Roschina, 'На Харківщині звільнили Куп'янськ-Вузловий, ще 6% області – під окупацією' ['Kupiansk-Vuzlovyi has been liberated in Kharkiv region, with 6% of the region still under occupation'], *Ukrainska Pravda* (27 September 2022), <https://www.pravda.com.ua/news/2022/09/27/7369277/>.

107 'В Бурятии формируется именное подразделение контрактников «Байкал»' ['A special unit of contract soldiers called "Baikal" is being formed in Buryatia'], *Baikal Daily* (27 July 2022) <https://www.baikal-daily.ru/news/16/439794/>.

108 'В Украине почти полностью уничтожили батальон «боевых бурят» из РФ' ['In Ukraine, a battalion of "combat Buryats" from the Russian Federation has been almost completely destroyed'], *Charter 97* (27 October 2022), <https://charter97.org/ru/news/2022/10/27/521672/>.

109 Poberezhnyi, 'Як Піски-Радьківські чинили опір окупації' ['How Pisky-Radkivski resisted the occupation'].

110 General Staff ZSU, 'Разом повинні тримати стрій…' ['Together we must keep the ranks…'] [Twitter post], 7:15 p.m., 4 May 2023, <https://x.com/GeneralStaffUA/status/1654187978384723996>.

111 Roman Petrenko, 'ЗСУ звільнили Борову на Харківщині' ['The Armed Forces of Ukraine liberated Borova in the Kharkiv region'], *Ukrainska Pravda* (3 October 2022), <https://www.pravda.com.ua/news/2022/10/3/7370187/>.

112 Solodovnik, Kryvko, and Kryvonis, '"Залужний обіцяв, що все буде добре"…' ['"Zaluzhny promised that everything would be fine"…'].

113 Komarov and Kruglyak, 'Контрнаступальна операція Збройних сил України на Харківському напрямку…' ['Counteroffensive operation of the Armed Forces of Ukraine in the Kharkiv direction in 2022…'], p.42.

114 Mark Townsend, Lorenzo Tondo, and Isobel Koshiw, 'Ukrainian counter-offensive in north-east inflicts a defeat on Moscow', *The Guardian* (10 September 2022), <https://www.theguardian.com/world/2022/sep/10/ukrainian-forces-kupiansk-advances-north-east-russia-izyum>.

115 'Decree of the President of the Russian Federation of 21.09.2022 No 647 "On the announcement of partial mobilization in the Russian Federation"', Official Publication of Legal Acts (Russia) (21 September 2022), <http://publication.pravo.gov.ru/Document/View/0001202209210001>.

116 'Шойгу: будут мобилизованы 300 тысяч резервистов' ['Shoigu: 300,000 reservists will be mobilised'], *Radio Liberty* (21 September 2022), <https://www.svoboda.org/a/shoygu-obyavil-o-mobilizatsii-300-tysyach-rezervistov/32044077.html>.

117 Katharina Krebs, Chris Liakos, and Lianne Kolirin, 'Russia suspends "partial mobilisation" of citizens for Ukraine war', CNN (1 November 2022), <https://edition.cnn.com/2022/10/31/europe/russian-mobilization-suspended-intl/index.html>.

118 Andrey Pertsev, 'Кремль «поставил на стоп» референдумы о «присоединении» оккупированных территорий к России, утверждают источники «Медузы» Их «отложили на неопределенный срок» из-за успешного украинского контрнаступления' ['The Kremlin has "put on hold" referendums

on the "annexation" of occupied territories to Russia, according to sources at Meduza'], *Meduza* (11 September 2022), <https://meduza.io/feature/2022/09/11/kreml-postavil-na-stop-referendumy-o-prisoedinenii-okkupirovannyh-territoriy-k-rossii-utverzhdayut-istochniki-meduzy>.

119 I. G. Yevseyev, V. R. Maraev, O. L. Skryabin, and K. Khalimanenko, *Харківська наступна опера 2022 року: Військово-історичний шедевр [Kharkiv Offensive Operation 2022: A Military-Historical Essay]* (Kyiv: Research and Development Centre of the Armed Forces of Ukraine, 2025), pp.64–65.

120 Angelica Baibak, 'Слобожанський контрнаступ: у ЗСУ пояснили, чому не вдалося втілити плани дійти до Сватового' ['Slobozhanshchyna counteroffensive: the Armed Forces of Ukraine explained why they failed to reach Svatove'], 24 Kanal (28 October 2023), <https://24tv.ua/slobozhanskiy-kontrnastup-zsu-poyasnili-shho-zupinilo-nastup_n2420719>.

121 Iryna Balachuk, 'In Izium 447 bodies exhumed, many women and children', *Ukrainska Pravda* (23 September 2022), <https://www.pravda.com.ua/news/2022/09/23/7368817/>.

122 'We must show that there will be a tough and principled reaction to every manifestation of Russian terror – address by the President of Ukraine', President of Ukraine Volodymyr Zelensky (15 September 2022), <https://www.president.gov.ua/news/mayemo-pokazati-sho-na-kozhen-proyav-teroru-rosiyi-bude-zhor-77825>.

123 'Рік тому Збройні Сили України звільнили Ізюм' ['A year ago, the Armed Forces of Ukraine liberated Izium'], *Christians for Ukraine* (10 September 2023), <https://media.c4u.org.ua/calendar/2236>.

124 'На Харківщині виявили тіла понад 760 загиблих під час окупації' ['The bodies of more than 760 people killed during the occupation were found in the Kharkiv region'], *Mykolaivksa Pravda* (30 October 2022), <https://www.nikpravda.com.ua/na-harkivshhyni-vyyavyly-tila-ponad-760-zagyblyh-pid-chas-okupatsiyi/>.

125 'Поліція повідомила про ексгумацію перших 20 тіл на місці масового поховання в Лимані' ['Police reported the exhumation of the first 20 bodies at a mass grave in Lyman'], *Radio Liberty* (9 October 2022), <https://www.radiosvoboda.org/a/news-politsia-ekshumatsia-lyman/32072127.html>.

126 Anton Stepura and Anastasia Galasyuk, 'У Лиманській громаді за рік після звільнення не встановили дані понад 50 людей, чиї тіла знайшли у похованнях' ['In the Lyman community, a year after liberation, more than 50 people whose bodies were found in the graves remain unidentified'], *Suspilne Donbas* (30 September 2023), <https://suspilne.media/donbas/582303-u-limanskij-gromadi-za-rik-pisla-zvilnenna-ne-vstanovili-dani-ponad-50-ludej-cii-tila-znajsli-u-pohovannah/>.

127 Anastasia Doroshenko and Victoria Alekseeva, 'У Лимані на Донеччині триває ідентифікація та встановлення причин смерті загиблих людей під час окупації — прокуратура' ['In Lyman, Donetsk Oblast, the identification and determination of the causes of death of people who died during the occupation is continuing, according to the prosecutor's office'], *Suspilne Donbas* (30 May 2024), <https://suspilne.media/donbas/757389-u-limani-na-doneccini-trivae-identifikacia-ta-vstanovlenna-pricin-smerti-zagiblih-ludej-pid-cas-okupacii-prokuratura/>.

128 Mikhalevska, 'ОКУПОВАНІ: Куп'янськ. Життя під загрозою повторної окупації' ['Occupied: Kupiansk. Life under threat of new occupation'].

129 Solodovnik, Kryvko, and Kryvonis, '"Залужний обіцяв, що все буде добре"...' ['"Zaluzhny promised that everything would be fine"...'].

130 Solodovnik, Kryvko, and Kryvonis, '"Залужний обіцяв, що все буде добре"...' ['"Zaluzhny promised that everything would be fine"...'].

131 'Удари по Харкову: все, що відомо про атаку Росії на енергосистему' ['Strikes on Kharkiv: everything we know about Russia's attack on the power grid'], BBC News Ukraine (12 September 2022), <https://www.bbc.com/ukrainian/news-62873359>.

132 'На Харківщині підірвався на міні і загинув тракторист' ['A tractor driver was killed when he hit a mine in the Kharkiv region'], *Ukrinform* (17 October 2023), <https://www.ukrinform.ua/rubric-regions/3775204-na-harkivsini-pidirvavsa-na-mini-i-zaginuv-traktorist.html>.

Conclusion

1 Viktor Kevlyuk, 'Український наступ. Що сталося на Слобожанщині?' ['Ukrainian offensive. What happened in Slobozhanshchyna?'], *LB.ua* (14 September 2022), <https://lb.ua/society/2022/09/14/529296_ukrainskiy_nastup_shcho_stalosya.html>.

ABOUT THE AUTHORS

Andrij Kharuk is a Doctor of Historical Sciences and Professor of Military History at the Hetman Petro Sahaidachnyi National Academy of Land Forces (Lviv, Ukraine). His academic interests include the history of wars and military conflicts of the twentieth and twenty-first centuries, as well as the history of armaments and military equipment. He has paid particular attention to the history of military aviation and the history of the Ukrainian armed forces in the twentieth and twenty-first centuries. In recent years, he has focused on studying the Russian-Ukranian War in its various strategic, military-technical, and social aspects. He is the author of numerous scholarly and popular science publications. Among his principal works are *Wings of Ukraine: The Air Forces of Ukraine, 1917–1920* (2009), *Combat Aircraft of the 21st Century* (2017), *Field Artillery of the Second World War: A Historical Survey* (2017), *Anti-Tank Artillery of the Second World War: A Historical Survey* (2021), *The Fighting Falcon: The History of the F-16* (2024), *History of the Armed Forces of Ukraine, 1991–2021* (2026). He is the Editor-in-Chief of the *Military Scientific Bulletin* (Lviv).

Daryna Kharuk is a PhD candidate in Political Science and Administration at the University of Opole, Poland. Her academic interests focus on civil society, democratic participation, civic engagement, and the role of non-governmental organisations in times of war and political crisis. She pays particular attention to Ukrainian civil society after the Revolution of Dignity, the transformation of civic activism since 2014, and the role of NGOs in wartime mobilisation, humanitarian response, commemoration, and post-war reconstruction.

Her research explores the relations between civil society organisations and state institutions in Ukraine, especially in the context of the Russian-Ukranian War. In recent years, she has focused on the social and political dimensions of wartime resilience, the mechanisms of civic participation, and the ways in which Ukrainian NGOs contribute to democratic continuity during armed conflict.

She has presented her research at international academic and public events, including the 'Faces of War' Conference at the University of Łódź, Democracy Week in Kristiansand, Civic Engagement Week in Sibiu, and the International Congress on Human Rights in Rzeszów. Her recent papers include 'Crisis and Community: Enhancing Civil Society Through Wartime in Ukraine, 2014–2023', and 'From Wartime Mobilization to Reconstruction: The Future Role of Civil Society in Ukraine'.